THE COPYWRITER'S HANDBOOK

ALSO BY ROBERT W. BLY

Secrets of a Freelance Writer

Selling Your Services

The Digital Marketing Handbook

The New Email Revolution

The Direct Mail Revolution

The Elements of Business Writing

The Elements of Technical Writing

Careers for Writers

Public Relations Kit for Dummies

How to Write and Sell Simple Information for Fun and Profit

THE COPYWRITER'S HANDBOOK

A Step-by-Step Guide to Writing Copy That Sells

4TH EDITION

Robert W. Bly

ST. MARTIN'S GRIFFIN
NEW YORK

Published in the United States by St. Martin's Griffin,
an imprint of St. Martin's Publishing Group

THE COPYWRITER'S HANDBOOK. Copyright © 1985, 2005, 2020 by Robert W. Bly.
All rights reserved. Printed in the United States of America. For information,
address St. Martin's Publishing Group, 120 Broadway, New York, NY 10271.

www.stmartins.com

Designed by Kelly S. Too

The Library of Congress Cataloging-in-Publication Data is available upon request.

ISBN 978-1-250-23801-6 (trade paperback)
ISBN 978-1-250-23800-9 (ebook)

Our books may be purchased in bulk for promotional, educational, or
business use. Please contact your local bookseller or the Macmillan Corporate
and Premium Sales Department at 1-800-221-7945, extension 5442,
or by email at MacmillanSpecialMarkets@macmillan.com.

Originally published in the United States by Dodd, Mead & Company

First St. Martin's Griffin Edition: April 2020

10 9 8 7 6

For David Justiss, Scott Martin, and Brian Croner

Advertise in some shape or other, because it is evident that if a man has a good article for sale, and nobody knows it, it will bring him no return.

—P. T. Barnum, *The Art of Getting Money*

CONTENTS

PREFACE TO THE FOURTH EDITION

In the digital age, readers perceive any book with a copyright date older than the expiration date on the chicken they bought at the supermarket last week as ancient and outmoded.

So when readers pointed out to me that the last revision of *The Copywriter's Handbook*, the third edition, had been published more than ten years ago, we knew it was time for a fourth edition.

Whether you already own an earlier edition of this book or are reading *The Copywriter's Handbook* for the first time, I think you will find this revised and updated fourth edition interesting and helpful.

While the core of copywriting, human psychology, has not changed in ten centuries, the world is changing at a dizzying pace, and that affects marketing. For instance, we used to say a disgruntled customer would tell ten other people about his dissatisfaction with a merchant. Now, with online reviews and social media, some can and do tell thousands.

Over the past decade, digital marketing has evolved at warp speed and now accounts for half or more of all dollars spent on marketing. With dozens of marketing channels to choose from online and offline, planning marketing strategy today is much more complex than when the first edition of *The Copywriter's Handbook* was published more than three decades ago.*

So . . . what's new in the fourth edition of *The Copywriter's Handbook* that makes it more useful and up-to-date than previous editions?

Well, there are new chapters written expressly for this fourth edition: chapter 12 on landing pages, chapter 14 discussing online ads, chapter 15 on social media, chapter 16 on video content, chapter 17 on content marketing, and chapter 18 on getting copy written. All other chapters have been revised—some with only minor corrections, others with substantial updates. In particular, the guidelines for a number of digital marketing tactics, among them online video, search engine optimization (SEO), online conversion, e-mail marketing, online advertising, social media, and content marketing, are updated to be as current, accurate, and useful as I could possibly make them.

---

* For an in-depth discussion of how to plan a multichannel marketing campaign, see my book *The Marketing Plan Handbook*, 2nd edition, published by Entrepreneur Press.

PREFACE TO THE FIRST EDITION

This is a book for everyone who writes, edits, or approves copy—ad agency copywriters, freelancers, ad managers, account executives, creative directors, publicists, entrepreneurs, sales and marketing managers, product and brand managers, Internet marketers, marcom professionals, content writers, and business owners. It is largely a book of rules, tips, techniques, and ideas.

Many big agency copywriters and creative directors will tell you that advertising writers don't follow rules and that "great" advertising breaks the rules.

Maybe so. But before you can break the rules, you have to know the rules. And the number of rules and restrictions on marketing has multiplied at a prolific rate.

This book is written to give you guidelines and advice that can teach you to write effective copy—that is, copy that gets attention, gets its message across, and convinces the customer to buy the product.

Beginners will learn all the basics they need to know: what copy is, what it can do, and how to write copy that gets results.

For people who have been in the business a few years, *The*

Copywriter's Handbook serves as a welcome refresher in writing clear, simple, direct copy. And the book contains some new "tricks," examples, and observations that can help these folks increase the selling power of their copy. Even "old pros" may find some new ideas—or some old ideas that they can use profitably for their own clients.

My approach is to teach through example. Copy excerpts from case histories and sample ads, commercials, mailers, Web pages, e-mails, and brochures illustrate the principles of effective copy. Guidelines are presented as easy-to-follow rules and hints.

Perhaps the copywriters who don't know the rules do produce great advertising—one time out of one thousand. But the rest of the time they create weak, ineffectual ads—ads that look pretty and read pretty but don't sell the product. (And the reason they produce bad ads is that they don't know what makes for a good ad!)

If you master the basics presented in this book, I can't guarantee that you'll go on to write "great" advertising or win prestigious advertising awards. But I can be fairly certain that you'll be writing good, clean, crisp, hardworking copy—copy that gives your customers reasons to dig into their wallets and buy your product . . . and not someone else's!

As you read *The Copywriter's Handbook*, you'll discover what you've suspected all along—that copywriters aren't "literary people," any more than they are coders, data analysts, or graphic designers. Copywriters are salespeople whose job is to convince people to buy products.

But don't be disappointed. When you begin to write copy that sells, you'll discover, as I have, that writing words that persuade can be just as challenging—and exciting—as journalism, fiction, or other writing. And it typically pays a lot better, too.

I do have one favor to ask: if you have a copywriting technique that has worked particularly well for you, why not send

it to me so I can share it with readers of the next edition? You
will receive full credit, of course. I can be reached at:

Robert W. Bly
Copywriter
31 Cheyenne Drive
Montville, NJ 07045
Phone: 973-263-0562
Fax: 973-263-0613
E-mail: rwbly@bly.com
Web site: www.bly.com

A NOTE ABOUT YOU, THE READER

Because this book has a dual audience—ad professionals who create advertising for clients as well as marketing managers who commission the creation of ads—I use "you" to talk with both audiences, and I believe it will be clear which of the two a particular comment is directed at based on the context. Of course, the majority of what is in this book should be useful to both audiences.

ACKNOWLEDGMENTS

I'd like to thank the following people and companies for contributing samples of their work or copywriting tips for publication in this book:

Jim Alexander, Alexander Marketing
Brian Croner
Casey Damachek
Mark Ford
Len Kirsch, Kirsch Communications
Wally Shubat, Chuck Blore & Don Richman Incorporated
Lori Haller
Brian Cohen, Technology Solutions
Len Stein, Visibility PR
Sig Rosenblum
Richard Armstrong
Herschell Gordon Lewis
John Tierney, The DOCSI Corporation
Sandra Biermann, Masonry Institute of St. Louis
Perry Marshall, Perry Marshall & Associates
Fred Gleeck

Andrew Linick
Clayton Makepeace
Milt Pierce
Nick Usborne
Caleb O'Dowd
And many others.

I'd also like to thank my editor, Madeline Jones, for her patient and dedicated work on this project; my agent, Dominick Abel, for his usual fine job in finding a home for the book; and Kim Stacey and Penny Hunt, for their valuable editorial and research assistance.

THE COPYWRITER'S HANDBOOK

1

AN INTRODUCTION TO COPYWRITING

"A copywriter is a salesperson behind a typewriter."*

That quote comes from Judith Charles, president of her own retail advertising agency, Judith K. Charles Creative Communication. And it's the best definition of the word *copywriter* I've ever heard.

The biggest mistake you can make as a copywriter is to judge advertising as laypeople judge it. If you do, you'll end up as an artist, entertainer, or, worse, a clown—but not a salesperson. And your copy will be wasting your client's time and money.

Let me explain a bit. When ordinary folks talk about advertising, they talk about the ads or commercials that are the funniest, the most entertaining, or the most unusual or provocative. A prime example is the annual creative TV commercial extravaganza broadcast during the Super Bowl. These are the ads people point to and say, "I really like that!"

But the goal of advertising is not to be liked, to entertain, or

---

* Yes, I know you use a PC, laptop, or tablet, and not a typewriter. But we were using typewriters when Judith said this back in 1982 or so, and I've decided to let the quote stand as is. Substitute "PC" or "mobile device" for "typewriter" in your own mind, if you like.

to win advertising awards; it is to sell products. The advertiser, if he is smart, doesn't care whether people like his commercials or are entertained or amused by them. If they are, fine. But commercials are a means to an end, and the end is increased sales—and profits—for the advertiser.

This is a simple and obvious thing, but the majority of copywriters and advertising professionals seem to ignore it. They produce artful ads, stunningly beautiful Web site design, and clever commercials whose artistic quality and creativity may rival the finest feature films. But they sometimes lose sight of their goals—more sales—and the fact that they are "salespeople behind keyboards," and not literary artists, entertainers, or movie directors.

Being creative by nature, advertising writers naturally like ads that are aesthetically pleasing, as do advertising artists. But just because an ad is pretty to look at and pleasant to read doesn't necessarily mean it is persuading people to buy the product. Sometimes cheaply produced ads, written simply and directly without a lot of fluff, do the best job of selling.

I'm not saying that all your ads should be "schlock" or that schlock always sells best. I am saying that the look, tone, and image of your advertising should be dictated by the product and your prospects—and not by what is fashionable in the marketing business at the time, or is aesthetically pleasing to some creative people who deliberately shun selling as if it were an unwholesome mental chore to be avoided at all costs.

Some people say (erroneously) that no one reads anymore and we live entirely in a visual age. To that, Carlin Twedt of Ragan Communications replied, "Sure visuals are gaining in popularity, but words are still a communicator's most precious commodity."

As a creative person, you naturally want to write clever copy and produce fancy promotions. But as a professional, your obligation to your client or employer is to increase sales and gain new customers at the lowest possible cost. If a banner ad online works better than a full-page magazine ad, use it. If a simple postcard gets more business than a four-color pop-up mailer with a sound chip, use the postcard.

Actually, once you realize that the goal of advertising is selling (and copywriter Luther Brock once defined selling as "placing 100 percent emphasis on how the reader will come out ahead by doing business with you"), you'll see that there is a creative challenge in writing copy that sells. This "selling challenge" is a bit different from the artistic challenge: instead of creating aesthetically pleasing prose, you have to dig into a product or service, uncover the reasons why consumers would want to buy the product instead of others in its category, and present those sales arguments in copy that is read, understood, and reacted to—copy that makes the arguments so convincingly that the customer can't help but want to buy the product being advertised.

One of the greatest advantages of digital marketing is that results can be measured quickly and accurately. This makes it difficult for copywriters to defend creativity or humor should the metrics—page views, time spent on page, click-throughs, conversion rates, opt-ins, and sales—underperform other e-mails and Web pages used by that same client.

Of course, Judith Charles and I are not the only copywriters who believe that salesmanship, not entertainment, is the goal of the copywriter. Here are the thoughts of a few other advertising professionals on the subjects of advertising, copywriting, creativity, and selling:

My definition says that an ad or commercial has a purpose other than to entertain. That purpose is to conquer a sale by persuading a logical prospect for your product or service, who is now using or is about to use a competitor's product or service, to switch to yours. That's basic, or at least it should be. In order to accomplish that, it seems to me, you have to promise that prospect an advantage that he's not now getting from his present product or service and it must be of sufficient importance in filling a need to make him switch.

—Hank Seiden, Vice President, Hicks & Greist, New York

For years, a certain segment of the advertising industry has been guilty of spinning ads out of whole cloth; they place a premium on advertising's appearance, not on the reality of sales. The result: too many ads and commercials that resemble third-rate vaudeville, desperately trying to attract an audience with stale jokes and chorus lines. On its most basic level, [the advertising] profession involves taking a product, studying it, learning what's unique about it, and then presenting that "uniqueness" so that the consumer is motivated to buy the product.

—Alvin Eicoff, Chairman, A. Eicoff & Company

Those of us who read the criticisms leveled at advertising around the world are constantly struck by the fact that they are not really criticisms of advertising as such, but rather of advertisements which seem to have as a prime objective finding their way into creative directors' portfolios. Possibly the best starting discipline for any creative man in any country is the knowledge that the average [consumer] does not even know that an advertising agency, creative director, art director, or copywriter even exists. What's more, she couldn't care less if they do. She's interested in buying products, not creative directors.

—Keith Monk, Nestlé, Vevey, Switzerland

Of course, I have never agreed that creativity is the great contribution of the advertising agency, and a look through the pages of the business magazines should dramatize my contention that much advertising suffers from overzealous creativity—aiming for high readership scores rather than for the accomplishment of a specified communications task. Or, worse, creativity for self-satisfaction.

—Howard Sawyer, Vice President, Marsteller, Inc.

When your advertising asks for the order right out front, with a price and a place to buy and with "NOW" included in the copy, that's hard-sell advertising, and it should invariably be tried before any other kind. Advertising is usually most beautiful when it's least measurable and least productive.

—Lewis Kornfeld, President, Radio Shack

Viewers are turned off by commercials that try so hard to be funny, which is the present product of so many agencies. The question that comes to mind is, "Why do these people have to have characters acting like imbeciles for thirty seconds or more just to get the product name mentioned once or twice?"

Are they afraid to merely show the product and explain why the viewer should buy it instead of another like product? Possibly the most stupid thing advertisers do is allow their agency to have background music, usually loud, rock-type music, played while the person is trying to explain the features of the product.

Frequently the music is louder than the voice, so the commercial goes down the drain. More and more people are relying on ads for information to help them decide which product to purchase. The entertainment-type ads on TV are ineffective.

—Robert Snodell, "Why TV Spots Fail," *Advertising Age*

Humorous ads are troubling because you have to create a link to the product and its benefit. Often, people remember a funny ad but they don't remember the product.

—Richard Kirshenbaum, Co-Chairman,
Kirshenbaum Bond & Partners

Direct marketing . . . is the only form of accountable advertising. It's the only kind of advertising you can ever do where you can trace every dollar of sales to every dollar of costs. Major corporations using traditional advertising have no idea which advertising is effective. If you employ direct marketing you can tell exactly what works.

—Ted Nicholas, *How to Turn Words into Money*
(Nicholas Direct, 2004)

Copy cannot create desire for a product. It can only take the hopes, dreams, fears, and desires that already exist in the hearts of millions of people, and focus those already-existing desires onto a particular product. This is the copywriter's task: not to create this mass desire—but to channel and direct it.

—Eugene Schwartz, *Breakthrough Advertising*
(Boardroom, 2004)

Ads are not written to entertain. When they do, these entertainment seekers are little likely to be the people whom you want. This is one of the greatest advertising faults. Ad writers abandon their parts. They forget they are salesmen and try to be performers. Instead of sales, they seek applause.

—Claude Hopkins, *Scientific Advertising*
(Bell Publishing, 1920)

The advertisements which persuade people to act are written by [copywriters] who have an abiding respect for the intelligence of their readers, and a deep sincerity regarding the merits of the goods they have to sell.

—Bruce Barton, Cofounder,
Batten, Barton, Durstine & Osborn (BBDO)

A good advertisement is one which sells the product without drawing attention to itself. It should rivet the reader's attention on the product. It is the professional duty of the advertising agent to conceal his artifice.

—David Ogilvy, *Confessions of an Advertising Man*
(Atheneum, 1963)

The "literary quality" of an advertisement, per se, is no measure of its greatness; fine writing is not necessarily fine selling copy. Neither is its daring departure from orthodoxy, nor its erudition, nor its imaginative conceits, nor its catchiness.

—James Woolf, *Advertising Age*

I contend that advertising people are too tolerant of fluff copy, too eager to produce the well-turned phrase to bother with the hard-fought sale.

—Eleanor Pierce, *Printer's Ink*

If there are two "camps" in advertising—hard-sell versus creative—then I side with the former. And so do the experts quoted above.

The Copywriter's Handbook is written to teach you how to write copy that sells. For copy to convince the consumer to buy the product, it must do four things:

1. Get attention.
2. Communicate.
3. Persuade.
4. Ask for a response.

Chapter 2 shows you how to write copy that gets attention. You'll learn to use both headlines and pictures as attention-getting tools. (And you'll learn to make them work together.)

Chapter 3 is a primer on writing to communicate. It provides rules for writing clear, concise, simple copy that gets your message across to the reader both online and offline.

Chapter 4 presents guidelines on persuasive writing. It will teach you to be a salesperson as well as a writer.

Chapter 5 presents step-by-step instructions that can help you prepare effectively for any copywriting assignment.

In chapters 6 through 17, you learn how to apply these copywriting principles to a variety of media both online and offline.

In chapters 18 and 19, we discuss various options for getting your copy written, designed, and produced, including graphics, visuals, and layout.

HAS THE INTERNET CHANGED COPYWRITING FOR BOTH WRITERS AND READERS?

The major event that has taken place since the publication of the first edition of *The Copywriter's Handbook* is the rise of the Internet as a marketing medium and channel of commerce.

Many readers of the first edition have asked me, "Are the copywriting techniques *The Copywriter's Handbook* teaches still applicable in the Internet era in general, and particularly to writing for the Web?"

The answer is: well, yes and no. The core of persuasion is pretty much the same. What has changed is what today is known as the "sales funnel" or "customer journey." Or as the great copywriter Gary Halbert astutely observed: "Fundamentals never change but current *variations* of how to best use those fundamentals are something you must always stay on top of."[1]

Undeniably, the Internet has revolutionized marketing because of its speed, accessibility, ease, and low cost: sending an e-mail marketing campaign is faster, easier, and less costly than distributing the same promotional material through the mail or running it as magazine ads or on TV. Facebook ads can directly target the prospects you want to reach through access to consumer ads. Also, you know the preliminary results within minutes of broadcasting your e-mail or your ads going live. In direct mail, it sometimes takes weeks before you know how well you've done.

THE THREE KEYS TO WRITING COPY THAT WORKS IN THE DIGITAL AGE

Here are three ways the Internet has affected the manner in which copy is written, evaluated, and tested today:

1—Human emotion. First, good copy used to be primarily driven by an understanding of human emotion. That was the main factor that guided good copywriters to create winning copy.

But today, there are not one but three key factors that influence how you create copy and make it work: human emotion, data, and compliance (fig. 1.1).

Fig. 1.1: Copywriting is based on three factors: human emotion, data, and compliance.

Copywriter Frank Joseph writes, "There's never been any marketing of any type that is not enhanced by emotion and sincerity." Tyler Kelley of SLAM! Agency says, "I think we're going to see the rise of digital marketing professionals who not only understand digital but understand people—how they think, what motivates them, and why they purchase."[2]

An important point is that the Internet has not changed human nature, nor does people's buying psychology change simply because they are reading your message online instead of offline. As Claude Hopkins wrote in his classic book *Scientific Advertising* (see appendix D):

> Human nature is perpetual. In most respects it is the same today as in the time of Caesar. So the principles of psychology are fixed and enduring. You will never need to unlearn what you learn about them.

2—Data analytics. Human emotion remains important, but copywriting is increasingly driven by data as reported by analytics.

A white paper from Signal notes, "Decision-makers can no longer depend on experience, intuition, and secondhand information. . . . Data . . . is the single source of truth—the north star guiding marketers in a world where change is the only constant."[3] Or, as Jordan Pritikin from HubSpot puts it, "Great marketers listen to their numbers."

Of the marketers surveyed by eMarketer, 55 percent said better use of data for more effective audience segmentation and targeting is among their three top priorities.[4]

You ignore data at your peril, because they show what's working today. Also, quantitative measurement based on live data and tests trumps subjective opinion every time.

As for data and information used as source material for copywriting projects, there is so much raw data and content on the Web on every subject imaginable, some of my clients send me new links every five minutes for the project I am writing for them.

For decades, I always told clients more is better than less. But now I am rethinking that position. Sometimes there are thousands of articles on the topic. (I just googled "weight loss" and in less than a second was given links to nearly two million pages.) If I gave all two million articles on weight loss a careful reading or even a quick scan, I could not possibly make my copy deadline.

Renowned journalist John McPhee says: *"Writing is selection."*[5] In an era of Information Overload, selectivity in writing is more important than ever.

Some marketers are so data-driven that they ignore strong emotional copy, which frequently generates higher response rates than the mediocre copy used in so many tests.

They also impose rules, based on their extensive testing of ads in their product category and preferred medium, which are contrary to what experienced copywriters think they know. For instance, one client in a niche industry finds that the optimal length for a half-page newspaper ad headline is 8 to 12 words. Longer or shorter and response drops. This is something I had never heard before writing for them, but their data trump my training, opinions, and instincts.

3—Digital compliance. You must follow the ad guidelines and rules for whatever search engine, social network, Web site, ad network, e-mail service provider, or other digital platform on which you want to run your ad. If you do not, your ad won't run, and no one will ever see it.

Compliance with these requirements often makes it difficult to create online advertising that says what you want it to say.

For instance, as of this writing, Facebook rejects ads that talk about weight loss with specific promises (e.g., lose 10 pounds in 7 days). So how is one to run an effective weight loss ad there? And in 2018, Google dropped *3.2 billion ads* that violated its advertising policies.[6]

Marketers are finding hacks around these restrictions. For weight loss and other health claims, product benefit ads have widely been replaced by food-based Facebook ads (e.g., "Top Doctors Say to Throw This Vegetable in the Garbage!").

Smart marketers are increasingly finding honest and clever ways to get their stronger, bolder, more specific ads approved by Facebook and other media controlling compliance.

Still, data and compliance restrict us in ways we didn't have to deal with back in the day. Copywriter Richard Armstrong sums up the debilitating effects of digital ad requirements #2 and #3 as follows:

"We've gone from 'They Laughed When I Sat Down at the Piano . . . But When I Started to Play' to 'It's Feasibly Possible that the Correspondence Course Being Sold in this Advertisement May Be of Some Assistance in Helping You Familiarize Yourself with Learning How to Play the Piano If You're Willing to Put in Many Hours of Study and Practice.'"

Although compliance is important, what constitutes compliance is sometimes open to interpretation. The rule of thumb, though, is this: for each 10 percent closer you get to perfect compliance, your response rates drop by 10 percent. The plain and simple truth is that overly zealous compliance in many cases results in weaker copy.

ONLINE ADVERTISING COMPLIANCE GUIDELINES

Amazon Advertising Policies
https://advertising.amazon.com/resources/ad-specs/en

Facebook, Instagram, Audience Network
https://www.facebook.com/business/help/223106797811279

Google Advertising Policies
https://support.google.com/adspolicy/answer/6008942?hl=en

Microsoft Advertising
https://about.ads.microsoft.com/en-us/resources/policies

SOME GOOD NEWS FOR OLD-SCHOOL COPYWRITERS

The good news for you is that the vast body of the copywriting techniques and selling principles you've learned throughout your career, including the ones in this book, remain viable and effective.

Well then, has the Internet changed anything for your *readers*? Yes, plenty—and here are the changes I see:

1. The Internet, computers, video games, and other screen-based electronic media have caused a reduction in the human attention span. Being concise has always been a virtue in writing, but now it is even more important. This does not mean that long copy doesn't work, that people don't read anymore (as some erroneously claim), or that all copy should be minimal (some of my video sales letter scripts run to sixty-five hundred words). It does mean you must follow the wise advice of Strunk and White in *The Elements of Style* and "omit needless words," keeping your copy clean and concise.

2. Readers are bombarded by more ad messages and information overload than at any time in human history. As Yale librarian Rutherford D. Rogers once said, "We are drowning in information and starving for knowledge." That means you must strive to make your copy relevant to the reader, understand what keeps him or her up at night, and address that need, desire, want, or fear in your ad.

3. The Internet has made consumers more savvy, training them to shun promotion, better able to spot hype, and become increasingly skeptical. Both in print and on the Web, buyers often prefer educational-type advertising material: advertising that respects their intelligence, does not talk down to them, and conveys useful and practical information they perceive as valuable in solving their problem or making a purchasing decision.

4. Copy that is mostly information rather than sales is today called "content marketing." Advertising that *looks* more like an article than a paid ad is called either an advertorial or "native advertising."

5. Your prospects are busy and are pressed for time. Convenience and speed of delivery are big selling points today for products and services, as is time saving.

6. Marketers now have the option of putting their product information in print material, online, or a combination of the two. "Multichannel marketing campaigns" typically alternate promotions between print and digital.

7. Because print and digital to a large degree have become integrated, the sales funnel and customer journey—the steps marketers take to generate leads and sales, as well as the buying process the customer goes through—are multistep and more sophisticated than they were before the advent of Internet marketing. Chapters 11 through 17 cover these changes in detail.

Here's good news for copywriters: because of the rapidly growing use of digital marketing and all the new channels it has spawned, copywriting is a critical skill—both online and offline.

Why? Consumers today are better educated and more skeptical. Thanks in part to the Internet, they have easier, faster access to product information and pricing for comparative shopping. There are more products and brands to choose from, and also more advertising messages—commercials, e-mails, banner ads, mailers—competing for our attention.

As a result, our prospects are bombarded by more communications than were previous generations of consumers. There are more than a billion Web sites they can visit, and over eight hundred channels of television they can watch. Not to mention the hundreds of e-mails and even a dozen or so telemarketing calls some of us get each day.

With all of that information competing for the prospect's attention, you have to work extra hard to make your promotion—whether print or online—stand out and grab the prospect's attention. And of course that means one thing primarily: strong copy with a message that readers actually care about.

Yes, lists, media, and offers are tremendously important. But you can identify, fairly quickly and easily, those lists and offers that work best for your product. Once you've found the right lists, ad networks, and offers, then the only additional leverage you have for boosting response is through—you guessed it—copy.

Writing is critical to success on the Web. As Nick Usborne points out in his book *Net Words*, "Go to your favorite Web site, strip away the glamour of the design and technology, and you're left with words—your last, best way to differentiate yourself online." In marketing, whether on the Internet or the printed page, copy is still king.

HOW ONLINE VIDEO HAS CHANGED COPYWRITING

Platforms including Vimeo and YouTube have flooded the Web with marketing videos ranging from twenty seconds to forty-five minutes or longer.

YouTube is the leading online video platform, with almost five billion videos watched daily, and three hundred hours of new videos uploaded every minute.[7,8]

Back in the day, marketing videos were burned onto DVDs and sent to prospects by mail, or else shown to prospects by salespeople on their laptops. Some DVDs and video are still used as inserts in direct-mail packages or in video brochures.

There are four basic modes of learning: watching, listening, reading, and doing—the latter also called "experiential learning." The problem is, it's difficult to segment your market by their preferred learning mode. Therefore, we produce our content in multiple formats:

- Video mp4 files for people who like to watch.
- Audio mp3 files for people who prefer to listen.
- Books and e-books for readers.
- Workshops, training exercises, and other live events for people who learn by doing.

(According to an article in *ClickZ* [May 1, 2019], 73 percent of people who participate in a brand's experiential marketing are more likely to purchase the brand involved.)

Chapter 16 shows you how to write both short-form and long-form online videos.

HOW SOCIAL MEDIA HAS CHANGED MARKETING

Social media has changed the Internet in general and online marketing in particular in four important ways.

First, no longer do you need a huge ad budget to communicate your messages to the world. All you need is a free account on one or more of the social media channels and then to start writing posts, though boosted posts and ads are not free. (A "boosted post" means you pay Facebook to distribute your post to more people.)

Second, while some communications between two parties on the Internet are private, whatever you post on Facebook, whether text or photos, is for public consumption. So social media lessens the degree of privacy Internet users have.

Third, social media is more interactive than most other digital channels. Users can comment on other users' posts at their whim. Also, social networking is at times a contentious medium, with online arguments in lengthy comment threads sometimes getting rude, mean, personal, or ugly. Apparently, people feel comfortable insulting you while hiding behind their keyboard, saying things they would never dare say to you face-to-face.

Fourth, most social media networks sell advertising, which is often their primary source of income. And because the social networks are controlled by their management, they can reject any ad without the need to explain or justify their decision. So rather than a universal medium for free exchange of information, the advertising side of the Web is restrictive and tightly controlled.

Chapter 15 presents guidelines on how marketers should write for and use social media to build brands, generate clicks and conversions, and ultimately sell products.

HOW MULTICHANNEL MARKETING HAS CHANGED COPYWRITING

The major event that has taken place since the publication of the first edition of *The Copywriter's Handbook* is the rise of the Internet as a marketing medium and channel for e-commerce.

The problem for marketing managers, brand managers, small business owners, and copywriters is the growing number of marketing channels, planning how to integrate them into a successful campaign, and then creating a sales funnel for maximum results. A "sales funnel" is a planned sequence of communications that takes people from being unfamiliar with you to doing business with you.

For instance, many clients ask their copywriters to boost conversion rates on their Web sites. When the copywriter asks what the current conversion rate is, some clients often don't know, because they don't measure. ("Conversion rate" is the percentage of users who land on a Web site or landing page and order a product, download free content, or otherwise respond to the call to action.) But without a metric by which to measure and evaluate results, you have no way of knowing which copy is working best.

The other challenge created by the proliferation of marketing channels is "attribution." In modern marketing parlance, attribution is knowing which promotion is the original source of the inquiry or order. In a multichannel world, proper attribution can be difficult, with clicks coming in from so many sources, often simultaneously. That's a problem because the less accurately you can track attribution and ad performance, the less you know about what's working for you and therefore which promotions you should continue to run versus which ads are bombing and should be cut off.

According to eMarketer, of the more than one thousand marketers surveyed, more than four out of ten identified "integration of marketing tools for greater efficiencies" as a top priority.[9]

2

WRITING TO GET ATTENTION: THE HEADLINE AND SUBJECT LINE

When you read a magazine, newspaper, or e-newsletter, you ignore most of the ads and look at or click only a few. Yet many of the ads you skip are selling products that may be of interest to you.

The reason you don't read more ads is simple: there are just too many advertisements competing for your attention. And you don't have the time—or the inclination—to read them all.

This is why you, as a copywriter, must work hard to get attention for your ad, e-mail, landing page, or podcast. Wherever you turn—the Web, magazines, television, or the e-mail inbox—there are just too many things competing for your reader's attention.

For example, each year American companies spend about half a trillion dollars on media advertising.[1]

Even worse, your ad competes with all of the other content that crosses the reader's desk or screen.

Let's say you're writing an ad to sell laboratory equipment to scientists. Your ad will compete with other ads in the scientific journal in which it is published. The scientist probably receives a dozen or more such journals every month. Each is filled with articles and papers he or she should read to keep up-to-date in his field.

And scientists are suffering from massive information overload: 2.5 million scientific articles are published annually[2]— and the total amount of knowledge in the world doubles *every twelve* days,[3] as incredible at that sounds.

This increased amount of information makes it difficult for any single piece of information to be noticed. Most Americans in urban areas are exposed to more than four thousand ad messages per day.[4]

Obviously, those ads that don't do something special to grab the reader's attention are not noticed and not read. Bob Donath, former editor of *Business Marketing*, says the successful ad is one that is able to "pop through the clutter."

Direct-mail advertisers know that a sales letter has only five seconds in which to gain the reader's attention. If the reader finds nothing of interest after five seconds of scanning the letter, she will toss the letter in the trash. Similarly, an ad or commercial has only a few seconds to capture the prospect's interest before the prospect turns the page or goes to the refrigerator. The average cold business e-mail ("cold" meaning sent to a rented e-list) has an open rate of between 14 and 23 percent.[5]

In advertising, getting attention is the job of the headline. "If you can come up with a good headline, you are almost sure to have a good ad," writes John Caples in his book *How to Make Your Advertising Make Money*. "But even the greatest writer can't save an ad with a poor headline."

HOW HEADLINES GET ATTENTION

In all forms of advertising, the "first impression"—the first thing the reader sees, reads, or hears—can mean the difference between success and failure. If the first impression is boring or irrelevant, the ad will not attract your prospect. If it offers news or helpful information or promises a reward for reading the ad, the first impression will win the reader's attention. And this is the first step in persuading the reader to buy your product.

What, specifically, is this "first impression"?

- In a print advertisement, it is the headline and the visual.
- On a Web site, it is the home page headline and copy.
- In a radio or TV commercial, it's the first few seconds of the commercial.
- In a direct-mail package, it's the copy on the outer envelope or the first few sentences in the letter.
- In a press release, it's the lead paragraph.
- In a sales brochure or catalog, it's the front cover.
- In a sales presentation, it's the first few PowerPoint slides.
- In an online video, it's the first twenty seconds of the video.
- In an e-mail marketing message, it's the From line and the Subject line.

No matter how persuasive your body copy or how great your product, your ad cannot sell if it does not attract your customer's attention. Most advertising experts agree that an attention-getting headline is a key ingredient in a successful advertisement.

Here's what David Ogilvy, author of *Confessions of an Advertising Man*, says about headlines:

> The headline is the most important element in most advertisements. It is the telegram which decides whether the reader will read the copy.
> On average, five times as many people read the headline as read the body copy. When you have written your headline, you have spent eighty cents out of your dollar.

If you haven't done some selling in your headline, you have wasted 80 percent of your client's money.

Ogilvy says that putting a new headline on an existing ad has increased the selling power of the ad tenfold. I have experienced similar results. What is it that makes one headline a failure and the other a success?

Many copywriters fall into the trap of believing that clever wordplay, puns, and "cute" copy make for a good headline. But think a minute. When you make a purchase, do you want to be amused by the sales clerk? Or do you want to know that you're getting quality merchandise at a reasonable price?

The answer is clear. When you shop, you want products that satisfy your needs—and your budget. Good copywriters recognize this fact and put sales appeal—not cute, irrelevant gimmicks and wordplay—in their headlines. When readers browse ad headlines, they want to know: "What's in it for *me*?"

The effective headline tells the reader: "Hey, stop a minute! This is something of interest to you!" As mail-order copywriter John Caples explains, "The best headlines appeal to people's self-interest, or give news."

Let's look at a few examples:

• A classic appeal to self-interest is the headline "How to Win Friends and Influence People," from an ad for the Dale Carnegie book of the same name. The headline promises that you will make friends and be able to persuade others if you read the ad and order the book. The benefit is almost irresistible. Who but a hermit doesn't want more friends?

• An ad for Kraft Foods appeals to the homemaker with the headline "How to Eat Well for Nickels and Dimes." If you are interested in good nutrition for your family but must watch your budget carefully, this ad speaks directly to your needs.

• The headline for a Duncan Hines ad hooks us with the question, "Know the Secret to Moister, Richer Cake?" We are promised a reward—the secret to moist cake—in return for reading the copy.

• "Geico can save you 15% on your auto insurance in 15 minutes" offers the most basic and appealing offer: saving time and money.

• "Dollar Shave Club: Shaving and Grooming Made Simple" stresses the main benefit of convenience: razors and other shaving supplies are shipped automatically, eliminating the need to go to the drugstore to purchase them.

Each of these headlines offers a benefit to the consumer, a reward for reading the copy. And each promises to give you specific, helpful information in return for the time you invest in reading the ad and the money you spend to buy the product.

THE FOUR FUNCTIONS OF THE HEADLINE

Headlines do more than get attention. The Dale Carnegie headline, for example, lures you into the body copy of the ad by promising useful information. The Duncan Hines ad also gets you interested in reading more. And it selects a specific type of reader—those people who are interested in baking cakes.

Your headline can perform four different tasks:

1. Get attention.
2. Select the audience.
3. Deliver a complete message.
4. Draw the reader into the body copy.

Let's take a look at how headlines perform each of these jobs.

1. Getting Attention

We've already seen how headlines get attention by appealing to the reader's self-interest. Here are a few more examples of this type of headline:

"Give Your Kids a Fighting Chance"   Crest

"Why Swelter Through Another   GE air conditioners
Hot Summer?"

"For Deep-Clean, Oil-Free Skin,   Noxzema moisturizer
Noxzema Has the Solution"

Another effective attention-getting gambit is to give the reader news. Headlines that give news often use words such as *new, discover, introducing, announcing, now, it's here, at last*, and *just arrived*.

"New Sensational Video Can Give   Exercise
You Thin Thighs Starting Now!"

"Discover Our New Rich-Roasted   Decaffeinated coffee
Taste"

If you can legitimately use the word *free* in your headline, do so. *Free* is one of the most powerful words in the copywriter's vocabulary. Everybody wants to get something for free.

Other powerful attention-getting words include *how to, why, you, sale, quick, easy, bargain, last chance, guarantee, results, proven,* and *save*. Do not avoid these words because other copywriters use them with such frequency. Other copywriters use these words because they work. You should, too. Grade your performance as a copywriter on sales generated by your copy, not on originality.

Headlines that offer the reader useful information are also

attention getters. The information promised in the headline can be given in the copy or in a free booklet the reader can send for. Some examples:

"Free New Report on 67 Emerging Growth Stocks"	Merrill Lynch
"Three Easy Steps to Fine Wood Finishing"	Minwax Wood Finish
"How to Bake Beans"	Van Camp's

Many advertisers try to get attention with headlines and gimmicks that don't promise the reader a benefit or are not related to the product in any way. One industrial manufacturer features a photo of a scantily clad woman in his ads, with an offer to send a reprint of the photo to readers who clip the coupon and write in for a brochure on the manufacturer's equipment. It bombed.

Does this type of gambit get attention? Yes, but not attention that leads to a sale or to real interest in the product. Attention getting for attention getting's sake attracts a lot of curious bystanders but precious few serious customers.

When you write a headline, get attention by picking out an important customer benefit or concern and presenting it in a clear, bold, dramatic fashion. Avoid headlines and concepts that are cute, clever, and titillating but irrelevant. They may generate some hoopla, but they do not sell.

2. Selecting the Audience

If you are selling life insurance to people over sixty-five, there is no point in writing an ad that generates inquiries from young families. In the same way, an ad for a $95,000 sports car should imply, "This is for rich folks only!" You don't want to waste time answering inquiries from people who cannot afford the product.

The headline can select the right audience for your ad and screen out those readers who are not potential customers. A good headline for a life insurance ad might read, "To Men and Women over 65 Who Need Affordable Life Insurance Coverage."

Here are a few more headlines that do a good job of selecting the right audience for the product:

"A Message to All Charter Security Life Policyholders of Single Premium Deferred Annuities"	Charter Security life insurance
"Is Your Electric Bill Too High?"	Utility ad
"Can you trust solar heating companies you never heard of who try to sell you solar roof panels over the phone?"	Solar panels

3. Delivering a Complete Message

According to David Ogilvy, four out of five readers will read the headline and skip the rest of the ad. If this is the case, it pays to make a complete statement in your headline.

That way, the ad can do some selling to those 80 percent of readers who read headlines only. Here are a few headlines that deliver complete messages:

"Caught Soon Enough, Early Tooth Decay Can Actually Be Repaired by Colgate!"

"Hitachi Chiller-Heater Cuts Cooling and Heating Costs Up to 50%"

"Allstate—with accident insurance, they guarantee your car insurance rates won't go up because of an accident."

Ogilvy recommends that you include the selling promise and the brand name in the headline. Many effective headlines don't include the product name. But put it in if you suspect most of your prospects won't bother to read the copy underneath. For instance, having the product name in the headline or subhead in a half-page newspaper ad for health offers typically boosts response.

4. Drawing the Reader into the Body Copy

Certain product categories—liquor, soft drinks, and fashion, for example—can be sold with an attractive photo, a powerful headline, and a minimum of words.

But many products—automobiles, computers, books, records, home study programs, life insurance, and investments—require that the reader be given a lot of information. That information appears in the body copy, and for the ad to be effective the headline must compel the reader to read this copy.

To draw the reader into the body copy, you must arouse his or her curiosity. You can do this with news, or intrigue, or mystery. You can ask a question or make a provocative statement. You can promise a reward, news, or useful information.

A sales letter offering motivational pamphlets was mailed to business managers. The headline of the letter was "What Do Japanese Managers Have That American Managers Sometimes Lack?" Naturally, American managers wanted to find out about the techniques the Japanese use to run their businesses so effectively.

A classic headline for an ad offering a facial lotion reads: "The $5 Alternative to Costly Plastic Surgery." The reader is lured into the ad to satisfy her curiosity about what this inexpensive alternative might be. The headline would not have been as successful if it said, "$5 Bottle of Lotion Is an Inexpensive Alternative to Costly Plastic Surgery."

EIGHT BASIC HEADLINE TYPES

It's only natural for a creative person to avoid formulas, to strive for originality and new, fresh approaches. To the creative writer, many of the headlines in this chapter might seem to follow rigid formulas: "How to . . . ," "Three Easy Ways . . . ," "Introducing the New . . ." And to an extent, copywriters do follow certain rules, because these formulas have been proven effective in thousands of letters, brochures, ads, e-mails, and online videos.

Remember, as a copywriter, you are not a creative artist; you are a salesperson. Your job is not to create literature; your job is to persuade people to buy the product. As the late John Francis Tighe, a top direct-mail copywriter, pointed out, "We are not in the business of being original. We are in the business of reusing things that work."

Of course, John didn't mean that copywriters spend their time deliberately copying the work of other writers. The challenge is to take what works and apply it to your product in a way that is compelling, memorable, and persuasive. Certainly, the best copywriters succeed by breaking the rules. But you have to know the rules before you can break them effectively.

Here, then, are eight time-tested headline categories that have helped sell billions of dollars' worth of products and services. Study them, use them well, and then go on to create your own breakthroughs in headline writing.

1. Direct Headlines

Direct headlines state the selling proposition directly, with no wordplay, hidden meanings, or puns. "Pure Silk Blouses—30 Percent Off" is a headline that's about as direct as you can get. Most retailers use newspaper ads with direct headlines to announce sales and bring customers into their stores.

2. Indirect Headlines

The indirect headline makes its point in a roundabout way. It arouses curiosity, and the questions it raises are answered in the body copy.

The headline for an ad for an industrial mixing device reads, "Ten Million to One, We Can Mix It." At first, this sounds like a wager; the company is betting ten million to one that its mixer can handle your mixing applications. But when you read the copy, you discover that the real significance of "ten million to one" is the mixer's ability to mix two fluids where one fluid is as much as ten million times thicker than the other. The headline has a double meaning, and you have to read the copy to get the real message.

3. News Headlines

If you have news about your product, announce it in the headline. This news can be the introduction of a new product, an improvement of an existing product ("new, improved Bounty"), or a new application for an old product. Some examples of headlines that contain news:

"Trump's Tougher Immigration Policies Has Democrats Seething."	Political
"Finally, a Caribbean Cruise as Good as Its Brochure"	Norwegian Cruise Line
"The Greatest Market Discovery Ever Made"	Commodities trading newsletter

The Norwegian Cruise Line headline, in addition to containing news, has added appeal because it empathizes with the reader's situation. We've all been disappointed by fancy travel brochures that promise better than they deliver. Norwegian gains credibility in our eyes by calling attention to this well-known fact.

4. How-to Headlines

The words *how to* can be pure magic in advertising headlines, magazine articles, and book titles. There are more than seven thousand books in print with *how to* in their titles. Many advertising writers claim if you begin with *how to*, you can't write a bad headline. They may be right.

How-to headlines offer the promise of solid information, sound advice, and solutions to problems: "How to Turn a Simple Party into a Royal Ball." "How to Write Better and Faster." "How to Stop Smoking in 30 Days . . . Or Your Money Back." "How to Use Webinars to Drive the Buying Cycle."

Whenever I'm stuck for a headline, I type "How to" on the page, and what follows those words is always a decent, hard-working headline: good enough to use until something better comes along.

5. Question Headlines

To be effective, the question headline must ask a question that the reader can empathize with or would like to see answered. Some examples:

"What in the World Is Wrong with Me?"	Health magazine
"When an Employee Gets Sick, How Long Does It Take Your Company to Recover?"	Life insurance
"Is Your Pump Costing You More to Operate Than It Should?"	Gorman-Rupp pumps

"Do You Close the Bathroom Door Even When You're the Only One Home?"	*Psychology Today*
"Have You Have Any of These Decorating Problems?"	Carpet store
"What Do Japanese Managers Have That American Managers Sometimes Lack?"	Business magazine

Question headlines should always focus on the reader's self-interest, curiosity, and needs, and not on the advertiser's. A typical self-serving question headline used by many companies reads something like, "Do You Know What the XYZ Company Is Up to These Days?" The reader's response is "Who cares?" and turns the page or exits from the Web page.

6. Command Headlines

Command headlines generate sales by telling your prospects what to do. Here are a few command headlines:

"Try Burning This Coupon"	Harshaw Chemical
"Subscribe Today and get a FREE Special Issue Instantly."	*Prevention*
"Aim High. Reach for New Horizons."	U.S. Air Force

Note that the first word in the command headline is a strong verb demanding action on the part of the reader.

7. Reason-Why Headlines

One easy and effective way of writing body copy is to list the sales features of your product in simple 1-2-3 fashion. If you write your ad this way, you can use a reason-why headline to introduce the list.

Examples of reason-why headlines include "Five Reasons Why You Can't Afford to Miss the MoneyShow Toronto" and "120 to 4,000 Reasons Why You Should Buy Your Fur During the Next Four Days."

Reason-why headlines need not contain the phrase "reason why." Other introductory phrases such as "6 ways," "7 steps," and "here's how" can do just as well.

8. Testimonial Headlines

In a testimonial advertisement, your customers do your selling for you. An example of a testimonial are the Publishers Clearinghouse commercials in which past winners tell us how they won big prize money in the sweepstakes. Testimonials work because they offer proof that a business satisfies its customers.

In print ad testimonials, the copy is written as if spoken by the customer, who is usually pictured in the ad. Quotation marks around the headline and the body copy signal the reader that the ad is a testimonial.

When writing testimonial copy, use the customer's own words as much as possible. Don't polish his statements; a natural, conversational tone adds believability to the testimonial.

THE "UNATTRIBUTED TESTIMONIAL"

Even if the words are not a testimonial or quotation, put quotation marks around your headline, if it is strong. Quotation marks catch the reader's eye and create the impression that the words are a quotation or at least factual, even though they are not attributed to any particular speaker or source.

---

38 MODEL HEADLINES FOR YOUR "SWIPE FILE"

A "swipe file" is a collection of promotions that you turn to for reference when creating your own marketing materials. The best way to get ideas for headlines when you are stuck is to keep a swipe file and consult it for inspiration when you sit down to write a new ad or mailing.

The best swipe samples are those that keep running. You know they are being repeated—because they are profitable. Put a red X on any swipe samples you see multiple times, so you can identify winners at a glance.

As a shortcut, here's a partial collection of such headlines from my vast swipe file, organized by category so as to make clear the approach being used:

1. *Ask a question in the headline.*
   "What Do Japanese Managers Have That American Managers Sometimes Lack?"
2. *Tie-in to current events.*
   "Stay One Step Ahead of the Stock Market Just Like Martha Stewart—But Without Her Legal Liability!"
3. *Create a new terminology.*
   "New 'Polarized Oil' Magnetically Adheres to Wear Parts in Machine Tools, Making Them Last Up to 6 Times Longer."
4. *Give news using the words "new," "introduction," or "announcing."*
   "Announcing a Painless Cut in Defense Spending."
5. *Give the reader a command—tell him to do something.*
   "Try Burning This Coupon."
6. *Use numbers and statistics.*
   "Who Ever Heard of 17,000 Blooms from a Single Plant?"
7. *Promise the reader useful information.*
   "How to Avoid the Biggest Mistake You Can Make in Building or Buying a Home."

8. *Highlight your offer.*
"You Can Now Subscribe to the Best New Books—Just as You Do to a Magazine."

9. *Tell a story.*
"They Laughed When I Sat Down at the Piano, But When I Started to Play . . ."

10. *Make a recommendation.*
"The 5 High-Yield Stocks You Must Own NOW."

11. *State a benefit.*
"Managing UNIX Data Centers—Once Difficult, Now Easy."

12. *Make a comparison.*
"How to Solve Your Emissions Problems—at Half the Energy Cost of Conventional Venturi Scrubbers."

13. *Use words that help the reader visualize.*
"Why Some Foods 'Explode' in Your Stomach."

14. *Use a testimonial.*
"After over Half a Million Miles in the Air Using AVBLEND, We've Had No Premature Camshaft Failures."

15. *Offer a free special report, catalog, or booklet.*
"New FREE Special Report Reveals Little-Known Strategy Millionaires Use to Keep Wealth in Their Hands—and Out of Uncle Sam's."

16. *State the selling proposition directly and plainly.*
"Surgical Tables Rebuilt—Free Loaners Available."

17. *Arouse reader curiosity.*
"The One Internet Stock You MUST Own Now. Hint: It's NOT What You Think!"

18. *Promise to reveal a secret.*
"Unlock Wall Street's Secret Logic."

19. *Be specific.*
"At 60 Miles an Hour, the Loudest Noise in This New Rolls-Royce Comes from the Electric Clock."

20. *Target a particular type of reader.*
"We're Looking for People Who Want a Higher-Paying Career."

21. *Add a time element.*
"Instant Incorporation While U-Wait."

22. *Stress cost savings, discounts, or value.*
"Now You Can Get $2,177 Worth of Expensive Stock Market Newsletters for the Incredibly Low Price of Just $69!"

23. *Give the reader good news.*
"You're Never Too Old to Hear Better."

24. *Offer an alternative to other products and services.*
"No Time for Yale—Took College at Home Online."

25. *Issue a challenge.*
"Will Your Scalp Stand the Fingernail Test?"

26. *Stress your guarantee.*
"Develop Software Applications Up to 6 Times Faster or Your Money Back."

27. *State the price.*
"Link 8 PCs to Your Mainframe—Only $2,395."

28. *Set up a seeming contradiction.*
"Profit from 'Insider Trading'—100% Legal!"

29. *Offer an exclusive the reader can't get elsewhere.*
"Earn 500+% Gains with Little-Known 'Trader's Secret Weapon.'"

30. *Address the reader's concern.*
"Why Most Small Businesses Fail—and What You Can Do About It."

31. *"As Crazy as It Sounds . . ."*
"Crazy as It Sounds, Shares of This Tiny R&D Company, Selling for $2 Today, Could Be Worth as Much as $100 in the Not-Too-Distant Future."

32. *Make a big promise.*
"Slice 20 Years Off Your Age!"

33. *Show ROI (return on investment) for purchase of your product.*
"Hiring the Wrong Person Costs You Three Times Their Annual Salary."

34. *Use a reasons-why headline.*
"7 Reasons Why Production Houses Nationwide Prefer Unilux Strobe Lighting When Shooting Important TV Commercials."

35. *Answer important questions about your product or service.*
"7 Questions to Ask Before You Hire a Collection Agency . . . and One Good Answer to Each."

36. *Stress the value of your premiums.*
"Yours Free—Order Now and Receive $280 in Free Gifts with Your Paid Subscription."

37. *Help the reader achieve a goal.*
"Now You Can Create a Breakthrough Marketing Plan Within the Next 30 Days . . . for FREE!"

38. *Make a seemingly contradictory statement or promise.*
"Cool Any Room in Your House Fast—Without Air Conditioning!"

Notice that many of these headline use numbers. Numbers attract the reader's eye. They should always be written as numerals. If you say "7 reasons why," prospects want to know the seven reasons and will read the ad to learn them. Also ads and content written as lists, or "listicles," which look more like editorial content, are easy to write and easy to read.

THE 4 U'S FORMULA FOR WRITING EFFECTIVE HEADLINES

When prospects see your ad, they make a quick decision, usually in a couple of seconds, to read it or turn the page, based largely on the subject line. But given the flood of commercial messages today, how can you convince a busy prospect—in just a few words—that your ad is worthy of attention?

The "4 U's" copywriting formula—which stands for *urgent*, *unique*, *ultra-specific*, and *useful*—can help.

Developed by my colleague Mark Ford for writing more powerful headlines, the 4 U's formula states that strong headlines are:

1. *Urgent.* Urgency gives the reader a reason to act now instead of later. You can create a sense of urgency in your headline by incorporating a time element. For instance, "Make $100,000 working from home this year" has a greater sense of urgency than "Make $100,000 working from home." A sense of urgency can also be created with a time-limited special offer, such as a discount or premium if you order by a certain date. Many digital marketers give prospects twenty-four hours or less to take advantage of the offer on their screen. Once the offer period is over, the offer is no longer available. However, I have found consumers find "offer extended" after the expiration deadline credible and acceptable.

2. *Unique.* The powerful headline either says something new or, if it says something the reader has heard before, says it in a new and fresh way. For example, "Why Japanese women have beautiful skin" was the headline in an e-mail promoting a Japanese bath kit. This is different from the typical "Save 10% on Japanese Bath Kits."

3. *Ultra-specific.* Bottom Line, Inc. (formerly Boardroom), a newsletter publisher, is the absolute master of ultra-specific bullets, known as "fascinations," that tease the reader into reading further and ordering the product. Examples: "What never to eat on an airplane," "Bills it's okay to pay late," and "Best time to file for a tax refund."

4. *Useful.* The strong subject line appeals to the reader's self-interest by offering a benefit. In the headline "An Invitation to Ski & Save," the benefit is saving money.

When you have written your headline, ask yourself how strong it is in each of the 4 U's. Use a scale of 1 to 4 (1 = weak, 4 = strong) to rank it in each category.

Rarely will a headline rate a 3 or 4 on all four U's. But if your headline doesn't rate a 3 or 4 on at least *three* of the U's, it's probably not as strong as it could be—and can benefit from some rewriting.

A common mistake is to defend a weak headline by pointing to a good response. A better way to think is as follows: if the ad generated a profitable response despite a weak headline, imagine how much more money you could have made by applying the 4 U's.

A marketer wrote to tell me he had sent out a successful e-mail marketing campaign with the subject line "Free Special Report." How does this stack up against the 4 U's?

• *Urgent.* There is no urgency or sense of timeliness. On a scale of 1 to 4, with 4 being the highest rating, "Free Special Report" is a 1.

• *Unique.* Not every marketer offers a free special report, but a lot of them do. So "Free Special Report" rates only a 2 in terms of uniqueness.

• *Ultra-specific.* Could the marketer have been less specific than "Free Special Report"? Yes, he could have just said "Free Bonus Gift." So we rate "Free Special Report" a 2 instead of a 1.

• *Useful.* I suppose the reader is smart enough to figure that the report contains some helpful information. On the other hand, the usefulness is in the specific information contained in the report, which isn't even hinted at in the headline. And does the recipient, who already has too much to read, really need yet another "free special report"? I rate it a 2. Specifying the topic would help (e.g., "Free special report reveals how to cut training costs up to 90% with e-learning").

I urge you to go through this exercise with every headline you write. You can also apply the formula to other copy, both online and offline, including e-mail subject lines, direct-mail envelope teasers, letter leads, Web page headlines, subheads, and bullets.

Rate the headline you've written in all 4 U's. Then rewrite it so you can upgrade your rating on at least two and preferably three or four of the categories by at least 1 point. This simple exercise can increase readership and response rates substantially with very little effort.

MORE HEADLINE TIPS

Here are a few points to consider when evaluating headlines:

- Does the headline promise a benefit or a reward for reading the ad?
- Is the headline clear and direct? Does it get its point across simply and quickly?
- Is the headline as specific as it can be? ("Lose 19 Pounds in Three Weeks" is a better headline than "Lose Weight Fast.")
- Does the headline reach out and grab your attention with a strong sales message, dramatically stated in a fresh new way?
- Does the headline relate logically to the product? (Avoid "sensationalist" headlines that lure you with ballyhoo and then fail to deliver what they promise.)
- Do the headline and visual work together to form a total selling concept?
- Does the headline arouse curiosity and lure the reader into the body copy?
- Does the headline select the audience?
- Is the brand name mentioned in the headline?

- Is the advertiser's name mentioned in the headline?
- Avoid blind headlines—the kinds that don't mean anything unless you read the copy underneath. ("Give It a Hand" is a blind headline used in a recent ad for facial powder.)
- Avoid irrelevant wordplay, puns, gimmicks, and other copywriter's tricks. They may make for amusing advertising, but they do not sell products.
- Avoid negatives. (Instead of "Contains No Sodium," write "100% Sodium-Free.")

A TECHNIQUE FOR PRODUCING HEADLINES

No two copywriters have identical methods for producing headlines. Some writers spend 90 percent of their writing time coming up with dozens of headlines before they write one word of body copy. Others write the body copy first and extract the headline from this copy. Many copywriters keep swipe files of published ads and use headlines from these ads as inspiration for their own advertisements (I gave you thirty-eight of these from my personal collection earlier).

Copywriters who work at big agencies often rely on art directors to help them develop the concept. But I believe professional copywriters should be able to generate headlines, concepts, and ideas on their own.

Let me tell you how I go about writing a headline. You may find these techniques useful in your own work. First, I ask four questions:

1. Who is my customer?
2. What are the important features of the product?
3. Which of these features do competing products lack?
4. Why will the customer want to buy the product? (What product feature delivers the benefit most important to him?)

When I have my answer to question number 3, I know the key selling proposition I want to feature in the headline. Then it's simply a matter of stating this benefit in a clear, compelling, interesting fashion, in a way that will make the reader take notice and want to know more about the product.

Sometimes I'll use a how-to headline. Sometimes I'll use a question or a reason-why format. Other times I do something that doesn't fit any of these categories. The point is, I don't try to force-fit the selling proposition into a formula. I start with a sales message and write headlines that do the best job of illuminating this message.

I usually write six to eight headlines out of which a winner or two emerges. Other copywriters I know write dozens of headlines for a single ad. If writing a lot of headlines works best for you, fine. You can always use some of the strongest discarded headlines as subheads or sentences in your body copy.

When writing a new ad for an existing product, I go through the file of previous ads to see what sales points were covered in those ads. Often, the sales message for my headline will be buried in the body copy of one of the existing ads.

Sometimes when I am unable to produce a lively headline, I make a list of words that relate to the product. I then mix and match the words from this list to form different headlines.

For instance, a client asked me to write an ad on a new type of dental splint used to keep loose teeth in place. The old-type splints were made of stiff strips of metal; the new splint was made of braided wire that could more easily twist to fit the patient's teeth.

My word list looked something like this:

Twist	Easy
Splint	Technology
Teeth	Invented

New	Revolutionary
Developed	Contour
Dental	Bend
Braided	Dentist
Wire	Introducing
Steel	Flexible
Fit	Loose

Mixing and matching words from this list produced half a dozen good headlines. The one I liked best was "Introducing a New Twist in Splint Technology." The client liked it and used it in a successful ad.

If you cannot come up with a headline, don't let it result in writer's block. Put it aside and begin to write the body copy. As you write the copy and go over your notes, ideas for headlines will pop into your head. Write them down as they come, and go back to them later. Much of this material will be inadequate, but the perfect headline might just be produced this way.

A FINAL WORD ON HEADLINES

The headline is the part of the ad that gets attention. And getting attention is the first step in persuading your reader to buy your product.

Showmanship, clever phrases, and ballyhoo do not, by themselves, make for a good headline. Creating headlines that are wonderfully clever is worthwhile only if the cleverness enhances the selling message and makes it more memorable. Unfortunately, many copywriters engage in creativity for creativity's sake, and the result is cleverness that obscures the selling message.

If you have to choose between being clever and obscure or simple and straightforward, I advise you to be simple and straightforward. You won't win any advertising awards. But at least you'll sell some merchandise.

Jim Alexander, president of Alexander Marketing Services, also believes that headlines should sell. Here are a few of Jim's thoughts on the subject:

> We believe in dramatizing a product's selling message with flair and excitement. Those are important ingredients of good salesmanship in print. But simple statements and plain-Jane graphics often make powerful ads.
>
> For example, the headline "Handling Sulfuric Acid" might sound dull or uncreative to you. To a chemical engineer who's forever battling costly corrosion, that simple headline implies volumes. And makes him want to read every word of the problem-solving copy that follows.
>
> So before we let our clients pronounce an ad dull, we first ask them, "Dull to whom?" Dull to you, the advertiser? Or dull to the reader, our potential customer? It's easy to forget that the real purpose of an ad is to communicate ideas and information about a product. Too many ads are approved because of their entertainment value. That's a waste of money.

Later in the book, we look at how to write effective headlines for specific digital media including Web sites, e-mail marketing campaigns, and online ads (see chapters 11, 13, and 14).

3

WRITING TO COMMUNICATE

An article published in the *Harvard Business Review* described experiments designed to measure advertising effectiveness. The experiments showed, not surprisingly, that advertising is most effective when it is easy to understand. In other words, you sell more merchandise when you write clear copy.

In theory, it sounds easy. Advertising deals, for the most part, with simple subjects—clothing, soda, beer, soap, CDs. But in practice, many advertisements don't communicate as effectively as they could. Here's an example from an ad that appeared in *Modern Bride* magazine:

THEY LOVED MY DRESS ON QUIRIUS 3
They smiled politely when Harry showed them our late model telestar, but when he opened the hood of our auto-drive one of their children burst into a shrill laugh and was boxed on his starfish-shaped ears. . . .

The students in my copywriting seminars call this one "What did she say?" This is an example of a "borrowed interest" ad:

The writer didn't have faith in her ability to make the product interesting, so she hid behind a made-up scenario involving a conversation on the planet Quirius 3. The result? Maximum confusion and minimum communication.

"Borrowed interest" is a major cause of confusing copy. There are others: lengthy sentences, clichés, big words, not getting to the point, a lack of specifics, technical jargon, and poor organization, to name a few.

The following tips will help you write copy that gets its message across to the reader.

11 TIPS FOR WRITING CLEAR COPY

1. Put the Reader First

In his pamphlet "Tips to Put Power in Your Business Writing," consultant Chuck Custer advises executives to think about their readers when they write a business letter or memo.

"Start writing to people," says Custer. "It's okay that you don't know your reader! Picture someone you do know who's like your reader. Then write to him."

Think of the reader. Ask yourself: Will the reader understand what I have written? Does he know the special terminology I have used? Does my copy tell her something important or new or useful? If I were the reader, would this copy persuade me to buy the product?

One technique to help you write for the reader is to address the reader directly as "you" in the copy, just as I am writing to *you* in this book. Copywriters call this the "you-orientation." Flip through a magazine, and you'll see that 90 percent of the ads contain the word *you* in the body copy.

On page 46, the column at left shows examples of copy written without regard to the reader's interests. The right gives revisions that make the copy more you-oriented.

Advertiser-Oriented Copy	You-Oriented Copy
Bank Plan is the state-of-the-art in user-friendly, sophisticated financial software for small-business accounts receivable, accounts payable, and general ledger applications.	Bank Plan can help you balance your books. Manage your cash flow. And keep track of customers who haven't paid their bills. Best of all, the program is easy to use—no special training is required.
The objective of the daily cash accumulation fund is to seek the maximum current income that is consistent with low capital risk and the maintenance of total liquidity.	The cash fund gives you the maximum return on your investment dollar with the lowest risk. And you can take out as much money as you like—whenever you like.
To cancel an order, return the merchandise to us in its original container. When we have received the book in salable condition, we will inform our Accounting Department that the invoice is canceled.	If you're not satisfied with the book, simply return it to us and tear up your invoice. You won't owe us a cent. What could be fairer than that?

2. Carefully Organize Your Selling Points

The managers at a bank in the Midwest wanted to know if people read booklets mailed by the bank. So they included an extra paragraph in a booklet mailed to a hundred customers. This extra paragraph, buried in forty-five hundred words of technical information, offered a free ten-dollar bill to anyone who asked for it.

So how many bank customers requested the free money? None. Obviously, the organization of your material affects how people read it. If the bank had put "FREE $10!" on the brochure cover and on the outside of the mailing envelope, many customers would have responded to the offer.

When you write your copy, you must carefully organize the points you want to make. In an ad, you might have one primary sales message ("This car gets good mileage") and several secondary messages ("roomy interior," "low price," "$500 rebate").

The headline states the main selling proposition, and the first few paragraphs expand on it. Secondary points are covered later in the body copy. If this copy is lengthy, each secondary point may get a separate heading or number.

The organization of your selling points depends on their relative importance, the amount of information you give the reader, and the type of copy you are writing (letter, ad, commercial, blog post, or news story).

Terry C. Smith, a former communications manager with Westinghouse, has a rule for organizing sales points in speeches and presentations. His rule is: "Tell them what you're going to tell them. Tell them. And then, tell them what you told them." The speechwriter first gives an overview of the presentation, covers the important points in sequence, and then gives a brief summary of these points. Listeners, unlike readers, cannot refer to a printed page to remind them of what was said, and these overviews and summaries help your audience learn and remember.

Burton Pincus, a freelance copywriter, developed a unique organizational pattern for the sales letters he writes. Pincus begins with a headline that conveys a promise, shows how the promise is fulfilled, and gives proof that the product is everything the copy says it is. Then he tells the reader how to order the product and explains why the cost of the product is insignificant compared to its value.

Before you create an ad or landing page, write down your sales points. Organize them in a logical, persuasive, clear fashion. And present them in this order when you write your copy.

3. Break the Writing into Short Sections

If the content of your ad can be organized as a series of sales points, you can cover each point in a separate section of copy. This isn't necessary in short ads of 150 or fewer words. But as length increases, copy becomes more difficult to read. Breaking the text into several short sections makes reading easier.

What's the best way to divide the text into sections? If you have a series of sections where one point follows logically from the previous point, or where the sales points are listed in order of importance, use numbers.

If there is no particular order of importance or logical sequence among the sales points, use graphic devices such as bullets, asterisks, or dashes to set off each new section. If you have a lot of copy under each section, use subheads (as I've done in this book).

Paragraphs should also be kept short. Long, unbroken chunks of type intimidate readers. A page filled with a solid column of tiny type says, "This is going to be tough to read!"

When you edit your copy, use subheads to separate major sections. Leave space between paragraphs. And break long paragraphs into short paragraphs. A paragraph of five sentences can usually be broken into two or three shorter paragraphs by finding places where a new thought or idea is introduced and beginning the new paragraph with that thought.

FOLLOW THE SIMPLE 4 S FORMULA

Here are 4 simple writing principles that can do more than any other writing techniques to make your copy clear and easy to read:

- Short words.
- Short sentences.
- Short paragraphs.
- Short sections.

4. Use Short Sentences

Short sentences are easier to read than long sentences. All professional writers—newspaper reporters, publicists, magazine writers, copywriters—are taught to write in crisp, short, snappy sentences.

Long sentences tire and puzzle your readers. By the time they have gotten to the end of a lengthy sentence, they don't remember what was at the beginning.

D. H. Menzel, coauthor of *Writing a Technical Paper*, conducted a survey to find the best length for sentences in technical papers. He found that sentences became difficult to understand beyond a length of about 34 words. And the consumer has far less patience with wordiness and run-on sentences than does the scientist studying an important report.

Rudolf Flesch, best known for his classic books *Why Johnny Can't Read* and *The Art of Plain Talk*, said the best average sentence length for business writing is 14 to 16 words. Twenty to 25 words is passable, he added, but above 40 words, the writing becomes unreadable.

Because ad writers place a premium on clarity, their

sentences are even shorter than Flesch's recommended: 14- to 16-word average.

Now, let's take a look at how you can reduce sentence length. First, you should break large sentences into two or more separate sentences whenever possible.

Today every penny of profit counts and Gorman-Rupp wants your pumps to work for all they're worth.	Today every penny of profit counts. And Gorman-Rupp wants your pumps to work for all they're worth.
This article presents some findings from surveys conducted in Haiti in 1977 that provide retrospective data on the age at menarche of women between the ages of 15 and 49 years.	This article presents some findings from surveys conducted in Haiti in 1977. These surveys provide retrospective data on the age at menarche of women between the ages of 15 and 49 years.

Another method of breaking up a long sentence is to use punctuation to divide it into two parts.

One purpose is to enable you to recognize and acknowledge the importance of people who handle people from the company president right down to the newest foreman.	One purpose is to enable you to recognize and acknowledge the importance of people who handle people—from the company president right down to the newest foreman.
The outcome is presentations that don't do their job and make others wonder whether you're doing yours.	The outcome is presentations that don't do their job . . . and make others wonder whether you're doing yours.

Copy becomes dull when all sentences are the same length. To make your writing flow, vary sentence length. By writing an occasional short sentence or sentence fragment, you can reduce the average sentence length of your copy to an acceptable length even if you frequently use lengthy sentences.

Over thirty thousand aerospace engineers are members now. To join them, send your check for $146 with the coupon below and become a member today.	Over thirty thousand aerospace engineers are members now. Join them. Send your check for $146 with the coupon below and become a member today.
Now, discover the Splint-Lock System, a simply beautiful, effective, and versatile chair-side splinting technique that helps you stabilize teeth quickly, easily, and economically.	Now, discover the Splint-Lock System . . . a simply beautiful, effective, and versatile chair-side splinting technique that helps you stabilize teeth. Quickly. Easily. And economically.

Train yourself to write in crisp, short sentences. When you have finished a thought, stop. Start the next sentence with a new thought. When you edit, your cursor should automatically seek out places where a long string of words can be broken in two.

5. Use Small, Simple Words

Simple words communicate more effectively than big words. People use big words to impress others, but they rarely do. More often, big words annoy and distract the reader from what the writer is trying to say.

Yet big words persist, because using pompous language makes the reader or speaker feel important. Some recent examples of big words in action:

In his sermon, a Unitarian minister says: "If I were God, my goal would be to maximize goodness, not to eternalize evil."

In a cartoon appearing in *Defense News*, a manager tells his staff: "I want you to focalize on your optionalizations, prioritize your parametrics, budgetize your expendables, and then schedualize your throughput." Fred Danzig, writing in *Advertising Age*, asks why an E. F. Hutton executive says the market might "whipsaw back and forth" when he could have said it "will go up and down."

In advertising copy, you are trying to communicate with people, not impress them or boost your own ego. Avoid pompous words and fancy phrases. Cecil Hoge, the mail-order expert, says the words in your copy should be "like the windows in a storefront. The reader should be able to see right through them and see the product."

The column at left lists some big words that have appeared over the years in ads, brochures, and articles. The column at right offers simpler—and preferable—substitutions.

Big Word	Substitute Word or Phrase
obtain	get
operate	run, use
optimum	best
parameters	factors
prioritize	set priorities, rank
procure	get
perspiration	sweat
purchase	buy
substantiate	prove
select	pick
superior	best
utilize	use
terminate	end, finish
visage	face

Small words are better than big words whether you're writing to farmers or physicists, fishermen or financiers. "Even the best-educated people don't resent simple words," says John Caples. "But [simple words] are the only words many people understand."

Ernest Hemingway famously said, "Poor Faulkner. Does he really think big emotions come from big words? He thinks I don't know the ten-dollar words. I know them all right. But there are older and simpler and better words, and those are the ones I use."

And don't think your copy will be ignored because you write in plain English. In Shakespeare's most famous sentence—"To be or not to be?"—the biggest word is three letters long.

6. Avoid Technical Jargon

Industrial copy isn't the only writing that uses technical jargon. Here's a sample from a Porsche ad that ran in *Forbes*:

> The new Porsche has a new 2.5-liter, 4-cylinder, aluminum-silicon alloy Porsche engine—designed at Weissach, and built at Zuffen-hausen.

> It achieves maximum torque of 137.2 ft-lbs as early as 3,000 rpm, and produces 143 hp at 5,500 rpm.

> The new model also has the Porsche transaxle design, Porsche aerodynamics, and Porsche handling.

Like many *Forbes* readers, I'm not an automotive engineer. I didn't know that torque is achieved in foot-pounds, or that 3,000 rpm is considered early for achieving it. I know hp is "horsepower" and rpm is "revolutions per minute," but I don't know whether 143 hp at 5,500 rpm is good, bad, or mediocre.

The point is: don't use jargon when writing to an audience that doesn't speak your special language. Jargon is useful for communicating within a small group of experts. But used in copy aimed at outsiders, it confuses the reader and obscures the selling message.

IT professionals have created a new language: machine intelligence, quantum computing, terabyte, gigahertz, raster image, and wireframe. But non-computer people may not know the vocabulary.

A business executive may know the meaning of "software" and "hardware," but not understand terms like "interprocess message buffer," "asynchronous software interrupt," and "four-byte integer data type." When you use jargon, you enjoy an economy of words, but you risk turning off readers who don't understand this technical shorthand.

Computer experts aren't the only technicians who baffle us with their lingo. Wall Streeters use an alien tongue when they speak of downside ticks, standstills, sideways consolidation, and revenue enhancements. Hospital administrators, too, have a language all their own: cost outliers, prospective payments, catchment areas, diagnostic-related groups, and ICD-9 codes.

Because advertisers are specialists, it is they—not their copywriters—who most often inflict jargon on readers. One of my clients rewrote some brochure copy so that their storage silo didn't merely dump grain; the grain was "gravimetrically conveyed."

When is it okay to use technical terms, and when is it best to explain the concept in plain English? I have two rules:

RULE #1: Don't use a technical term unless 95 percent or more of your readers will understand it. If your client insists you use jargon that is unfamiliar to your readers, be sure to explain these terms in your copy.

RULE #2: Don't use a technical term unless it precisely communicates your meaning. I would use *software* because there is no simpler, shorter way to say it. But instead of using *deplane*, I would just say, "Get off the plane."

7. Be Concise

Good copy is concise. Unnecessary words waste the reader's time, dilute the sales message, and take up space that could be put to better use.

Rewriting is the key to producing concise copy. When you write your first draft, the words just flow, and you can't help being chatty. In the editing stage, unnecessary words are deleted to make the writing sparkle with vigor and clarity.

One copywriter I know describes her copy as a "velvet slide"—a smooth path leading the prospect from initial interest to final sale. Excess words are bumps and obstacles that block the slide.

For example, a writing consultant's Web site says his clients receive "informed editorial consideration of their work." As opposed to *uninformed*? Delete *informed*.

An ad in a writer's magazine refers to "incomplete manuscripts still in progress." Obviously, a manuscript still in progress is incomplete.

Make your writing concise. Avoid redundancies, run-on sentences, wordy phrases, the passive voice, unnecessary adjectives, and other poor stylistic habits that take up space but add little to meaning or clarity. Edit your writing to remove unnecessary words, phrases, sentences, and paragraphs.

Here are some examples of wordy phrases and how to make them more concise.

Wordy Phrase	*Concise Substitute*
at first glance	at first
the number 20	20
free gift	gift
whether or not	whether
a general principle	a principle
a specific example	an example
he is a man who	he
they managed to use	they used
from a low of 6 to a high of 16	from 6 to 16
a wide variety of different models	a variety of models
approximately 17 tons or so	approximately 17 tons
expert specialists	specialists
simple and easy to use	easy to use
can help you	helps you
can be considered to be	is
most unique	unique
the one and only	the only
comes to a complete stop	stops
the entire issue	the issue
dull and boring	boring
on an annual basis	yearly
in the form of	as
exhibits the ability to	can
as you may or may not know	as you may know
a substitute used in place of	a substitute for
features too numerous to mention	many features
John, Jack, Fred, Tom, etc.	John, Jack, Fred, and Tom
feminine hygiene products for women	feminine hygiene products

where you were born originally	where you were born
your own home	your home
a product that you can use	a product you can use
RAM memory*	RAM

8. Be Specific

Advertising persuades us by giving specific information about the product being advertised. The more facts you include in your copy, the better. Copywriters who don't bother to dig for specifics produce vague, weak, meaningless copy.

"If those who have studied the art of writing are in accord on any one point," write Strunk and White in *The Elements of Style*, "it is this: the surest way to arouse and hold the attention of the reader is by being specific, definite, and concrete. The greatest writers—Homer, Dante, Shakespeare—are effective largely because they deal in particulars and report the details that matter."

When you sit down at the PC, your file of background information should have at least twice as much material as you will end up using in the final version of your ad. When you have a warehouse of facts to choose from, writing copy is easy: you just select the most important facts and describe them in a clear, concise, direct fashion.

But when copywriters have little to say, they fall back on fancy phrases and puffed-up expressions to fill the empty space on the page. The words sound nice but say nothing of value. And the ad doesn't sell because it doesn't inform.

9. Go Straight to the Point

If the headline is the most important part of an ad, then the lead paragraph is surely the second most important part. It is

---

* RAM stands for "random access memory." So a RAM memory is a "random access memory memory."

this lead that either lures the reader into the text by fulfilling the promise of the headline, or bores the reader with uninteresting, irrelevant, unnecessary words.

The first piece of copy I ever wrote was a brochure describing an airport radar system. Here's the lead:

> Times change. Today's airports handle a far greater volume of traffic than the airports of the late 1960s.
>
> Radars of that era were not built with an eye toward the future and could not handle the rapidly increasing demands placed upon terminal air traffic control systems.
>
> The air traffic handled by today's airports continues to increase at a tremendous rate. An airport surveillance radar must be built to handle not only today's airport traffic but also the more complex air traffic control requirements of tomorrow's airports.

All this is true, and as a layman I found it interesting. But the person reading the brochure is in charge of air traffic control at a large or medium-size airport. Doesn't he already know that air traffic volume is increasing? If so, I am wasting his time by repeating the obvious. Many novice copywriters fall into this trap. They spend the first few paragraphs "warming up" before they get to the sales pitch. By the time they do start talking about the product, most readers have fled.

Start selling with the very first line of copy. Here's how I should have written the lead to that radar brochure:

> The X-900 radar detects even the smallest commercial aircraft out to a range of 145 miles. What's more, the system's L-band operating efficiency makes it 40 times more efficient than S-band radars.

If you feel the need to "warm up" as you set your thoughts on paper, do so. But delete these warm-ups from your final draft. The finished copy should sell from the first word to the last.

Here's another example of copy that fails to get to the point:

> **AIM HIGH. REACH FOR NEW HORIZONS**
> It's never easy. But reaching for new horizons is what aiming high is all about. Because to reach for new horizons you must have the vision to see things not only as they are, but as they could be. . . .

Why write vague copy like this? The ad tries to be dramatic, but the result is empty rhetoric; the copy does not give a clue as to what is being advertised.

This copy appeared in a U.S. Air Force recruitment ad. The benefits of joining the air force are travel, vocational training, and the chance to fly jets. Why not feature these points right off?

10. Write in a Friendly, Conversational Style

Ann Landers was one of the most widely read columnists in the country. Why was she so popular? Said Ann, "I was taught to write like I talk."

People enjoy reading clear, simple, easy-to-understand writing. And the simplest, clearest style is to write the way you talk. (The writing experts call this "conversational tone.")

Conversational tone is especially important in advertising, where the printed page is an economical substitute for a salesperson. (The only reason companies advertise is that advertising can reach more people at less cost than a traveling salesperson can.) A light, conversational style is much easier to read than the stiff, formal prose of business, science, and academia. And when you write simply, you become the reader's friend. When you write pompously, you become a bore.

In the 1980s, IBM's famous Charlie Chaplin ads and commercials launched IBM's first PC and helped make it a bestseller. This ad series was a model of friendly, helpful, conversational copy. Here's a sample:

> There's a world of information just waiting for you. But to use it, study it, enjoy it and profit from it, you first have to get at it. Yet the facts can literally be right at your fingertips—with your own telephone, a modem, and the IBM Personal Computer.

Note the use of colloquial expressions ("a world of information," "at your fingertips") and the informal language ("just waiting for you," "you first have to get at it"). IBM seems to want to help us on a person-to-person level, and its copy has the sound of one friend talking to another.

So how do you go about it? In an article in the *Wall Street Journal*, John Louis DiGaetani recommends this simple test for conversational tone: "As you revise, ask yourself if you would ever say to your reader what you are writing. Or imagine yourself speaking to the person instead of writing."

My former boss once wrote a sales letter that began, "Enclosed please find the literature you requested." I asked him, "If you were handing this envelope to me instead of mailing it, what would you say?"

"Well, I'd say, 'Here is the information you asked for' or 'I've enclosed the brochure you requested' or something like that."
"Then why not write it that way?" I replied. He did.

And to help you write the way you talk, here are some tips for achieving a natural, conversational style:

- Use pronouns—*I, we, you, they.*
- Use colloquial expressions—*a sure thing, turn-on, rip-off, okay.*
- Use contractions—*they're, you're, it's, here's, we've, I'm.*

- Use simple words.
- If you must choose between writing naturally and being grammatically correct, write naturally.

11. Editing to Avoid Sexist Language

The day of the advertising man, salesman, and Good Humor man are over. Now it's the advertising *professional*, sales*person*, and Good Humor *vendor*.

Copywriters must avoid sexist language. Like it or not, sexist language offends a large portion of the population, and you don't sell things to people by getting them angry at you.

In this age of LGBTQ, handling gender in writing is a sensitive issue. Here are a few tips:

- *Use plurals.* Instead of "the doctor receives a report on his patients," write, "the doctors receive reports on their patients."
- *Rewrite to avoid reference to gender.* Instead of "the manager called a meeting of his staff," write, "the manager called a staff meeting."
- *Alternate gender references.* In the past, I used *his* and *he* throughout my copy. Now, I alternate *he* with *she* and *his* with *her*.
- *Use "he and she" and "his and her."* This works in simple sentences. But it can become cumbersome in such sentences as, "When he or she punches his or her time card, he or she is automatically switched to his or her overtime pay rate." When you use *he and she* and *his and her*, alternate these with *she and he* and *her and his*.
- *Do not use the awkward constructions he/she or his/her.* Instead, write "he or she" or "his or her."
- *Create an imaginary person to establish gender.* For example: "Let's say Doris Franklin is working overtime. When she punches her time card, she is automatically switched to her overtime pay rate."

Sexist Term	Nonsexist Substitute
anchorman	anchor
advertising man	advertising professional
chairman	chairperson
cleaning woman	domestic
Englishmen	the English
fireman	firefighter
foreman	supervisor
a man who	someone who
man the exhibit	run the exhibit
man of letters	writer
mankind	humanity
manpower	personnel, staff
man-made	artificial, manufactured
man-hours	work hours
Mrs., Miss	Ms.
newsman, newspaperman	reporter
postman	mail carrier
policeman	police officer
salesman	salesperson
stewardess	flight attendant
weatherman	meteorologist
workman	worker

A FEW TRICKS OF THE TRADE

Copywriters use a number of stylistic techniques to pack a lot of information into a few short paragraphs of smooth-flowing copy. Here are a few tricks of the trade.

End with a Preposition

Ending a sentence with a preposition adds to the conversational tone of the copy. And it's a perfectly acceptable technique endorsed by William Zinsser, Rudolf Flesch, Henry Fowler, and most other authorities on modern writing. Some examples:

He's the kind of fellow with whom you love to have a chat.	He's the kind of fellow you love to have a chat with.
Air pollution is something of which we want to get rid.	Air pollution is something we want to get rid of.
For what are we fighting?	What are we fighting for?

Use Sentence Fragments

Sentence fragments help keep your average sentence length to a respectable number of words. And sentence fragments can add drama and rhythm to your copy.

> Basic Eye Emphasizer does it all. It's the one eye makeup everyone needs. The only one.

> Not one of the Fortune 1000 companies even comes close to our rate of growth. And no wonder. Smartphones are the hottest product of the 2020s, with no end to demand in sight.

> It doesn't take much to block the door to success. A flash of an idea that slips your mind. A note that never gets written.

Begin Sentences with Conjunctions

Beginning a sentence with *and, or, but*, or *for* makes for a smooth, easy transition between thoughts.

Use these simple words instead of more complex connectives. *But* is a shorter, better way of saying *nevertheless*, *notwithstanding*, and *conversely*. And don't use such antiquated phrases as *equally important*, *moreover*, and *furthermore* when *and* will do just as well.

> The first lesson is free. But I can't call you. You have to take the first step.
>
> The choice is simple. Be a pencil pusher. Or get the Messenger. And move ahead at the speed of sound.
>
> ECS phones the first two numbers you've selected until someone answers. It announces the emergency. Gives your address. And repeats it.

Use One-Sentence Paragraphs

An occasional one-sentence paragraph provides a change of pace that can liven up a piece of copy. When all sentences and paragraphs are pretty much the same, the reader is lulled into a stupor, just as a driver can be hypnotized by a long stretch of straight road. A one-sentence paragraph is like a sudden curve in the road—it can shock your reader to wakefulness again. Here's an example from a sales letter pitching freelance copywriting services:

> For many ad agency people, industrial advertising is a difficult chore. It's detailed work, and highly technical. To write the copy, you need someone with the technical know-how of an engineer and the communications skills of a copywriter.
>
> That's where I can help.

Use Graphic Techniques to Emphasize Words or Phrases in the Copy

College students use yellow markers to highlight sentences in their textbooks. This saves time in studying, since the highlights allow them to reread only the important material and not the entire book.

Highlighting and underlining can make words and phrases stand out in print advertising and promotion as well as in schoolbooks. Many readers skim copy without reading it carefully, so an underline or highlight can be useful in calling out key words, phrases, paragraphs, and selling points.

Of course, underlines and other mechanical devices should be used sparingly. If you underline every other word in your sales letter, nothing stands out. On the other hand, if you underline only three words in a one-page letter, you can be sure most readers will read those words. Here is a list of mechanical techniques copywriters use to call attention to key words and phrases:

> underlines
> capital letters
> indented paragraphs
> boldface type
> italics
> colored type
> simulated handwriting fonts
> arrows and notes in margins
> yellow highlighting
> reverse type (white type on black background)
> boxed copy
> call-outs
> P.S. (in letters)

Use Bullets
One of the most effective techniques for writing copy is to present the content as a list of bulleted items (e.g., "7 ways

to reduce your heating bill this winter"). Many copywriters rattle off the bullets quickly—and as a result settle for bullets that are ordinary and therefore not engaging.

It takes a bit more energy and creativity to come up with a bullet item that is as strong and compelling as this classic from Boardroom: "What Never to Eat on an Airplane."

One of the most common mistakes with bullets is not including the right level of information. "Tell too much, and you give away the information free, and there is no need to order the product to find the answer," says copywriter Parris Lampropoulos. "For example, if your bullet says 'how to erase pain by using an over-the-counter lotion called capsaicin,' no curiosity is generated because you've already told the secret."

On the other hand, says Parris, if your bullet contains too little information, or not enough specific information, it fails to grab attention. "If you say 'why B vitamins are an absolute must for people predisposed to this disease,' you fail to hook me, because I don't know what 'this disease' is," says Parris.

His rule of thumb for writing strong bullets: Be specific about the *problem*; be vague and mysterious about the solution. Plus, do it with a twist, hook, or unusual angle.

Parris gives as an example a copywriter who had to write a promotion for a book on natural health. One of the tips in the book was that sitting on bulky objects can cause back pain. So if you have a big, bulging wallet, take it out of your back pocket and keep it in your front pocket to prevent back stress. The bullet that the copywriter came up with: "How a pickpocket can make your back pain better." He is specific about the problem (back pain), but mysterious about the solution (how can a pickpocket help with back pain?).

A COPYWRITER'S CHECKLIST

Before you release copy to the client or the art department, ask yourself these questions:

• *Does the copy fulfill the promise of the headline?* If the headline is "How to Win Friends and Influence People," the copy should tell you how to win friends and influence people. Copy that doesn't fulfill the promise of the headline cheats the reader—and the reader knows it.

• *Is the copy interesting?* Your copy can't generate enthusiasm for the product if the reader yawns as she reads it. Tell a story, give news, improve the reader's life. Make it *interesting*. You can't bore people into buying your product.

• *Is it easy to read?* When a person reads your copy, it is not his job to try to figure out what you mean. It is your job to explain what you mean in plain, simple English. Use short sentences, short paragraphs, small words. Be clear.

• *Is it believable?* Once a teacher said of a phrase I had written, "Bob, this has all the sincerity of a three-dollar bill." People mistrust advertising and advertising professionals. You must work hard to convince the reader that what you say is true. One way to establish credibility is to include testimonials from satisfied customers. Another is to offer a demonstration or scientific evidence that proves your claim. But the best way to get people to believe you is to tell the truth.

• *Is it persuasive?* Clear, readable prose is not enough. Your copy must sell as well as communicate. To sell, your copy must get attention . . . hook the reader's interest . . . create a desire for the product . . . prove the product's superiority . . . and ask for action. (Chapter 4 covers the basics of salesmanship in print.)

• *Is it specific?* To persuade people to buy, you have to give them specifics—facts, features, benefits, savings—reasons why they should buy the product. The more specific you are, the more informative and believable your copy.

• *Is it concise?* Tell the whole story in as few words as possible. When you are finished, stop.

• *Is it relevant?* Freelance copywriter Sig Rosenblum explained: "One of the rules of good copy is: Don't talk about yourself. Don't tell the reader what you did, what you achieved, what you like or don't like. That's not important to him. What's important to him is what he likes, what he needs, what he wants." Make sure your copy discusses facts that are relevant to the reader's self-interest.

• *Does it flow smoothly?* Good copy flows smoothly from one point to the next. There are no awkward phrases, no confusing arguments, and no strange terms to jar the reader and break the flow.

• *Does it call for action?* Do you want the consumer to switch to your brand, send for a free brochure, call your sales representative, send you a check? Find the next step in the buying process and tell the reader to take it. Use coupons, reply cards, toll-free numbers, and other such devices to increase response.

WRITING FOR PRINT VS. WEB

Chapters 11 through 17 go into greater detail on the differences between writing for print versus writing for the Web. For example:

• Serif type, with little curls at the ends of the letters, is preferred for print. San serif type, without the curls, is more readable on screens. **Times Roman** is a serif type and **Arial** is a sans serif type.
• E-mail marketing is easier to read when the paragraphs

are just one or two sentences each; the proof is in the greater open and click-through rates. And each line should be no longer than 60 characters; longer than that makes the e-mails look more foreboding.

- On Web sites, the topics are conveniently divided among multiple Web pages, each focusing on just one topic in no more than three hundred to four hundred words. Breaking writing into bite-size chunks has long been a strategy for more readable writing, and multipage Web sites are an ideal medium in which to employ this writing method.

- Most offline documents have a single communication mode: black ink printed on white paper. But the Web extends to more varied formats and media including audio, video, color, and animation.

- A book can reference other books in its bibliography. On the Web, you can hyperlink to pages within your site as well as to content on a billion other sites. So added detail is quickly accessible to the reader.

- The Web is a two-way communication channel. Example: You write a blog post. Your readers comment. Similarly, you go to a Web site and have a conversation with a chat bot.

- When your reader gets your catalog in the mail, he can place it on a shelf for future reference, where he probably sees it every day. When your reader is finished browsing your Web site, he clicks away and has nothing tangible in his hands.

- Thanks to Google's search engine, it is much easier to quickly find the information you are looking for. Google has access to over a million terabytes, all delivered to your screen within a second. Libraries hold a minuscule fraction of that, often buried in stacks and so time-consuming to locate.

- Writing for the Web means using keywords people would search for to find your content or product (chapter 11), as well as avoiding words in e-mails that trigger spam filters (chapter 13).
- First drafts of Web pages do not have to be perfect. Reason: because they are digital, they are easy to correct, change, and update.

4

WRITING TO SELL

"The object of advertising is to sell goods," said Raymond Rubicam of Young & Rubicam. "It has no other justification worth mentioning."

For the beginning copywriter, this may be a new idea. If you've done other kinds of writing—magazine articles, news reporting, fiction, technical writing—you know how to express yourself in clear, simple English. You know how to write words that inform, and maybe even words that amuse or entertain. But now, you're faced with a new challenge: writing words that convince the reader to *buy your product*.

This puts most writers on uncertain ground. There are many choices you have to make, and unless you're experienced in sales or advertising, you don't know how to make them.

For example, should you write a lot of copy, or is it better to write short copy? (If you write a lot of copy, will people read it? Or is it true that people won't read ads with more than a couple of paragraphs?)

Do you need some clever gimmick, slogan, or sexy model to

get the reader's attention? Or should you concentrate on the product when you write?

If your product has a minor advantage over the competition, should you focus on that advantage? Or should you concentrate on the general benefits of using the product (which the reader gets from both your product and your competitor's)? What do you do if there is no difference between your product and the competition's?

How do you know whether what you're writing will be convincing or interesting to the reader? If you think of two or three ideas for an ad, how do you pick the best one?

Let's start finding out the answers to these questions.

FEATURES AND BENEFITS

The first step in writing copy that sells is to write about benefits and not about features.

A *feature* is a descriptive fact about a product or service; it's what the product is or has. A *benefit* is what the product does; it's what the user of the product or service gains as a result of the feature.

For example, I'm writing this book on a PC. A feature of the machine is that it allows me to edit and revise what I'm typing electronically, so I can move a sentence or add a word without retyping the whole page. The benefit of this feature is that I save a lot of time and can increase my productivity (and make more money) as a result.

Another example: A second feature of my PC is that it has a keyboard connected to the main unit with a coil cable. The benefit is that I can position the keyboard for maximum typing comfort.

In its pamphlet "Why Don't Those Salespeople Sell," Learning Dynamics Incorporated, a sales training firm, cites poor ability to present benefits as one of ten reasons why sales-people fail to make the sale. "Customers don't buy products or services," the firm explains. "They buy what these products and services are going to do for them. Yet many salespeople describe only the features, assuming the customer knows the benefits. Salespeople need to know how to translate features into benefits, and then present them in a customer-centered language."

The same goes for copywriters. Novices tend to write about features: the facts, figures, and statistics at hand. Experienced copywriters turn those features into customer benefits: reasons why the reader should buy the product.

Here's a simple technique for digging out a product's benefits. Divide a sheet of paper into two columns. Label the left-hand column "Features" and the right-hand column "Benefits."

In the left-hand column write down all the features of the product. Some of these you'll find in the background material you've collected on the product (chapter 5 tells you what background material to collect). The rest you can learn by examining and using the product or by talking with people involved with the product: customers, salespeople, distributors, engineers.

Then, go down the list of features and ask yourself, "What benefit does this feature provide to the customer? How does this feature make the product more attractive, useful, enjoyable, or affordable?"

When you complete the list, the right-hand column will contain all the benefits the product offers the customer. These are the sales points that should be included in your copy.

Try this exercise with a common household product that you have nearby. Below is my features/benefits checklist for a No. 2 pencil. Can you add to this list or think of a stronger way to state the benefits?

Features	Benefits
Pencil is a wooden cylinder.	Can be resharpened as often as you like to ensure clear writing.
Cylinder is hexagonal.	Won't roll off your desk.
One end is capped by a rubber eraser.	Convenient eraser lets you correct writing errors cleanly and quickly.
Eraser is attached with a tight-fitting metal band.	Holds eraser snugly in place; no pencils ruined by eraser coming loose.
Pencil is 7½ inches long.	7½-inch graphite core ensures long writing life.
Pencil is ¼ inch in diameter.	Slender shape makes it easy to hold and comfortable to write with.
Pencil is No. 2.	Graphite core is blended for just the right hardness—writes smoothly yet crisply.
Yellow exterior.	Bright, attractive exterior—stands out in a pencil holder or desk drawer.
Sold by the dozen.	One stop to the store gives you enough pencils to last for months.
Also available in a box containing a gross.	Easier purchasing and lower price per unit for large-volume users such as business offices and schools.
Made in the U.S.A.	A quality product. (Also, buying American-made strengthens U.S. economy.)

Now that you have a list of customer benefits, you must decide which sales point is the most important, the one you will feature in your headline as the "theme" of the ad. You also have to decide which of the other points you will include and which you will not use. And you have to arrange these points in some sort of logical order.

Let's take a look at a handy five-step sequence that can help you put your sales points in an order that will lead the reader from initial interest to final sale.

THE MOTIVATING SEQUENCE

Over the years, many advertising writers have developed "copy formulas" for structuring ads, commercials, and sales letters.

The best known of these formulas is AIDA, which stands for Attention, Interest, Desire, Action.

According to AIDA, the copy must first get the reader's *attention*, then create an *interest* in the product, then turn that interest into a strong *desire* to own the product, and finally ask the reader to buy the product or take some other *action* that will eventually lead to a sale.

A second well-known formula is ACCA: Awareness, Comprehension, Conviction, Action. In ACCA, consumers are first made *aware* that the product exists. Then they must *comprehend* what the product is and what it will do for them. After comprehension, the readers must be *convinced* to buy the product. And finally, they must take *action* and actually make the purchase.

A third famous formula is the 4 P's: Picture, Promise, Prove, Push. The copywriter creates a *picture* of what the product can do for the reader, *promises* the picture will come true if the reader buys the product, *proves* what the product has done for others, and *pushes* for immediate action.

A fourth and my personal favorite is the "motivating sequence," a five-step formula for writing copy that sells.

1. Get Attention

This is the job of the headline and the visual. The headline should focus on the single strongest benefit you can offer the reader.

Some copywriters try to hook the reader with clever phrases, puns, or irrelevant information, then save the strongest benefit for a big windup finish. A mistake. If you don't hook the reader with the strongest benefit—the most important reason why he or she should be interested in what you're selling—the reader won't get past the headline. (For more tips on headline writing, see chapter 2.)

2. Show a Need

All products, to some degree, solve some problem or fill a need. A car solves the problem of getting to and from work. An air conditioner prevents you from sweltering in summer heat. Toothpaste with fluoride keeps your teeth from getting holes in them. And mouthwash saves you the embarrassment of having bad breath.

However, with most products, the need for the product may not be obvious or it may not be ingrained in the reader's mind. The second step of writing copy that sells, then, is to show the reader why she needs the product.

For example, many small-business owners do their own taxes and haven't thought about hiring an accountant. But an accountant, with his or her superior knowledge of taxes, can take advantage of the latest tax regulations and save the business owner hundreds or even thousands of dollars in income tax.

So one tax reduction firm's TV commercial promises: if

you owe the IRS $10,000 or more, we can help you settle the unpaid taxes you owe for pennies on the dollar.

3. Satisfy the Need and Position Your Product as a Solution to the Problem

Once you've convinced readers that they have a need, you must quickly show them that your product can satisfy this need, answer their questions, or solve their problems.

An ad for a CPA firm might begin like this:

WOULD YOU PAY $1,000 TO SAVE $5,500?
Last year, a local flower shop decided to hire an accountant to do their income tax returns. They worried about the seemingly high fee, but realized they didn't have the time—or the expertise—to do it themselves.

You can imagine how delighted they were when they hired an accountant who showed them how they could pay thousands of dollars less in income tax than they originally thought they would owe.

I am their accountant, and I'd like to tell you how the flower shop—and dozens of other firms whose taxes I prepare—have saved $2,000 . . . $3,500 . . . even $5,500 a year or more by taking advantage of legitimate tax regulations, deductions, and shelters.

This copy isn't perfect. It needs some work. But it does get attention, highlights a major benefit (saving money), and shows that the service being advertised can satisfy the need.

4. Prove Your Product Can Do What You Say It Can Do

It isn't enough to say you can satisfy readers' needs—you've got to prove you can. You want the readers to risk their hard-earned money on your product or service. You want them to buy from or hire you instead of your competitors. How do you demonstrate your superiority over the competition? How do you get the readers to believe what you say?

Here are a few proven techniques for convincing the readers that it's to their advantage to do business with you:

• Talk about the benefits of your product or service (use the features/benefits list as the source of your discussion). Give the readers reasons to buy by showing the benefits they'll get when they own your product.

• Use testimonials. In testimonials, others who have bought the product praise the product in their own words. This third-party endorsement is much more convincing than manufacturers praising their own product.

• Compare your product to the competition's. Show, benefit for benefit, how you are superior. But have documentation supporting your claim in case your copy is challenged.

• If you have conducted studies to prove your product's superiority, cite this evidence in the copy. Offer a free reprint of the study to interested readers. For dietary supplements, the proof is clinical studies—preferably randomized, double-blind, controlled clinical trials—published in peer-reviewed medical journals.

• Show that your company is reliable and will be in business a long time. Talk about number of employees, size of distributor network, annual sales, number of years in business, growth rate.

5. Ask for Action

The last step in any piece of copy should always be a call for action. If the product is sold by mail, ask readers to mail in an order form, or go online to buy. If the product is sold retail, ask readers to clip the ad and bring it into the store.

If your ad doesn't sell the product directly, then find out the next step in the buying process and tell your readers about it. For example, you might offer a free brochure on the product, a demonstration, or a sample. At the very least, encourage the readers to look for the product in the future if they are not going to buy it today.

Make it easy for the readers to take action. Include your company name, address, and phone number in every piece of copy you write.

If you're writing retail copy, include store hours and locations.

If you're writing copy for a hotel or tourist attraction, include easy-to-follow instructions on how to get there, along with a clearly drawn map of the area.

If you want the readers to send in an order or write for a free brochure, include a handy coupon they can clip and mail.

If you want the readers to call, highlight your toll-free number in large boldface type. And, if you take credit-card orders, be sure to say so and indicate which cards you accept.

Put order forms in catalogs, reply cards in mailers, dealer lists in industrial sales literature, and response forms at the top of landing pages. Make it easy for your readers to respond.

Offer a Web response option, where the ad hyperlinks to an online form the prospects can use to request more information or place an order.

And, if possible, give the readers an incentive for responding now: a price-off coupon, a time-limited sale, a discount to the first one thousand people who order the product. Don't be afraid to try for immediate action and sales as well as long-range "image building." Ask for the order, and ask for it right away.

USE "FALSE LOGIC" TO MAKE THE FACTS SUPPORT YOUR SALES ARGUMENTS

False logic, a term coined by master copywriter Mark Ford, is copy that, through skillful writing, manipulates (but does not lie about or misrepresent) existing facts. The objective: to help readers come to conclusions that these facts, presented without the twists of the copywriter's pen, might not otherwise support.

A catalog for Harry & David says of its pears, "Not one person in 1,000 has ever tasted them." The statistic, as presented by the catalog writer, makes the product sound rare and exclusive—and that's how the average reader interprets it, just as the copywriter intended.

But a logician analyzing this statement might say that it indicates that the pears are not very popular—almost no one buys them.

It's possible to argue that some false logic borders on deception, but the marketer has to make that call for himself. A metals broker advertised "95 percent of orders shipped from stock" to indicate ready availability. But he ran his business out of an office and had a very small warehouse. How could he claim he shipped from stock?

"We do ship 95 percent of orders from stock," the marketer explains. "But not from *our* stock—from the *metal supplier's stock*. We are just a broker. But we do not advertise that, since being a broker is perceived as a negative."

A promotion selling a stock market newsletter to consumers compares the $99 subscription price to the $2,000 the editor would charge if he were managing your money for you, based on a 2 percent fee and a minimum investment of $100,000.

The copy implies that the subscriber is getting Mr. Editor to give him $2,000 worth of money management services for

$99, and quickly glosses over the fact that the newsletter is not precisely the same as a managed account.

A similar example is the promotion done by my friend Don Hauptman for *American Speaker*, a loose-leaf service for executives on how to give good speeches. In his promotion, he points out that this product can help you with your speeches all year long (it has periodic supplements), in contrast to the $5,000 it costs to have a professional speechwriter write just one speech. Of course, *American Speaker* is not actually writing your speech for you.

There is an ongoing debate over whether people buy for emotional or for logical reasons, but most successful marketers know that the former is more dominant as a buying motive than the latter. It is commonly said, "People buy based on emotion, then rationalize the purchase decision with logic."

"Only five percent of our thought processes are fully conscious," writes Dan Hill, president of Sensory Logic. "There's neurological evidence that we make an emotional response—in effect, a decision—about a product or service within three seconds. So businesses need to make an emotional connection with consumers."

Because buying decisions are based on strong feelings and ingrained beliefs, marketers should provide justification and support for what the consumer already wants to do. Therefore, as long as the logical argument seems credible and sensible, your readers will accept it. They do not probe into it as scientifically or deeply as would, say, Ralph Nader, Michael Moore, or an investigative reporter for *Consumer Reports* or the *LA Times*.

Some critics view direct marketing as a step below general marketing in respectability, ethics, and honesty. And perhaps they might reason that my advocating the use of false logic adds fuel to their argument. But in fact false logic is not just the purview of direct marketers: general marketers use it routinely, some with great success.

McDonald's advertises "billions sold"[1] to promote its hamburgers—leading customers to the false conclusion that just because something is popular, it is necessarily good. Publishers use similar logic when they trumpet a book as "a *New York Times* best seller."

Is all this unethical? You can draw your own conclusion, but in my opinion, no.

Copywriters, like lawyers, are advocates for the client (or employer). Just as lawyers use all the arguments at their disposal to win cases, so do copywriters use all the facts at their disposal to win consumers over to the product.

Certainly, we should market no products that are illegal, dangerous, or immoral, although one man's Victoria's Secret catalog is another man's soft porn. But to not use all the tools at our disposal to persuade the buyer is either incompetence, failure to discharge fiduciary duties, or both—and false logic is among the most effective of those tools.

THE UNIQUE SELLING PROPOSITION

Samuel Johnson said, "Promise, large promise, is the soul of an advertisement."

But how do you make a big promise in your advertising that is powerful enough to convince the consumer to buy your product instead of competing brands?

One way is to develop a compelling USP, or Unique Selling Proposition.

What is a USP? Rosser Reeves, author of *Reality in Advertising*, coined this term to describe the major advantage of your product over the competition. The idea is this: If your product is no different from or better than other products of the same type, there is no reason for consumers to choose your product over someone else's. Therefore, to be promoted effectively, your product must have a Unique Selling Proposition: a major benefit that other products in its category don't offer.

According to Reeves, there are three requirements for a USP (and I am quoting, in the italics, from *Reality in Advertising*):

1. *Each advertisement must make a proposition to the consumer. Each must say, "Buy this product, and you will get this specific benefit."* Your headline must contain a benefit—a promise to the reader.

2. *The proposition must be one that the competition either cannot, or does not, offer.* Here's where the *unique* in Unique Selling Proposition comes in. It is not enough merely to offer a benefit. You must *differentiate* your product from other, similar products. The USP for M&M's is that the chocolate is surrounded by a hard candy shell so it won't melt in your hand.

3. *The proposition must be so strong that it can move the mass millions (i.e., pull over new customers to your product).* The differentiation cannot be trivial. It must be a difference that matters to the reader.

Why do so many advertisements fail? One reason is that the marketer has not formulated a strong USP for his product and built his advertising upon it. When you start creating advertising without first thinking about what your USP is, your marketing is weak because there is nothing in it to compel the reader to respond. It looks and sounds like everyone else, and what it says isn't important to the reader.

In general advertising for packaged goods, marketers achieve differentiation by building a strong brand at a cost of millions or even billions of dollars.

Coca-Cola has an advantage because of its brand. If you

want a cola, you can get it from a dozen soda makers. But if you want a Coke, you can only get it from Coca-Cola.

Intel has achieved a similar brand dominance, at an extraordinary cost, with its Pentium line of microprocessors.

Most businesses are too small, and have too strong a need to generate an immediate positive return on investment (ROI) from their marketing, to engage in this kind of expensive brand building. So we use other means to achieve the differentiation in our USP.

One popular method is to differentiate your product or service from the competition based on a feature that your product or service has and they don't.

The common error here is building the USP around a feature that, while different, is unimportant to the prospects, and therefore unlikely to move them to try your product or service.

For example, in the chemical equipment industry, it is common for pump manufacturers to attempt to win customers by advertising a unique design feature. Unfortunately, these design twists often result in no real performance improvement, no real advantage that customers care about.

In a classic industrial ad that ran in the twentieth century, Blackmer Pump, realizing that it could not differentiate based on a technical design principle, took a different approach: to create a USP based upon *application* of the product.

Blackmer's trade ads showed an ad ripped out of an industrial buying guide, full of listings for pump manufacturers, including Blackmer. The company name was circled in pen. The headline of the ad read, "There are only certain times you should call Blackmer for a pump. Know when?"

Body copy explained (and I am paraphrasing here), "In many applications, Blackmer performs no better or worse than any pump, so we are not a particularly advantageous choice."

But, the ad went on, for certain applications (viscous fluids, fluids containing abrasives, slurries, and a few other situations) Blackmer has been proven to outperform all other pumps and is the logical brand of choice. Blackmer closed the ad by offering a free technical manual proving the claim.

My old friend Jim Alexander of Alexander Marketing in Grand Rapids, Michigan, created this campaign and told me it worked extremely well. ·

The easiest situation in which to create a strong USP is when your product has a unique feature—one that competitors lack—that delivers a strong benefit. This must be an advantage the customer really cares about. Not one that, though a difference, is trivial.

But what if such a proprietary advantage does not exist? What if your product is basically the same as the competition, with no special features?

Reeves has the answer here, too. He said the uniqueness can stem either from a strong brand (already discussed as an option 95 percent of marketers can't use) or from "a claim not otherwise made in that particular form of advertising"—that is, other products may also have this feature, but advertisers haven't told consumers about it.

Going back to our example from packaged goods advertising: "M&M's melt in your mouth, not in your hand." Once M&M established this claim as its USP, what could the competition do? Run an ad that said, "We *also* melt in your mouth, not in your hand!"?

To be successful marketers, we must create advertising that generates net revenues in excess of its cost. Reeves believed all advertising had to do this. He defined advertising as "the art of getting a USP into the heads of the most people at the lowest possible cost." If I were to modify his definition, I would change it to "getting a USP into the heads of the people *most likely to buy the product* at the lowest possible advertising cost."

Herb Ahrend, founder of Ahrend Associates, Inc., once said, "A copywriter has to create perceived value. He has to ask, 'What is the nature of the product? What makes the product different? If it isn't different, what attribute can you stress that hasn't been stressed by the competition?'"

Malcolm D. MacDougall, former president and creative director of SSC&B, said there are four ways to advertise seemingly similar products:

1. *Stress an underpublicized or little-known benefit.* Once a copywriter visited a brewery in the hopes of learning something that could set the brewery's beer apart from other beers. He was fascinated to discover that beer bottles, like milk containers, are washed in live steam to kill the germs. Although all brands of beer are purified this way, no other manufacturer had stressed this fact. So the copywriter wrote about a beer so pure that the bottles are washed in live steam, and the brew's Unique Selling Proposition was born.

Study your list of product features and benefits. Then look at the competition's ads. Is there an important benefit that they have ignored, one you can embrace as the Unique Selling Proposition that sets your product apart from all others?

2. *Dramatize and demonstrate a big benefit in a compelling fashion.* Flex Tape's USP is that the tape makes watertight bonds. The company ran a TV commercial in which a metal boat was sawed in half. After taping the two halves together with Flex Tape, the boat was taken out on a lake. And it ran at high speeds without a leak.

3. *Dramatize the product name or package.* Remember Pez, the candy that came in plastic dispensers made to resemble Mickey Mouse, Pluto, and other cartoon characters? Pez was an ordinary candy, but the package made it special.

In the same way, the most unusual feature of the original L'eggs pantyhose was not its design, fabric, or style but the egg-shaped package it was sold in.

Making your product name or package famous is one sure way to move merchandise off the shelves. But it's also expensive. Unless your client is a major marketer with a million-dollar budget, this tactic will be tough to pull off.

4. *Build long-term brand personalities.* Another tactic used by the manufacturers of major national brands is to create advertising that gives their brand a "personality."

Sarah Jessica Parker's commercials for Stella Artois beer position it as a sophisticated alternative to a cosmopolitan, martini, or other cocktail.

Similarly, using *Jeopardy!* host Alex Trebek as a spokesperson for Colonial Penn Life Insurance conveys an image of a financial product that intelligent people would want to have.

If you have millions to spend, you can use advertising to give your product a unique "personality" in the mind of the consumer. But even if your advertising budget is more modest, you can still use features and benefits to create a Unique Selling Proposition that sets your product apart from the rest.

THE SECONDARY PROMISE

Samuel Johnson was right: to break through the clutter and generate a profitable response, marketing must make a big promise. Some examples of big promises from classic promotions:

"Retire overseas on $600 a month."
"Free money reserved for you."
"John F. Kennedy had it. So did Princess Diana. Michael Jordan

has it now. It's the reason why millions of people adore them. Look inside to find out what it is and how you can get it."

Testing shows that, at least in consumer direct marketing, small promises don't work. To get attention and generate interest, you have to make a large, powerful promise.

But there's a problem. What happens if the reader is skeptical . . . because the big promise is so fantastic, it sounds too good to be true? In that case, use a *secondary promise*.

The secondary promise is a lesser benefit that the product also delivers. Although not as large as the big promise, the secondary promise should be big enough so that, by itself, it is reason enough to order the product—yet small enough so that it is easily believed.

This way, even if readers are totally skeptical about the big promise, they can believe the secondary promise and order on that basis alone.

For instance, an investment promotion had a big promise in its headline: "Crazy as It Sounds, Shares of This Tiny R&D Company, Selling for $2 Today, Could Be Worth as Much as $100 in the Not-Too-Distant Future."

That's a really big promise—having a stock go from $2 to $100 is a gain of 4,900 percent. On a thousand shares, your profit would be $98,000.

The problem is, in a bear market, this gain may, to some readers, be too high to be believable. Yet, in this case, it was the truth: if the company's medical device won FDA approval, a fifty-fold increase in share price was not out of the question.

The solution: a subhead, placed directly under the big promise in the headline, made a secondary promise:

> I think this new technology for treating liver disease is going to work. And if it does, the stock price could easily increase 50-fold or more.

But even if it doesn't . . . and the company's treatment is a total failure . . . the stock could still earn early-stage investors a 500% gain on their shares within the next 24 months.

The catch was this: even if the treatment did not win FDA approval, the company would still make a lot of money (though not as much as with the treatment being approved) using the same technology in a different application. So even if the big promise didn't pan out, the secondary promise was enough to make the stock worth owning.

There are many techniques you can use to prove your big promise when your reader is skeptical. These include testimonials, case studies, test results, favorable reviews, superior product design, track record, system or methodology, reputation of the manufacturer.

All are good. But the trouble is this: if the big promise is so strong that readers are inclined to dismiss it as false, you find yourself arguing with them and going against their ingrained belief when you introduce all this proof.

I would still present the proof, but an easier way to overcome doubt concerning the big promise is always to accompany it with a secondary promise that is also desirable yet smaller and more credible.

The secondary promise is your "backup" promise. In a package with both a big promise and a secondary promise, the big promise will attract readers because it is so large— and if you offer enough proof, many of those readers will believe it.

What about those prospects who are not convinced? Without a secondary promise, they simply toss your ad or mailing without responding.

But when you add a secondary promise and make it prominent (which means featuring it in the headline or the lead), many of those who reject the big promise as being unbelievable will find the secondary promise credible—and appealing enough to sell them all on its own.

Actually, with a secondary promise, prospects who don't fully believe your big promise can still be sold by it. They think: "Hey, if this big promise happens to be true, this is a good product to buy; but even if it isn't true, the product is more than worth the price just for the secondary promise—which I am sure *is* true—by itself. So either way, I can't lose."

KNOW YOUR CUSTOMER

Psychology Today reported on a study designed to uncover the characteristics of successful salespeople.

"The best salespeople first establish a mood of trust and rapport by means of 'hypnotic pacing'—statements and gestures that play back a customer's observations, experience, or behavior," wrote the author of the study. "Pacing is a kind of mirror-like matching, a way of suggesting: 'I am like you. We are in sync. You can trust me.'"

In other words, successful salespeople empathize with their customers. Instead of launching into a canned sales pitch, the successful salesperson first tries to understand the customer's needs, mood, personality, and prejudices. By mirroring the customer's thoughts and feelings in their sales presentations, successful salespeople break down resistance to sales, establish trust and credibility, and highlight only those product benefits that are of interest to the customer.

Copywriters, too, must get to know the customers. Understanding the customers and their motivations for buying the product is the key to writing copy that sells.

Too much advertising is created in a vacuum. The advertiser and the agency write copy based on the product features that catch their fancy, not on the features that are important to the customer. The result is copy that pleases the agency and the advertiser, but leaves the customer cold.

In a survey published in a marketing newsletter, advertising agencies and buyers of high-tech products were asked which product features they considered important. The results showed that advertising agencies stressed features that were not important to buyers. The agencies also omitted information that was vital to the buyers. For example, both purchasing agents and engineers ranked price as the number two consideration when buying high-tech equipment. But the agencies said price was unimportant as a copy point. Agencies said high-tech ads should stress how the product saves the buyer time. But engineers and purchasing agents said this is far less important than product specifications and limitations.

When you write copy, don't write in a vacuum. Don't just sit down at the keyboard and pick the features and benefits that suit your fancy. Instead, find out which benefits and features your readers care about—and write about the sales points that will motivate readers to buy the product.

A good example of copy that "hits home" with the reader is a subscription letter I received some years ago from *Inc.* magazine. Here's the opening of the letter:

A special invitation to the hero of American business

Dear Entrepreneur:
You're it!

You're the kind of person free enterprise is built on. The ambition, vision, and guts of small business people like yourself have always been the driving force behind the American economy.

Unfortunately, that's a fact which the general business press seems to have forgotten. In their emphasis on everything big, like conglomerates, multinationals, and oil companies the size of countries, most business publications pay very little attention to the little guy.

The letter is effective because it speaks directly to the pride entrepreneurs feel in being "self-made." The letter writer has done a good job of empathizing with the reader and understanding how an entrepreneur thinks of himself.

You, too, must get to know your reader. One way of doing this is to start paying close attention to your own behavior as a consumer.

Once you start thinking as a consumer rather than a writer, you'll have more respect for your reader. And you'll write copy that provides useful product information and sales appeals rather than empty hype.

Another way to understand your prospect is to observe consumers and be an active student of the marketplace. When you're in the supermarket, watch other buyers. Which type of person picks the sale items and which type goes for the name brand?

When you visit an automobile dealer, observe how the successful salespeople deliver their pitches and handle their customers. Listen to the pitch you receive and think about why it did or didn't sway you.

Take an active interest in the world of e-commerce. When you are served an ad on Facebook, pay attention to subject matter, offer, and design.

And talk to the businesspeople you trade with—store owners, the plumber, your lawyer, the gardener, the person who repairs your hot-water heater—to find out the techniques they use to promote their services and products. People who are close to their customers—and many small business people are—know more about the reality of selling than most ad agency account executives or corporate brand managers do. Listen to these people, and you'll learn what makes the customer tick. (Chapter 5 provides additional tips on getting to know your reader.)

There's an old saying: "You can't be all things to all people." And it certainly applies to advertising and selling. You can't create one ad or commercial that appeals to everybody, because different groups of buyers have different needs. So, as a copywriter, you must first identify your audience—the segment of the market you are selling to—and then learn which product benefits interest these buyers.

Tailor both the content and the presentation of your information to the group of customers you're selling to. Take frozen foods as an example. When you sell frozen foods to a dad or mom who does the cooking, he or she is most interested in nutrition and price.

But a young, single professional person is primarily interested in convenience: he or she doesn't want to spend too much time in the kitchen. Price is not as much of a factor because the young professional has more disposable income than the homemaker.

Take photocopiers as another example. The large corporation buying a copier wants a machine that is fast and offers a variety of features such as color copies, collating, and two-sided copying. But the self-employed professional who works at home has different needs. His budget is limited, so the copier must be inexpensive. And, since he's working from home, space is at a premium, so compactness is an important feature. But speed and capacity are not as crucial, since the work-at-home professional makes fewer copies than the corporate user.

Sometimes, the benefits to stress to various groups of buyers are obvious. In other cases, you must ask the advertiser or his customers which features should be stressed. I once had the assignment of selling a water purification system to two different types of customers: marine users (mostly commercial fishing vessels) and chemical industry users (chemical plants). Same product, two different buyers.

By talking with a few customers in each group, I discovered that marine users put a premium on reliable operation, since they can't afford to be without fresh water while at sea. Weight is also important, because the larger the equipment, the more fuel the boat consumes in hauling the equipment around.

Chemical industry buyers, on the other hand, don't care about weight, because the machine is placed on the plant floor. And, because they have many sources of water, reliability is not as crucial. The chemical industry buyers—all engineers by training—were more interested in technical features. They wanted to know every product specification down to the last nut, bolt, pump, and pipeline. I wouldn't have known these differences existed unless I asked. Which is why it's vital that you get to know your buyer.

But how well do you really know your customers? Knowing that you are writing to farmers, information technology (IT) professionals, or plumbers is just the start. You have to dig deeper. But how?

To write powerful copy, you have to go beyond the demographics to understand what really motivates these people: who they are, what they want, how they feel, and what their biggest problems and concerns are that your product can help solve. Your copy should reach prospects on three levels: *intellectual*, *emotional*, and *personal*.

Intellectual is the first level and, while effective, not as strong as the other two. An intellectual appeal is based on logic, for example, "Buy the stocks we recommend in our investment newsletter and you will beat the market by 50 to 100 percent."

More powerful is to reach the prospect on an *emotional* level. Emotions that can be tapped include fear, greed, love, vanity, and, for fund-raising, benevolence. Going back to our example of a stock market newsletter, the emotional appeal might be, "Our advice can help you cut your losses and make much more money, so you become much wealthier than your friends and neighbors. You'll be able to pay cash for your next car—a Lexus, BMW, or any luxury automobile you care to own—and you'll sleep better at night."

The most powerful way you can reach people is on a *personal* level. Again, from our example of a stock market newsletter: "Did you lose a small fortune in the 2008 stock market crash? So much that it put your dreams of retirement or financial independence on hold? Now you can gain back everything you lost, rebuild your net worth, and make your goal of early retirement or financial independence come true. A lot sooner than you think."

THE BDF FORMULA

To reach your prospects on all three levels—intellectual, emotional, and personal—you must understand what copywriter Mark Ford calls the buyer's "Core Complex." These are the emotions, attitudes, and aspirations that drive them, as represented by the BDF formula, which stands for *beliefs*, *desires*, and *feelings*.

• *Beliefs*. What does your audience believe? What is their attitude toward your product and the problems or issues it addresses?

• *Desires*. What do they want? What are their goals? What change do they want in their lives that your product can help them achieve?

• *Feelings*. How do they feel? Are they confident and brash? Nervous and fearful? What do they feel about the major issues in their lives, businesses, or industries?

For instance, a marketing team did this exercise using IT people, for a company that gives seminars in communication and interpersonal skills for IT professionals. Here's what they came up with in a group meeting:

• *Beliefs.* IT people think they are smarter than other people, technology is the most important thing in the world, users are stupid, and management doesn't appreciate them enough.

• *Desires.* IT people want to be appreciated and recognized. They also prefer to deal with computers and avoid people whenever possible. And they want bigger budgets.

• *Feelings.* IT people often have an adversarial relationship with management and users, both of whom they service. They feel that others dislike them, look down upon them, and do not understand what they do.

Based on this analysis, particularly the feelings, the company created a direct-mail letter that was its most successful ever to promote a seminar, "Interpersonal Skills for IT Professionals." The rather unusual headline: "Important news for any IT professional who has ever felt like telling an end user, 'Go to hell.'"

Before writing copy, write out in narrative form the BDF of your target market. Share these with your team and come to an agreement on them. Then write copy based on the agreed-upon BDF.

Occasionally insights into the prospect's desires and concerns can be gleaned through formal market research. For instance, a copywriter working on a cooking oil account was reading a focus group transcript and came across this comment from a user: "I fried chicken in the oil and then poured the oil back into a measuring cup. All the oil was there except one teaspoon."

This comment, buried in the appendix of a focus group report, became the basis of a successful TV campaign dramatizing the selling point that food did not absorb the oil and therefore was not greasy when cooked in it.

Veteran adman Joe Sacco once had an assignment to write a campaign for a new needle used by diabetics to inject insulin. What was the key selling point?

The diabetics Sacco talked to all praised the needle because it was sharp. A nonuser would probably view being sharp as a negative. But if you have ever given yourself or anyone else an injection, you know that sharper needles go in more smoothly, with minimal discomfort. Sacco wrote a successful ad campaign based on the claim that these needles were sharp, therefore enabling easier, pain-free insulin injections.

Copywriter Don Hauptman advises, "Start with the prospect, not the product." With BDF, you can quickly gain a deeper understanding of your prospects before you attempt to sell them something. Stronger marketing campaigns usually follow.

A CHECKLIST OF "COPY MOTIVATORS"

As I've pointed out, different people buy products for different reasons. If I buy a car, I buy reliable transportation to get me where I want to go, and a used economy car suits me just fine. But the buyer of a Porsche or Mercedes-Benz is buying more than transportation—she's buying status and prestige as well.

Before you write your copy, it's a good idea to review the reasons why people might want to buy your product. To help you, I've compiled the following checklist of "copy motivators": twenty-two motivations people have for making purchases. This list is not comprehensive. But it will get you thinking about who you're writing to and why you're writing to them.

Here, then, are twenty-two reasons why people might buy your product. Don't just read the list; think about each of the reasons and how it might apply to the products you handle.

- ❑ To be liked
- ❑ To be appreciated
- ❑ To be right
- ❑ To feel important
- ❑ To make money
- ❑ To save money
- ❑ To save time
- ❑ To make work easier
- ❑ To be secure
- ❑ To be attractive
- ❑ To be sexy
- ❑ To be comfortable
- ❑ To be distinctive
- ❑ To be happy
- ❑ To have fun
- ❑ To gain knowledge
- ❑ To be healthy
- ❑ To gratify curiosity
- ❑ For convenience
- ❑ Out of fear
- ❑ Out of greed
- ❑ Out of guilt

Think about the things you buy—and why you buy them.

You buy cologne to smell nice. And you want to smell nice to attract a mate.

You buy sports equipment to have fun. You join a spa to become healthy. You buy a gold-plated money clip to be distinctive and feel important.

You buy insurance to be secure. You buy slippers to be comfortable. You buy a refrigerator with an ice maker for convenience.

Once you understand what makes people buy things, you know how to sell—and how to write copy. The rest is just organization and good editing and a few simple techniques.

LONG COPY VS. SHORT COPY

The slogan from an old cigarette commercial was, "It's not how long you make it; it's how you make it long." And that's a good rule of thumb for determining the length of the copy you write.

In other words, the question isn't how many words you should write; it's how much information to include for the copy to accomplish its sales mission.

In general, the length will depend upon three things: the product, the audience, and the purpose of the copy. First, consider your product. Is there a lot you can say about it? And will giving these facts help convince the reader to buy it?

Some products have a lot of features and benefits you can highlight in your copy. These include computers, Bluetooth speakers, cars, books, insurance policies, investment opportunities, courses and seminars, resorts and vacation trips, digital watches, smartphones, and home-exercise equipment.

Many other products don't have a lot of features and benefits, and there isn't too much you can say about them. These include soft drinks, fast food, candy, chewing gum, beer, wine, liquor, jewelry, lingerie, cologne, perfume, soap, laundry detergent, cosmetics, linens, pet food, and shampoo.

For example, there isn't much you can say about a new ginger ale, other than it tastes good and costs less.

But an automatic food processor has a lot of benefits you can highlight. It saves time. It eliminates messy chopping and cutting. It makes cooking easier and more pleasant. It can slice, dice, mash, peel, whip, blend, chop, and crush virtually any food. You can use it for desserts, appetizers, salads, and main courses. It can process fruits, vegetables, meats, nuts, cheeses.

So the length of the copy depends on the product and what there is to say about it.

Second, the length of the copy depends upon the audience. Some customers don't need a lot of information and are not accustomed to reading long text. Others seek out all the facts they can get and will devour as much as you can provide.

A book club wanted to know how much copy to include in the direct-mail package it used to get new members to join the club. It tested sales letters of various lengths: one, two, four, eight, and twelve pages. The twelve-page letter pulled the most orders. Why? One of the reasons is that people who will join a book club are readers—and they will read twelve pages of text if it interests them.

Businesspeople whose service or product revolves around intellectual property or technical methodology often write books outlining their approach to their service (e.g., investment management). Many have told me the same thing: "A prospect who has actually read the book becomes a better potential client and is much more likely to become a client. We prefer an educated client. They are easier to deal with and more likely to accept our recommendations."

The third factor in determining copy length is the purpose of the copy. If you want your copy to generate a sales lead, then there's no need to go into complete detail because you'll get a chance to provide more information when people respond to the lead. On the other hand, an ad that asks for the order by mail must give all of the facts the reader needs to make a buying decision and order the product.

"This is all very nice," you say, "but how do I determine the length that's best for my product, my audience, and my purpose?"

Fortunately, there's an answer. I've developed a tool, which I call the Copy Length Grid (fig. 4.1), that can enable us to determine copy length in a somewhat more scientific and semiquantitative fashion.

The Copy Length Grid says there are two major factors determining whether long or short copy will work best for your promotion: emotion and involvement.

Emotion refers to the degree to which the purchase is emotional. Buying a diamond engagement ring is a highly emotional purchase. But you are moved very little emotionally when deciding which brand of paper clips to buy.

Fig. 4.1: Copy Length Grid

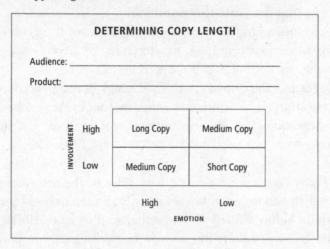

Involvement refers to how much time, effort, and thought goes into the product purchase. As with most large purchases, a lot of consideration goes into the selection and purchase of a diamond engagement ring. But most of us grab the first box of paper clips on the shelf of the stationery store without giving it a second thought.

To use this system for determining copy length, rate these

two criteria—emotion and involvement—as high or low. This dictates what quadrant of the Copy Length Grid you end up in, which in turn gives you at least a rough guideline for copy length.

For instance, the highly emotional purchase of a diamond engagement ring is a "considered purchase"—something you give a lot of thought to—so it rates high in involvement. As you can see in the diagram, this puts us firmly in the upper left quadrant of the grid, indicating that long copy is appropriate for this offer.

On the other hand, paper clips are more of an impulse purchase: we go to the store and pick up the first box we see, providing it's the right size. There's no emotion and very little thought that goes into this purchase.

This puts us in the lower right quadrant of the grid, which indicates that writing long, passionate copy about paper clips probably isn't going to sell more of them.

Of course, the Copy Length Grid is only a rough guide, not a precise analyzer. A number of other factors must also be taken into account when determining copy length. These factors include:

• *Price.* The more expensive a product is, the more copy you generally need to sell it. Lots of copy is needed to build the case for value before asking for the order, so that when the price is finally given, it seems like a drop in the bucket compared to what the buyer is getting in return.

• *Purpose.* Copy that sells the product directly off the printed page or screen (known as "one-step" or "mail-order" copy) usually has to be long, because it must present all product information and overcome all objections. Copy designed to generate a lead ("two-step copy") can be short, since a catalog, brochure, or salesperson will have the opportunity to present product details and overcome objections later.

• *Audience*. People who are pressed for time, such as busy executives and professionals, often respond better to short copy. (Business-to-business copywriter Steve Slaunwhite notes: "The B2B writing style tends to be clear, fact-based, conversational, and focused on down-to-earth performance expectations rather than overblown promises."[2]) Prospects with more time on their hands, such as retirees, as well as those with a keen interest in your offer, such as hobbyists, are more likely to read long copy.

• *Importance*. Products that people *need* (a refrigerator, an air conditioner) can be sold with short copy because . . . well, the prospect *has* to buy them. Products that people *want* but don't *have* to buy (exercise videos, self-help audio programs, financial newsletters) must be "sold," and require long copy to do so.

• *Familiarity*. Short copy works well with products the prospect is already familiar with and understands. This is why vouchers and double postcards are used so frequently to sell subscriptions to popular, well-known magazines (*Newsweek*, *Businessweek*).

Based on the Copy Length Grid and these other factors, it's clear that long copy is not always better, and there are many instances when short or almost no copy works best. This is the case with items that "sell themselves," such as staplers or garden hoses.

But for items that have to be "sold"—life insurance policies, luxury automobiles, IT systems, collectibles, high-end jewelry, career training—long copy is often required because of the high degree of emotion and involvement.

Don't be afraid of long copy. Include as many facts as it takes to make the sale.

At the same time, other factors also affect copy length. For instance, in a banner ad or Google pay-per-click ad, you are limited to short copy. When the user clicks the ad, he is taken to an online sales page where now you have room to say as much as you need to close the deal.

GENERATIONAL MARKETING

Today, perhaps more than ever, advertisers are targeting their marketing to specific generations, the most prevalent being baby boomers and millennials. Table 4-1 provides a quick overview of the various generations including their ages, interests, attitudes, and lifestyles.[3, 4, 5]

Because of the accelerated pace at which technology is developing, the volatile economy, geopolitical instability, and longer life spans, the generations perhaps differ even more sharply than in decades past—and for that reason, marketing targeting specific generations has become commonplace and extremely effective.

Table 4-1. Generational marketing.

Characters	Matures (pre-1945)	Baby Boomers (1945–1960)	Generation X (1961–1980)	Generation Y (1981–1995)	Generation Z (born after 1995)
Formative experiences	Second World War	Cold War	End of Cold War	9/11 terrorist attacks	Economic downturn
	Rationing	Postwar boom	Fall of Berlin Wall	PlayStation	Global warming
	Fixed-gender roles	"Swinging Sixties"	Reagan/ Gorbachev	Social media	Global focus
	Big-band music	Apollo Moon landings	Thatcherism	Invasion of Iraq	Mobile devices
	Nuclear families	Youth culture	Live Aid	Reality TV	Energy crisis
	Defined gender roles–particularly for women	Woodstock	Introduction to the first PC	Google Earth	Arab Spring
		Family-oriented	Early mobile technology	Glastonbury	Produce own media
		Rise of the teenager	Latchkey kids		Cloud computing
			Rising levels of divorce		WikiLeaks
Aspiration	Home ownership	Job security	Work-life balance	Freedom and flexibility	Security and stability

Attitude toward technology	Largely disengaged	Early information technology (IT) adapters	Digital Immigrants	Digital Natives	"Technoholics"— entirely dependent on IT, limited grasp of alternatives
Attitude toward career	Jobs are for life	Organizational— careers are defined by employers	Early "portfolio" careers—loyal to profession, not necessarily to employer	Digital entrepreneurs— work "with" organizations not "for"	Career multitaskers—will move seamlessly between organizations and "pop-up" businesses
Signature product	Automobile	Television	Personal Computer	Tablet/ Smartphone	Google Glass, graphene, nano-computing, 3-D printing, driverless cars
Communication media	Formal letter	Telephone	E-mail and text message	Text or social media	Handheld (or integrated into clothing) communication devices
Communication preference	Face-to-face	Face-to-face ideally, but telephone or e-mail if required	Text message or e-mail	Online and mobile (text messaging)	Facetime
Preference when making financial decisions	Face-to-face meetings	Face-to-face ideally, but increasingly will go online	Online—would prefer face-to-face if time permits	Face-to-face	Solutions will be digitally crowd-sourced

POSITIONING

Al Ries and Jack Trout, authors of *Positioning: The Battle for Your Mind*, write: "Today, positioning is used in a broader sense to mean what the advertising does for the product in the prospect's mind. In other words, a successful advertiser today uses advertising to position his product, not to communicate its advantages or features."

For instance, Coors is positioned as a fresh, pure beer made from the water of the Rocky Mountains. Heineken is positioned as a premium beer "crafted by connoisseurs."

Positioning does not take the place of features and benefits and sales arguments; it *complements* them. If your product fills a special niche, positioning it against a well-known brand is a quick and effective way of establishing the product's identity in the consumer's mind.

But your copy must do more than get the consumer to think about the product; it must also persuade him to buy it. And you can't persuade consumers to buy unless you tell what the product can do for them and why the product does it better than other products can.

5

GETTING READY TO WRITE

Helmut Krone, the art director who helped create such classic campaigns as Avis's "We Try Harder," Volkswagen's "Think Small," and Mennen's "Thanks, I Needed That," had a basic approach to tackling advertising assignments: "I start with a blank piece of paper and try to fill it with something interesting."

But what exactly should the copywriter do to prepare himself for facing that blank piece of paper or empty screen? What information do you need before you're ready to write your copy? How do you go about collecting this information? How do you develop advertising ideas?

This chapter provides answers to these questions and outlines specific techniques you can use to gain familiarity with a product and its market before you tackle your copywriting assignment.

COPYWRITING RESEARCH

There are three basic steps I take to do research on the product, technology, competition, and market for my copywriting assignments.

Step #1—Start with the client.

Most have a wealth of material they can share with you. You simply have to know what to ask for . . . and it starts with this: https://www.bly.com/newsite/Pages/documents/HTPFAC.html

Step #2—Hire an online researcher.

Not to do all of your online research—but to save you time finding both ordinary statistics and obscure data.

My online researcher has written an inexpensive e-book on this topic: http://www.fastonlineresearch.com/

Step #3—Then do your own online research.

In some cases, you don't know that an article or paper provides useful information for your copywriting until you find it or even stumble across it—similar to browsing shelves at your local library and bookstore.

Are there other steps you can take and resources you can explore to find great source material for copywriting assignments? Yes, many. But start with the three listed here.

Note: The Word References feature makes it easy to add footnotes to all information you took from other sources, so if a statement in your copy is questioned, you have backed it up with proper attribution.

ONLINE RESEARCH: A QUICK OVERVIEW

The major search engines are those that have large indexes, are better known and heavily used. For researchers, well-known search engines generally mean more dependable results. When you find similar results in multiple sources, you have a higher degree of confidence. Because these major search engines are commercially backed, they are more likely to be well maintained, updated often, and keep pace with the ever-growing amount of online data.

I assume that you have some familiarity with Google, Yahoo!, Bing, and other major search engines. So in this section, I'm not going waste your time on the basics. Rather, let's focus on how to find information on the Web *that you can trust as accurate and reliable.*

The Stanford (University, California) Persuasive Technology Lab and Makovsky Company Study about Web credibility[1] defines credibility as believability, and it points out that credibility is a perceived quality rather than a piece of information.

Credibility perception results from evaluating multiple criteria simultaneously. These criteria reside within two categories: expertise of the Web site and its trustworthiness. Many considerations go into each of them.

Some of the characteristics of a credible site are[2]:

- It acknowledges author's name, institution, or organization with which the author is associated (if any), and *current* contact information.
- It gives author's credentials and qualifications.
- It provides a complete list of citations. Additionally, you should ask yourself if the sources are authoritative.
- Its information is current (updated, no dead links, no old news, etc.).
- Clues of author's bias are minimal: the author does not try to sell the product or service he's talking about, and advertising on the Web site is minimal or absent.
- "Coverage" is not conditional: you can view the information without limitation of fees, browser technology for pay, or software requirement.

Some of the most reliable sources on the Web include[3] sites that are maintained by institutions or professional associations. The professional Web site may include research, resources, fact sheets, white papers, reports, surveys, press releases, and more. These Web sites are usually credible, especially when the institution or the association is legitimate and even prestigious.

When an online article provides only links to other sources, the credibility should be judged for each linked source separately, as it no longer reflects the original organization's credibility. Among other trustworthy sources for researching market, application, and technology for writing assignments:

- Articles from peer-reviewed scientific and medical journals, found mostly with the aid of scholarly search engines
- Financial sites such as Yahoo!'s
- Major news sources such as the *New York Times*, *USA Today*
- Major business news sources such as *Businessweek*, *Kiplinger's*
- Official government sources for statistical data
- Professional sites

HOW TO PREPARE FOR A COPYWRITING ASSIGNMENT

Here's a four-step procedure you can use to get the information you need to write persuasive, fact-filled copy for your clients:

Step 1: Get All Previously Published Material on the Product

For an existing product, there's a mountain of content the client can send to the copywriter as background material. This information includes:

- Tear sheets of previous ads
- Brochures
- Annual reports
- Catalogs
- Article reprints
- Technical papers
- Copies of speeches and presentations
- Audiovisual scripts
- Press kits
- Market research
- Advertising plans
- Web sites
- Letters from users of the product
- Back issues of e-newsletters
- Files of competitors' ads and sales literature
- Internal memos
- Letters of technical information
- Product specifications, blueprints, plans
- Illustrations and photos of product prototypes
- Engineering drawings
- Business and marketing plans
- Reports
- Proposals
- Customer reviews

Ask the client to provide this background material before you attend any briefings or write the copy. One way to simplify this request for information is to create a checklist of the background material you need.

And, of course, extract as much product information as you can from the Internet. You should spend a lot of time printing out and reading the client's Web site, or at least the pages pertaining to the product you are promoting.

Ask the client who its major competitors are, and study the content on those Web sites as well. Finally, a Google search on key words related to the product can unearth a lot of valuable information that may find its way into your copy.

By studying this background material, the copywriter should have 90 percent of the information he or she needs to write the copy. The copywriter can get the other 10 percent by asking the right questions, either in person or via e-mail, Skype, or telephone. Steps 2 through 4 outline the questions the copywriter should ask the marketer about the product, the audience, and the objective of the copy.

Step 2: Ask Questions About the Product

- What are its features and benefits? (Make a *complete* list.)
- Which benefit is the most important?
- How is the product different from those of the competition? Which features are exclusive? Which are better than the competition's?
- If the product isn't different, what attributes can be stressed that haven't been stressed by the competition?
- What technologies does the product compete against?
- What are the applications of the product?
- What problems does the product solve in the marketplace?
- How is the product positioned against competing products?
- How does the product work?
- How reliable is the product? How long will it last?
- How efficient is the product?
- How economical?
- How much does it cost?
- Is it easy to use? Easy to maintain?
- Who has bought the product and what do they say about it?
- What materials, sizes, and models is it available in?
- How quickly does the manufacturer deliver the product?

- If they don't deliver, how and where can you buy it?
- What service and support does the manufacturer offer?
- Is the product guaranteed?

Step 3: Ask Questions About Your Audience

- Who will buy the product? (What markets is it sold to?)
- What exactly does the product do for them?
- Why do they need the product? And why do they need it now?
- What is the customer's main concern when buying this type of product (price, delivery, performance, reliability, service, maintenance, quality, efficiency, availability)?
- What is the character of the buyer? What type of person is the product being sold to?
- What motivates the buyer?
- How many different buying influences must the copy appeal to? (A toy ad, for example, must appeal to both the parent and the child.)
- If you are writing an ad, read issues of the magazines in which the ad will appear.
- If you are writing direct mail, find out what mailing lists will be used and study the list descriptions.
- If you are writing online ads, study the Web sites and e-newsletters in which they will appear.

Step 4: Determine the Objective of Your Copy

This objective may be one or more of the following:

- To generate traffic
- To generate conversions
- To generate inquiries
- To generate sales
- To answer inquiries
- To qualify prospects

- To generate store traffic
- To introduce a new product or an improvement of an old product
- To keep in touch with prospects and customers
- To build an opt-in e-list of prospects
- To get prospects to purchase the product
- To transmit news or product information
- To build brand recognition and preference
- To build company image
- To provide marketing tools for salespeople

Before you write the copy, study the product you're writing about: its features, benefits, past performance, applications, and markets. Digging for the facts will pay off, because in copywriting, specifics sell.

USING INTERVIEWS TO GATHER FACTS

Of course, collecting background material doesn't always give you all the answers to the questions listed above. At times you must get additional facts from product experts employed by your client: engineers, designers, salespeople, product managers, and brand managers.

Journalists will tell you that a face-to-face interview is better than a phone interview. When you sit across the table from people, you can observe their manner, their dress, their appearance. And you can learn a lot about people from their surroundings.

But the kind of interview you conduct as a copywriter is different from the interview conducted by a reporter. You are not interested in the subject's colorful personality or history. You are seeking only straight facts and product information of an informational nature. Therefore, there's no need to get "up close" to the subject, and a telephone, Skype, or Zoom interview will serve your purpose just as well as an in-person conference.

Actually, there are a number of advantages to doing interviews by phone. First, although the experts have intimate knowledge of the product, advertising is usually not their area of responsibility and, since they are busy, they don't want to get involved with it. A phone interview takes less of their time and busy managers appreciate the efficiency of this method.

Second, it's easier to take notes by phone. Some people get jittery when they see you clicking away on your laptop. But your note taking can be invisible (turn off your Webcam); and the subject can talk in a relaxed, natural manner without being aware that his words are being transcribed.

Third, the copywriter eliminates a trip to and from the client's office. If you're billing by the job, this increases your profit on the assignment. If you're billing by the hour, the time saving is passed on to the client as less time spent on research. Either way, money is saved.

A question beginning copywriters ask is, "Should I use a digital recorder or take notes on my keyboard device?" My answer is that it depends on the situation and on the assignment. By the way, if you do decide to tape the interview, be sure you let the subject know your intention before you begin.

At times, you will be forced to go to a briefing without much background material on the product or the market. In this case, new information will be given to you at a frantic rate. It may help to use a digital recorder, like a smartphone app, in these situations, unless you are fast enough at the keyboard to get it all down.

If, on the other hand, you have been thoroughly briefed and are familiar with the product, you should go into the meeting or the phone conference with a list of specific questions: gaps in your product knowledge that the background material didn't fill. Here you are looking for short, specific answers, and taking notes with PC or pencil does the job.

I almost always e-mail that list of questions to the subject matter expert prior to our interview. About 20 percent of the time, they will type out answers and send them to me via return e-mail.

In an article in the *Writer*, author Dorothy Hinshaw Patent gives these tips for arranging and conducting a successful interview (the basic tips are Dorothy's, but I've added some elaboration to tailor them to the needs of the copywriter).

1. When you call a person to arrange an interview, immediately say who you are, who suggested you get in touch with the person, and why you want to interview him or her.

For example: "Jim Rosenthal? Good morning. My name is Bob Bly, and I'm handling the writing of the ground radar brochure for your ad agency, Anderson & Associates. Lansing Knight at the agency suggested I give you a call and says you know a lot about the design of the radar dish. I'd like to ask you a few questions, if that's convenient."

At times, you will encounter resistance from the person. Here are a few tactics to overcome this:

• *Explain that the interview won't take much time.* ("Well, I've got a small list of just six questions in front of me, and the interview will take but ten minutes to complete. I know you're busy, but do you think we might chat for just ten minutes sometime in the next few days?")

• *Flatter the subject, but be sincere.* ("I suppose I could talk to someone else in your department. But they told me you designed the antenna, and I'd really like to make sure I get the right information for this ad, since it's appearing in *Machine Design*, *Design News*, and *Electronics Digest*.")

• *Explain the importance of your assignment.* ("The article

I'm putting together will be published in this year's annual report, so you can see why I'm trying to get the most accurate information possible.")

• *Use authority as leverage.* ("Shirley Parker, your department head, is working closely with the agency on this one and she felt it would be really important to get your input.")

2. Let the subject select the time and date for the interview. Offer to do the interview in the morning, during lunch, after work, in the evening, or any time that's convenient and comfortable for the person. Some people are too busy during office hours to talk with you, and would prefer to do it after 5:00 or 6:00 P.M., when they can relax. Others may find lunch to be the best time. Schedule the interview at the subject's convenience.

And, just as important, set a firm date and time for the interview, whether it's a face-to-face meeting or a phone call. If you're doing a phone interview, make sure the subject understands that you are setting aside time to be by your phone on that date; the phone interview should be considered as firm a commitment as a meeting.

3. Arrange for interviews well in advance of your deadline. With advertising's short deadlines, this isn't always possible. So it's best to arrange interviews the day you get the assignment. That way, if a key interview subject is out of town or unavailable to meet, you can notify your client and work around it (by extending the deadline or finding someone else to take the subject's place).

4. Do your homework. Come prepared. Read all of the background information before the interview. Know in advance specifically what you want to find out during the interview. Prepare a written list of questions you want to ask.

The subject's time—and your time—is money spent by the client. Don't waste it by asking your subject to give you an education in the basics. Instead, use this valuable time with the expert to get specific, detailed product and marketing facts that the product literature and other background material didn't provide.

5. Be on time for the interview. Many businesspeople are impatient types, and if you miss your appointment, you may never get a second chance. If you can't avoid being late, call in advance and explain the situation.

6. If you are taking notes, type only the information you need to get the facts straight.

7. Establish a rapport with the subject. You two may not have a lot in common, but by showing an interest in and understanding of the subject's problems, you win that person over as a friend. And friends give better interviews than hostile or indifferent subjects.

Maybe you really don't care how difficult it was to manufacture the world's first fiber-optic fishing pole. But the engineer you're interviewing does. So, when he turns to you and says, "Boy, you don't know the problems we had in adjusting tensile strength to the right length-to-diameter ratio," give an understanding nod and a smile. Maybe even say, "I can imagine the problems you've had. But it sure is a great fishing pole." This is just common courtesy, and it helps make the interview go smoothly.

8. Keep a list of the people you interviewed. Also save your notes until the copy is accepted and published and for many months after that. Refer to the list and notes if the client wants to know where you got your information or questions the accuracy of the copy.

9. Show your appreciation. You should always say "thank you" at the close of the interview. A short follow-up e-mail is an even nicer way of showing your gratitude.

ORGANIZING YOUR INFORMATION

At this point, you've read mounds of product literature and have taken notes or underlined key passages, or both. You also have notes or audio files of interviews with product experts. The next step in getting ready to write copy is to type up your notes on your PC and print them out for quick and easy reference.

There are two benefits to this. First, by filtering the information through your brain, to your fingers, and onto the typewritten page, you gain more familiarity with your facts.

When I was in elementary school in the 1960s, teachers often assigned simple reports that could be based entirely on articles found in the encyclopedia. Not much research was involved, and as students, we thought we were pulling the wool over the teacher's eyes by cribbing from the *World Book* or *Encyclopaedia Britannica*.

But the teachers were smart. They knew that, by re-forming the encyclopedia essay in our own words, we would think through the ideas and come to our own conclusions about the subject.

So it is with the copywriter. As you retype interviews and previous copy in your own words, you gain a perspective on the product and generate your own ideas on how to sell it.

Now, to be fair, I know many copywriters who don't go through this step. All I can tell you is that it works for me, and I wouldn't tackle an assignment without first reprocessing all the information I've collected through my brain and keyboard and onto the printed page.

The second advantage of typing up and printing out your

notes is that, by single-spacing, you can reduce hours of interviews and mounds of Web pages, white papers, and product brochures to three to ten or so sheets of paper. Instead of searching through a huge pile of research material to find a key fact, you can quickly locate it in your typed notes using the Word Find feature.

You can also use the notes as a checklist, checking off facts you have used in your copy, circling those facts you must include but haven't yet, and crossing out information that will not be used in the copy. Also, looking at the notes is a lot easier on the eye than trying to decipher page after page of your handwriting.

Convenient as these notes are, I must tell you that once you've gone through the process of keying them into your PC or laptop, the material will be so fresh in your mind that you will probably be able to write the copy with only an occasional glance at the pages to confirm a fact or search for a missing bit of data.

I've written complete ads and e-mail marketing messages without once looking at my notes. After the copy was finished, I used the notes as a checklist to make sure all important facts were included.

SHOULD YOU MAKE AN OUTLINE FIRST?

Many copywriters debate the usefulness of preparing an outline before they write the copy. Again, this depends on your individual approach to writing, and you should make an outline only if it is helpful to you.

With most short pieces of copy—online ads, e-mails, blog posts—the number of separate sales points to be covered is small enough that I can hold the outline in my head. And so there's no need to write it down. But if the copy has an unusually large number of sales points, or if an organizational scheme hasn't popped into my head (as it usually does), I will open a new Word file and work up an outline.

For longer pieces—video sales letters, landing pages, white papers, Web sites—an outline is always helpful to me. I pin the outline to a cork board next to my desk and use it to guide me through the assignment. As first drafts of each section are completed, I check off the section on the outline. This gives me a sense of accomplishment and motivation to go on to the next step.

For decades, I have made a practice of showing at least a rough outline of the promotion to the client and getting approval before I proceed to a first draft. The outline consists of a working headline and a description, either in a numbered or bullet list or in paragraph form, of the theme and contents I intend to cover in the body copy.

Also called a "copy platform," this type of outline ensures that the client agrees with your approach before you write. Without submitting a copy platform and getting it approved, you risk writing an entire promotion on a theme or concept that the client is going to reject, forcing you to write the whole thing over again. This is far less likely to occur when you are writing from an approved copy platform.

How do you organize your outline? The "motivating sequence" presented in chapter 4 is a general outline for all pieces of persuasive writing. Examples of organizational schemes for specific writing tasks—ads, brochures, YouTube videos, Facebook boosted posts, press releases, sales letters, and e-mails—are presented later in the book.

SOCIAL MEDIA AS AN INFORMATION RESOURCE

As you build your network of LinkedIn contacts, Facebook friends, and Twitter followers, you gain access to a large audience of people, some of whom may prove useful to you as you research copywriting projects.

In particular, LinkedIn has many specialty groups that focus on various disciplines, industries, and areas of knowledge. Join the groups related to the subjects you write about since their members are ideally experts in those fields, members of your target markets, or both.

You can conduct informal research just by posing questions to the groups and listening to and keeping a record of the answers. See chapter 15 for more details on how to build your social media presence, use it as a research tool, and write copy for the different ad networks.

ONLINE SURVEYS

Another way to conduct primary research online is to build an opt-in e-list. One of the best ways to do this is by adding a registration box to your Web site in which you offer a subscription to a free online newsletter published by your company.

Once you have your own e-list, you can survey your readers using an online survey tool such as SurveyMonkey. While social media research yields qualitative answers, online surveys also give you quantitative data; for instance, you can determine that X percent of the people you surveyed intend to buy a new widget in the next twelve months, or that Y percent of the list eat kale.

In addition to conducting your own surveys, a Google search can yield many surveys by others on your topic. Surveys give results as percentages, as well as ranking results in order from most to least popular answer, and numbers strengthen copy: they are specific and numbers attract the reader's attention.

THE WRITING PROCESS

Now comes the fun part: the actual writing of the promotion.

Each writer has his or her own way of creating drafts, and you should use the method that's most productive for you.

Some writers start with a headline and rough drawing of the visual, then fill in the body copy. They cannot write a word of body copy until they have a headline and visual concept that pleases them.

Others write the body copy first. Then they extract the headline from the body copy or from their rough notes. Some writers like to start with the longest or most difficult section of a brochure or annual report. Others prefer to "warm up" by writing the easy sections first (e.g., the order form in a direct-mail package, the About page on a Web site).

Whatever your approach to copywriting, one thing you must realize is that you'll rarely get it right the first time. The key to writing great copy is rewriting two, three, four, five, six, seven drafts, or as many as it takes to get it right. Beginning copywriters tend to "freeze up" when faced with having to produce copy. They get nervous because they're afraid to write bad sentences or generate lousy ideas.

But nobody has to see your first efforts, and you don't have to get it right the first time. So don't be afraid to write down all the ideas, phrases, slogans, headlines, sentences, and fragments that come to you. You can always delete words that don't work. But once you have an idea or think of a way to say something, it is lost unless you write it down.

Many copywriters write much more copy than they will need in the final version. This lets them trim the fat and save only the prime cut. In the same way, you should collect much more information than you will use in the final version. This lets you be more selective in the facts you include in your copy.

Basically, copywriting can be divided into a three-stage process, although there may be several rewrites in each stage.

In the first stage, you "get it all down" on your computer. Just let the ideas flow. Don't edit yourself; don't stop ideas from forming. Don't go back and fix up the words you've put on the page, but instead go on and keep writing as long as you have a flow of ideas and phrases you want to put down on paper.

Some writers have trouble letting their thoughts flow freely. They become inhibited and intimidated because they are "writing copy," and that sounds like a difficult and challenging thing to do. If that's the case with you, try pretending you're writing a letter or e-mail to a friend to convince this friend to buy a new product you've become excited about. This technique seems to work, perhaps because letter and e-mail writing, unlike ad writing, are familiar, everyday tasks.

In the second stage, you edit your work. You delete unnecessary words. You rewrite awkward phrases and sentences. You read the copy aloud to make sure that it flows smoothly. And you rearrange and reorder material into a more logical sequence.

Also, you read what you've written to see if it conforms to your criteria for effective, persuasive copy. If it doesn't, you rewrite to strengthen its selling power. This may involve more facts, a better headline, a stronger closing, or a different visual.

In the third stage, you "clean up" your copy by proofreading for spelling and grammar and checking the accuracy of your facts. Here's where you make sure you are consistent in your copy. For example, you don't want to write the company name as "GAF" in the headline and "G.A.F." in the body copy.

Skill in copywriting, and in any type of writing, comes only with practice. As you write copy, you will learn to overcome poor stylistic habits, become more comfortable with your writing, and gain greater control over the English language.

DOCUMENTING YOUR SOURCES

As the copywriter, you are responsible for documenting the sources for all of the information you use in your copy. For instance, if you are writing a brochure for a fertility clinic and say, "One out of six couples in the U.S. is infertile," you need to document the source.

The best method is simply to use the Word footnote or end-note feature so that every quote and fact is easily verified by the client.

After you write a promotion, keep copies of all the source documents on file for at least six to twelve months. You may even want to give a set of these documents to the client for their own files.

A TECHNIQUE FOR PRODUCING PROFITABLE ADVERTISING IDEAS

The copywriter's job is to come up with words and ideas that sell the product or service being advertised. Where do these ideas come from? They come from an understanding of the product, the market, and the mission of the copy—which is to generate sales.

However, even the best copywriters get stuck for ideas at times. Here is a proven nine-step procedure you can follow to come up with ideas for ads, headlines, marketing campaigns, or anything else under the sun:

1. Identify the Problem

The first step in solving a problem is to know what the problem is. But many of us forge ahead without knowing what it is we are trying to accomplish. Moral: don't apply a solution before you have taken the time to accurately define the problem.

2. Assemble Pertinent Facts

In crime stories, detectives spend most of their time looking for clues. They cannot solve a case with clever thinking alone;

they must have the facts. You, too, must have the facts before you can solve a problem or make an informed decision.

Professionals in every field know the importance of gathering specific facts. A scientist planning an experiment checks the abstracts to see what similar experiments have been performed. An author writing a book collects everything he can on the subject: newspaper clippings, photos, official records, transcripts of interviews, diaries, magazine articles, and so on. A consultant may spend weeks or months digging around a company before coming up with a solution to a major problem.

Keep an organized file of the background material you collect on a project. Review the file before you begin to formulate your solution. Use your PC to take notes on your research materials. This step increases your familiarity with the background information, and can give you a fresh perspective on the problem. Also, when you type up notes you condense a mound of material into a few neat pages that show all the facts at a glance.

3. Gather General Knowledge

In copywriting, specific facts have to do with the project at hand. They include the product, the market, the competition, and the media. General knowledge has to do with the expertise you've developed in business and in life, and includes your storehouse of information concerning life, events, people, science, technology, management, and the world at large.

Become a student in the many areas that relate to your job. Trade journals and association Web sites are two valuable sources of industry knowledge. Subscribe to e-newsletters and trade journals that relate to your field. Scan them all, and clip and save articles that contain information that may be useful to you. Organize your clipping files for easy access to articles by subject.

Read books in your field and start a reference library. If a copywriter with twenty years of experience writes a book on radio advertising, and you buy the book, you can learn in a day or so of reading what it took him twenty years to accumulate. Take some night school courses. Attend seminars, conferences, trade shows. Make friends with people in your field and exchange information, stories, ideas, case histories, technical tips.

Most of the successful professionals I know are compulsive information collectors. You should be one, too.

4. Look for Combinations

It has been said more than once, "There's nothing new in the world. It's all been done before." Maybe. But an idea doesn't have to be something completely new. Many ideas are simply a new combination of existing elements. By looking for combinations, for new relationships between old ideas, you can come up with a fresh approach.

The Apple watch, for example, was invented by a team who combined multiple technologies including a digital watch, a smartphone, a blood pressure and heart rate monitor, apps, wireless power charging, and many others. Niels Bohr combined two separate ideas—Rutherford's model of the atom as a nucleus orbited by electrons and Planck's quantum theory—to create the modern view of the atom.

Look for synergistic combinations when you examine the facts. What two things can work together to form a third thing that is a new idea? If you have two devices, and each performs a function you need, can you link them together to create a new product?

5. Sleep on It

Putting the problem aside for a time can help you renew your idea-producing powers just when you think your creative well has run dry.

But don't resort to this method after only five minutes of puzzled thought. First, you have to gather all the information you can. Next, you need to go over the information again and again as you try to come up with that one big idea. You'll come to a point where you get bleary-eyed and punch-drunk, just hashing the same ideas over and over. This is the time to take a break, put the problem aside, sleep on it, and let your unconscious mind take over.

A solution may strike you as you sleep, shower, shave, or walk in the park. Even if it doesn't, when you return to the problem, you will find you can attack it with renewed vigor and a fresh perspective. I use this technique in writing—I put aside what I have written and read it fresh the next day. Many times the things I thought were brilliant when I wrote them can be much improved at second glance.

6. Use a Checklist

Checklists can be used to stimulate creative thinking and as a starting point for new ideas. There are several checklists in this book you can use. But the best checklists are those you create yourself, because they are tailored to the problems that come up in your daily routine.

For example, Jill is a salesperson well versed in the technical features of her product, but she has trouble when it comes to closing a sale. She could overcome this weakness by making a checklist of typical customer objections and how to answer them. (The list of objections can be culled from sales calls made over the course of several weeks. Possible tactics for overcoming these objections can be garnered from fellow salespeople, from books on selling, and from her own trial-and-error efforts.) Then, when faced with a tough customer, she doesn't have to reinvent the wheel but will be prepared for all the standard objections because of her familiarity with the checklist.

However, no checklist can contain an idea for every situation that comes up. Remember, a checklist should be used as a tool for creative thinking, not as a crutch.

7. *Get Feedback*

Sherlock Holmes was a brilliant detective. But even he needed to bounce ideas off Dr. Watson at times. As a professional writer, I think I know how to write an engaging piece of copy. But when I show a draft to my assistant, she can always spot at least a few ways to make it better.

Some people prefer to work alone. I'm one of them, and maybe you are, too. But if you don't work as part of a team, getting someone else's opinion of your work can help you focus your thinking and produce ideas you hadn't thought of.

Take the feedback for what it's worth. If you feel you're right, and the criticisms are off base, ignore them. But more often than not, feedback will provide useful information that can help you come up with the best, most profitable ideas.

Of course, if you ask others to "take a look at this report," you should be willing to do the same for them when they solicit your opinion. You'll find that reviewing the work of others is both educational and fun; it's easier to critique someone else's work than to create your own. And you'll be gratified by the improvements you come up with—things that are obvious to you but would never have occurred to the other person.

8. *Team Up*

Some people think more creatively when working in groups. The people on your team ideally have skills and thought processes that balance and complement your own. For example, in advertising, copywriters (the word people) team up with art directors (the picture people) and software engineers (the computer people).

In entrepreneurial firms, the idea person who started the company will often hire a professional manager from one of the Fortune 500 companies as the new venture grows; the entrepreneur knows how to make things happen, but the manager knows how to run a profitable, efficient corporation.

As an engineer, you may invent a better microchip. But if you want to make a fortune selling it, you should team up with someone who has a strong sales and marketing background.

9. Give New Ideas a Chance

Many businesspeople, especially managerial types, develop their critical faculties more finely than their creative faculties. If creative engineers and inventors had listened to these people, we would not have personal computers, electric cars, airplanes, lightbulbs, smartphones, or hydroelectric power.

The creative process works in two stages. The first is the idea-producing stage, when ideas flow freely. The second is the critical or "editing" stage, where you hold each idea up to the cold light of day and see if it is practical.

Many of us make the mistake of mixing the stages together, especially during the idea-producing stage, when we are too eager to criticize an idea as soon as it is presented. As a result, we shoot down ideas and make snap judgments when we should be encouraging the production of ideas. Avoid making this mistake, as many good ideas are killed this way.

The tasks and procedures outlined in this chapter may seem like a tall order. But don't worry. You can do it. Heed this advice from Lou Redmond, a former Ogilvy & Mather copywriter: "Advertising is one of the minor arts, so don't be intimidated by it."

TYPES OF ADS

Are all print advertisements basically the same? Or are there different techniques for writing ads in different media or ads designed to achieve different goals?

The basics of good print advertising are the same in all media, and the next chapter outlines the nine characteristics of the successful ad. But the tone, content, and focus of the ad can vary with the purpose and the medium in which is appears.

6

WRITING PRINT ADVERTISEMENTS

Despite the downward trend of the newspaper industry, nearly $16 billion annually in the United States is still spent on newspaper ads.[1] So while newspaper readership is certainly on the decline, the death of newspapers is somewhat exaggerated.

Today's print ads perform several marketing missions, chief among them:

1. To sell products directly (mail-order advertising)
2. To generate sales leads (ads that invite you to send for a free brochure or white paper)
3. To build awareness of a product (ads for packaged goods and most consumer products of low unit cost)
4. To drive traffic to brick-and-mortar stores and e-commerce Web sites to increase sales

How do these four categories differ?

Ads that ask for the order—generate a sale directly—do a *complete* selling job. There is no salesperson, no showroom, no retail display, no explanatory brochure to add to the sales pitch. The ad must get attention, hook the reader, and then convince her to send in an order for a product she has never seen.

Mail-order ads are usually lengthy (a half-page newspaper ad can run 1,000 words or more), because they must give complete information. They must answer all of the buyer's questions, lay his fears to rest, and overcome all of his objections in order to close the sale. They must also devote space to the mechanism used in placing the actual order: a Web site link, coupon, toll-free number, or other device.

Ads appealing to buyers in business and industry usually try to generate a sales lead: a response from an interested buyer asking for more information. This is because most products sold to business and industry cannot be sold directly, but require a salesperson to give a presentation and close the sale in person.

Ads that generate leads may give a lot of information or a little, but they never give the full story. To get complete information, the reader must respond to the ad by writing, phoning, mailing in a coupon, or going to a URL. To write a successful lead-generating ad, you must understand the steps in the buying process and where the ad fits in.

Some consumer products are not sold by mail or by salespeople; instead, you can buy them at supermarkets, in department stores, in automobile showrooms, and at fast-food chains. And you usually buy them only when you need them, not when you read an ad about them.

Therefore, the ads for these products don't sell them directly; they seek to generate an awareness of the product and a desire to use it. The ad campaign builds this awareness and desire over an extended period. Burger King knows you don't always rush out to buy a Whopper after viewing a Burger King commercial. The goal of its advertising is to make Burger King the first place you think of when you want a hamburger, so you will eat their product instead of McDonald's or Wendy's.

Some ads promote companies instead of products. This type of advertising, known as corporate advertising, seeks to create a certain image of the company in the mind of the reader. Sometimes these campaigns are aimed at the general public to clear up a misconception about a firm or promote the firm in a general sense. More often they are aimed at stockholders, investors, and the business community. You can find examples of corporate advertising in any issue of *Forbes*, *Fortune*, or *Businessweek*.

Ads also differ according to the type of medium in which they appear: newspaper, magazine, directory, or online ad. Newspapers have long been the backbone of retail advertising campaigns. Retailers run what is called "price and where to buy" advertising—simple display ads that emphasize the price of the merchandise and then direct local consumers to a nearby retail outlet to make the purchase. Such ads usually center around a storewide sale or price-off deal for certain items.

Of course, newspapers attract many other advertisers besides retailers: banks, insurance companies, real estate agents, theaters, restaurants, book publishers, exercise products, and dietary supplements. Some use the simple price-and-where-to-buy format of retailers. Others run more sophisticated campaigns closer to magazine advertisements.

Magazines are different from newspapers in two important ways. First, newspapers are written for a general readership, whereas magazines are published for specialized audiences: women, teens, Christians, business executives, techies, plumbers, engineers, geologists, writers. As a result, magazines are effective for reaching small segments of the market, whereas newspapers are a medium of mass advertising.

Second, the reproduction quality of magazines is far superior to newspapers. Plus, magazines offer the advertiser the use of full color in their advertisements.

Manufacturers use magazines for campaigns that build product awareness and company image. Many consumer magazines have special sections for mail-order advertisements.

There are several advertising options on the Internet. Once the most prevalent was banner advertising, but the response to banner ads has been declining for years. A growing number of PC users have filters that prevent pop-up ads from cluttering their screens. In a 2016 survey of desktop Internet users, 26 percent said that they use ad blockers so they do not see online ads.[2]

An alternative to banner advertising is to run small ads in online newsletters, also known as "e-zines." These ads consist of short text (50 to 100 words is typical) with a hyperlink to a Web site giving more information about the product being advertised.

Whether it is published in a newspaper or a magazine, on a Web site or in an online newsletter, your ad has to work hard to get the reader's attention. The reader, after all, bought the publication or clicked to the Web site for the articles and content, not for the ads. In most major newspapers, for example, your ad competes with hundreds of other ads. And most readers read only a few of the ads in a typical magazine. So the headline and visual must stop the reader in her tracks with an attention-getting concept centered around a strong reader benefit or the promise of a reward.

The size of your ad also affects your approach to writing the copy. A full-page magazine or newspaper ad gives you great flexibility in the size of the illustrations and the amount of copy you use. (Although it is usually shorter, a magazine ad consisting of solid text can contain more than 1,000 words.)

Brand advertisers frequently use full-page ads as the "core" of their campaign for building image and awareness; smaller ads are used for generating sales leads. Many mail-order advertisers have also had great success with smaller ads.

HOW TO WRITE A GOOD ADVERTISEMENT

The techniques used in different advertising situations—magazines versus newspapers, mail order versus image, business versus consumer—are important, to be sure. But the basics of good print advertising are pretty much the same no matter what medium you're writing for.

Here are nine criteria that an ad must satisfy if it is to be successful as a selling tool:

1. The headline contains an important consumer benefit, or news, or arouses curiosity, or promises a reward for reading the copy.

An ad for a long-distance network had the headline, "How to Cut Your Company's Long-Distance Phone Bill 50% or More." The benefit and the reward are clear: you will find out how to cut your phone bill in half if you read the ad.

A savings or discount is one of the most powerful benefits you can feature in a headline. An example is the headline for a mail-order ad offering a podcast on "assertiveness skills." The headline reads: "For $30 you can acquire the same Assertiveness Skills that are now being taught to Fortune 500 managers for up to $5,000 a day."

Never mind that streaming mp3 audio is different from live seminars; this headline creates the impression that you can acquire new knowledge for $4,770 less than others have paid for it: a good bargain, simply but powerfully stated.

Century 21's recruitment ad for real estate agents is also direct: "You Can Make Big Money in Real Estate Sales Right Now." No clever copy. No puns. No fancy photography or special effects. Just an irresistible promise stated in plain, straightforward language.

2. The visual (if you use a visual) illustrates the main benefit stated in the headline.

Note that I said "if you use a visual." Contrary to what some folks may tell you, it is the words, not the pictures, that do most of the selling in many advertisements. Hundreds of successful ads have used words alone to get their message across. Thousands of other successful ads are adorned only with simple photos, spot drawings, and plain-Jane graphics.

If possible, the visual should illustrate the benefit stated in the headline. One of the most effective visual techniques for doing so is the use of before-and-after photos.

DuPont's ad for Teflon explains how coating industrial-process equipment with Teflon protects it from acid. There are two photos. One shows an uncoated mixing blade reduced to scrap by industrial acids. The other shows a Teflon-coated blade used in the same corrosive chemicals; the Teflon blade is in perfect condition. What better way to illustrate and prove the benefit of using Teflon?

A Johnson & Johnson ad headline contains a strong benefit: "Now, from Johnson & Johnson, Toys That Allow Babies to Master New Skills." The photo shows a toddler playing with and obviously enjoying one of the toys. The visual illustrates the benefit of the product and offers proof that babies like these toys.

A visual doesn't have to be elaborate to illustrate the benefit. An ad for homeowners insurance can show the safe, cozy home the insurance helped pay for after the family's first home burned down.

Visuals benefit from captions. The caption either explains what you want the reader to pay attention to in the photo or emphasizes an important fact (e.g., the product is so popular, the factory can barely keep up with the orders, using scarcity as an act-now incentive).

3. *The lead paragraph expands on the theme of the headline.*
A few examples:

> **THE WORSE YOUR CORROSION PROBLEMS, THE MORE YOU NEED DUPONT TEFLON**
> In harsh, highly corrosive chemical process environments, fluid handling components lined or made with DuPont TEFLON® resins and films consistently outlast other materials.

> **YOU CAN MAKE BIG MONEY IN REAL ESTATE SALES RIGHT NOW**
> Business is booming at CENTURY 21. And so are careers. CENTURY 21 offices have helped more people to achieve rewarding careers in real estate than any other sales organization in the world.

> **NOW, FROM JOHNSON & JOHNSON, TOYS THAT ALLOW BABIES TO MASTER NEW SKILLS**
> Your child is growing bigger. Brighter. More curious and eager to learn every day. That's why Johnson & Johnson Child Development Toys are designed to change and grow with your child. To encourage his skill development every step of the way.

4. *The layout draws readers into the ad and invites them to read the body copy.*
Copywriters must consider the graphic elements of the ad and how these graphics will affect readership of their copy. Will the copy be broken up by subheads into many short sections? Will there be a coupon? Should the phone number be in larger type to encourage call-ins? Should the product or process be illustrated using a number of small secondary photos with captions? These are all the concerns of the writer.

The key to getting the ad read is a layout that is clean,

uncluttered, and easy on the eyes. The layout should catch the reader's eye and move it logically from headline and visual to body copy to logo and address.

Chapter 19 covers graphics in detail. But here are some factors that enhance the readability and eye appeal of a layout:

- Use one central visual.
- Headline set in large, bold type.
- Body copy set underneath headline and visual.
- Body copy set in clear, readable type.
- Space between paragraphs increases readability.
- Subheads help draw the eye through the text.
- Copy should be printed black on a white background. Copy printed in reverse, on a tint, or over a visual is difficult to read.
- Short paragraphs are easier to read than long ones.
- The lead paragraph should be very short—less than three lines of type, if possible.
- Simple visuals are best. Visuals with too many elements in them confuse the reader.
- The best layout is a simple layout: headline, large visual, body copy, logo. Additional elements—a subhead, a sidebar, secondary photos—can enhance the ad's readability, but too many make it cluttered and unappealing to the eye.
- Many art directors believe that ads must have a large amount of "white space" (blank space) or else they will look cluttered and people won't read them. But if your typography is clean and readable, you can set a solid page of text and people will read every word of it.

In the same way, there are certain visual techniques that make ads unappealing to readers. These techniques give ads an "addy" look and should be avoided. They include:

- Headlines and blocks of copy set on a slant
- Reverse type (white letters on a black background)
- Tinting of black-and-white photographs with a second color (usually blue or red)
- Tiny type (smaller than 8-point type)
- Long, unbroken chunks of text
- A long listing of company locations and addresses crammed in under the logo
- Type set in overly wide columns
- Poorly executed or reproduced artwork and photography

The look of your ad—its appearance, its layout, how the elements are set up on the page—won't make an ad with poor copy effective. But an unappealing layout can discourage interested consumers from reading brilliant copy that has a lot to offer them. Again, chapter 19 covers the basics of what copywriters need to know about designing ads.

5. The body copy covers all important sales points in logical sequence.

The effective ad tells an interesting, important story about the product. And, like a novel or short story, the copy must be logically organized, with a beginning, a middle, and an end.

If you are describing a product and its benefits, you will probably organize your sales points in order of importance, putting the USP in the headline and taking the reader from the major benefits to minor features as you go through the body copy. In this format, the ad resembles the "inverted pyramid" style used by journalists in news stories.

If the sales points are not related in any way, you might prefer to use a list format, in which you simply list the sales points in simple 1-2-3 fashion.

If you are writing a case history or testimonial ad, you can use chronological order to relate the story as it happened. Or you might use a problem/solution format to show how the product solved a problem.

6. *The copy provides the information needed to convince the greatest number of qualified prospects to take the next step in the buying process.*

The length and number of sales points to be included in the copy depends on what you're selling, who you're selling it to, and what the next step is in the buying process.

Here are some observations on ad length that come from flipping through a single issue of *Good Housekeeping* magazine:

• A full-page ad for Sophia perfume shows a color photo of the perfume bottle superimposed against a background of fireworks. The ad contains no body copy, just a headline and tagline.

SOPHIA IS DESIRE.

SOPHIA IS MYSTERY.

SOPHIA IS FANTASY.

SOPHIA BY COTY. WEAR IT WITH A PASSION.

Apparently, there is not a lot to say about perfume; it is sold on the mystique of what wearing perfume does to enhance your sex appeal.

• An ad for Caltrate 600, a calcium supplement, contains a diagram, a chart, more than four hundred words of body copy, and a straightforward headline announcing, "New Caltrate 600 Helps Keep Bones Healthy." Apparently, there is a lot to say about health products. The ad also invites the reader to write in for a price-off coupon for the product and a "calcium counter."

• Many food ads contain recipes that center around the

product being advertised. The food advertiser hopes the reader will like the recipe and, as a result, purchase the product every time he or she makes the dish.

• The ads for more expensive items—blenders, juicers, flooring, DNA test kits, dentures, real estate—all invite the reader to write or phone for additional information. The advertiser knows there is more to say about these products than can be put in a newspaper or magazine ad; brochures, Web sites, and salespeople will have to augment the efforts of the ad.

When you sit down to write your ad, ask yourself: "What do I want the reader to do? And what can I tell him that will get him to do it?"

7. *The copy is interesting to read.*

"You cannot bore people into buying your product," writes David Ogilvy in *Ogilvy on Advertising*. "You can only interest them in buying it."

People will read your ad only as long as it is interesting to them. They will not read copy that is boring, in content or in style.

As a writer and a reader, you know when writing is interesting to read and when it is dull. The style should be crisp, lively, and light. The copy should have rhythm and clarity.

But great style won't save an ad without substance. The copy must appeal to the reader's self-interest. It must contain benefits, or news, or it must solve the reader's problem. It cannot entertain for entertainment's sake; it must present compelling reasons why the product is desirable to the reader.

Here are a few things that add interest to advertisements:

• Copy that speaks directly to the reader's life, the reader's emotions, the reader's needs and desires
• Copy that tells a story

- Copy about people
- Copy written in a personal style, so that it sounds like a letter from a friend: warm, helpful, and sincere
- Testimonials from celebrities
- A free offer (of a gift, a pamphlet, a brochure, or a sample)
- Copy that contains important news, especially practical advances in health care and medical science
- Copy that addresses major issues: beauty, health, old age, parenting, marriage, home, security, family, careers, education, social issues
- Copy that answers questions readers have in their minds
- Copy about a subject that interests the reader

Here are some things that make ads boring:

- Copy that centers on the manufacturer—that talks about the company, its philosophy, its success
- Copy that talks only about how the product is made or how it works rather than what it can do for the reader
- Copy that tells readers things they already know
- Long-winded copy with big words, lengthy sentences, and large unbroken chunks of text
- Copy in which all sentences are the same length (varying sentence length adds snap to writing)
- Copy that gives only product features and not benefits
- Copy without a point of view—without a strong selling proposition or a cohesive sales pitch (such copy presents the facts without really showing the reader how these facts relate to his needs)
- Ads with cluttered layouts and poorly reproduced visuals that look boring and turn the reader off

8. The copy is believable.

"Cynicism and suspicion abound today," said ad agency owner Amil Gargano, "much of it with good reason. That's why advertising won't work unless it is trusted, no matter how clever it might seem. And the way to be trusted is to be honest and sensitive to the people you want to reach."

The copywriter's task is not an easy one. In addition to getting attention, explaining the product, and being persuasive, you must overcome the reader's distrust and get her to believe you.

We've already discussed a number of techniques for building credibility: testimonials, demonstrations, research tests. But these are just techniques. The key to being believed is to tell the truth.

This is not as radical as it sounds. Contrary to the image of advertising executives as slick hucksters, many are honest, professional businesspeople who believe in the products they're selling. They would not create advertising for a product that is harmful or inferior. And, although ethics plays a part, the real reason for this is a simple fact about advertising.

Clever advertising can convince people to try a bad product once. But it can't convince them to buy a product they've already tried and didn't like.

So you see, there's no percentage in writing ads that tell lies. Besides being unethical, it's unprofitable for the agency and the advertiser, and it gives advertising a bad name.

Fewer and fewer practitioners engage in such unethical behavior. The majority believe that the product they are advertising can do you a lot of good. When you believe in your product, it's easy to write copy that is sincere, informative, and helpful. And when you are sincere, it comes across to readers and they believe what you've written.

9. *The ad asks for action.*

The ad should ask the reader to take the next step in the buying process, whether that step is to send in an order, call a sales office, visit a store, try a sample, see a demonstration, or go to a Web site or landing page.

You are already familiar with coupons, toll-free numbers, and other devices used to urge the reader to respond to the ad. Barry Kingston, merchandising director of *Opportunity* magazine, gave these tips on getting the best response to your ad:

- Use a street address instead of a post office box number. A street address gives the impression that your firm is large, stable, and well established.
- If most of the magazine's readers qualify for your offer, use a toll-free number to increase response. But if you want to qualify your leads, use a regular company phone number.
- If the product can be ordered directly with a credit card, include a toll-free number.
- Use a company phone number to add credibility to both e-commerce and print advertising.
- A coupon boosts response between 25 and 100 percent.
- Asking the reader to send in a letter reduces response but produces highly qualified leads (people with genuine interest in the product).

DOES YOUR AD NEED A SLOGAN?

A slogan, also known as the tagline, is a phrase or sentence that appears beneath the company logo in an ad or series of ads. The slogan is used to sum up the central message of the ads, or to make a broad statement about the nature of the company.

Some well-known slogans:

WE'RE AMERICAN AIRLINES: DOING WHAT WE DO BEST

MAXWELL HOUSE: GOOD TO THE LAST DROP

LIKE A GOOD NEIGHBOR, STATE FARM IS THERE

NOTHING BEATS A GREAT PAIR OF L'EGGS

PRUDENTIAL: GET A PIECE OF THE ROCK

IF THEY COULD JUST STAY LITTLE TILL THEIR CARTER'S WEAR OUT

LONG DISTANCE: THE NEXT BEST THING TO BEING THERE

AMERICAN EXPRESS: DON'T LEAVE HOME WITHOUT IT

These slogans have built consumer awareness of brand-name products because they are pithy and memorable, and because they sum up the nature of the product or service. However, there are hundreds of slogans that have been used for a few months and then dropped from ads, never to be written or uttered again.

Should you use a slogan in your ad?

It depends on whether your product lends itself to this technique. In copywriting, the rule should be "Form follows function." In other words, use a technique if it works and seems natural. But don't force-fit a copy technique in an ad where it doesn't belong.

Applying this rule to slogans, I'd say use a slogan if your product's key selling proposition or its nature can be summed up in a single, catchy statement. But if the essence of your product or business can't be captured in a one-liner, don't force it, or the result will be an artificial slogan that detracts from the ad and makes you, your ad agency, your employees, and your customers embarrassed and uncomfortable.

For example, let's say your company manufactures flypaper. The company president says, "Our slogan should be: The Leader in Quality Flypaper." But this slogan restricts you to a narrow product category. If you decide to expand and manufacture flyswatters, you'll have a hard time because people will think of you as a flypaper company only.

Then your ad agency says, "Let's think big. You're not just in flypaper; you're in 'pest control.' How about 'Leaders in the Science of Pest Control' as a slogan?" But this is too general. Pest control can be anything from spraying termites to catching rats. And your company really doesn't plan to get involved in these areas.

So the danger with slogans is that some are too narrow and pigeonhole you in a specialty, while others are so broad-based that they lose any real meaning or applicability to your business.

Slogans work best when they are memorable and when they are repeated to the target audience numerous times over a prolonged period. For instance, Allstate's slogan has been "You're in Good Hands" since 1950.

MANUSCRIPT FORMAT FOR AD COPY

Today most of my copy is sent to clients via e-mail as attached Microsoft Word files, a Dropbox folder, or Google Docs. If your clients are PC literate, they can use the Word "Track Changes" feature to make their comments on your copy, eliminating the need to print it out and mark it up by hand.

Some copywriters include labels in their copy that indicate whether the text the reviewer is reading is for a headline, subhead, body copy, caption, boxed material, or the description of a visual. Some writers type these descriptions in parentheses in the left margin. I type them in capital letters flush against the left margin, with a colon following the label but with no parentheses. This way, my manuscript looks very neat because everything is flush with the left margin.

A sample page of manuscript is shown here:

ThermoPal ad—page 1

HEADLINE:
How to Keep Your Iced Tea on Ice

VISUAL:
Tall glass of iced tea sitting next to an open ThermoPal thermos.

COPY:
Nothing quenches thirst like a cold iced tea on a hot summer's day.

But the tea in a can or a carton won't stay cool in summer heat. And an ordinary thermos won't fit in your briefcase or bag or lunch box.

Introducing ThermoPal, the pint-size thermos that makes sure your cool summer drinks stay cool . . . and is small enough to go where you go.

SUBHEAD:
A big gulp in a tiny bottle

COPY:
ThermoPal is tiny enough to fit in the slimmest briefcase or in a tightly packed backpack. But it's big enough to hold a frosty 8 ounces of tea, lemonade, or fruit juice. That's as much as you get in a tall, cool glass at home or from a machine.

But by carrying your lunchtime drink in ThermoPal, your refreshment costs a few pennies instead of a dollar or more, as it would from a vending machine or fast-food stand. So ThermoPal pays for itself in just a few weeks . . . and brings big savings over the long, hot summer.

We know you'll be delighted with ThermoPal for years to come. If not, just send the lid back in the mail for a full refund—no questions asked.

To order ThermoPal, clip and mail the reply coupon. Or visit www.thermopal.com/offer. But hurry—supplies are limited, and we usually sell out by the middle of spring.

COUPON:

❏ *YES*, I want to keep cool. Please send me ___ ThermoPals at $8.95 each plus $1.00 each for shipping and handling. My check is enclosed. If not satisfied, I'll send back the top of the thermos for a full refund of my money.

Name _____

Address City State Zip _____

Mail coupon to: ThermoPal

                              Box XXX

                              Anytown, USA XXXXX

A CHECKLIST OF ADVERTISING IDEAS

Copywriters don't sit down with an assignment and say, "I want to do a testimonial ad" or "Let's make it a how-to ad." They first study the product, the audience, and the purpose of the advertisement. Then they use the technique that fits the assignment.

Still, it helps to be familiar with the various types of ads that have been successful over the years: how-to, testimonials, before-and-after, and others.

Below is a checklist of many of these categories. When you're stuck for an idea, a quick review of the list might give you inspiration—you might scan the list and say, "Hey, here's an approach that works with what I'm selling!" Turn to this checklist not as a crutch but as an aid in producing selling ideas:

❏ QUESTION AD—asks a question in the headline and answers it in the body copy.

❏ QUIZ AD—copy presents a quiz. Reader takes quiz. Her

answers determine whether she is a prospect for the product or service being offered.

❑ NEWS AD—announces a new product or something new about an existing product.

❑ DIRECT AD—gives a straightforward presentation of the facts.

❑ INDIRECT AD—has an obscure headline designed to arouse curiosity and entice the reader to read the body copy.

❑ REWARD AD—promises a reward for reading the ad.

❑ COMMAND AD—commands the reader to take action.

❑ PRICE-AND-WHERE-TO-BUY AD—announces a sale. Describes the product, gives the price and discount, and tells where to buy it.

❑ REASON-WHY AD—presents reasons why you should buy the product.

❑ LETTER AD—an ad written in letter form.

❑ BEFORE-AND-AFTER—shows the improvements gained by using the product.

❑ TESTIMONIAL—a user of the product or a celebrity speaks out in favor of the product.

❑ CASE HISTORY—a detailed product success story.

❑ FREE INFORMATION AD—offers free brochure, pamphlet, or other information. Ad concentrates on getting the reader to send for free literature rather than on selling the product directly.

❑ STORY—tells a story involving people and the product.

❑ "NEW WAVE"—relies on far-out graphics to grab attention.

❑ READER IDENTIFICATION—headline is used to select the audience.

❑ INFORMATION AD—ad gives useful information relating to the use of the product in general rather than pushing the product directly.

❑ LOCATION AD—features the product used in an unusual location to highlight its versatility, usefulness, convenience, or ruggedness.

- ❑ FICTIONAL CHARACTERS—ad centers around a fictional character such as Mr. Whipple or the Green Giant.
- ❑ FICTIONAL PLACES—ad centers around a fictional place such as Marlboro Country.
- ❑ CARTOONS AND CARTOON STRIPS.
- ❑ ADVERTISER IN AD—the advertiser appears in the ad to speak about his own product.
- ❑ INVENT A WORD—the advertiser invents a word to describe his product or its application. (The term "athlete's foot" was invented by adman Obie Winters to sell his client's product, a horse liniment that could also cure ringworm of the foot; Gerard Lambert popularized "halitosis" to sell Listerine.)
- ❑ COMPARATIVE ADVERTISING—shows how your product stacks up against the competition.
- ❑ CHALLENGE—challenges the reader to find a better product than yours.
- ❑ GUARANTEE AD—focuses on the guarantee, not the product.
- ❑ OFFER AD—focuses on the offer, the sale, and not the product.
- ❑ DEMONSTRATION—shows how the product works.
- ❑ PUN—headline attracts attention with clever wordplay. The pun is explained in the copy.
- ❑ CONTESTS AND SWEEPSTAKES.
- ❑ TIE-IN WITH CURRENT EVENTS—to add timeliness and urgency to the selling proposition.

WRITING FRACTIONAL DISPLAY ADS

As a copywriter, you will mostly be writing full-page ads in magazines and newspapers. But many mail-order advertisers get better results from half-page ads, usually but not always in a vertical layout to resemble a column of type in the paper.

These are often designed and written as advertorial or native advertising, which means they are designed to look like articles and not advertisements. The logic of this approach is sound, as "editorial" content (articles) get higher readership and are trusted more than items that are obvious ads.

To get prospects for the product to notice your ad, state in the headline either who the reader is (e.g., "prescription drug users") or what their problem is (e.g., "wet basement").

Sales appeals that work in classified mail-order advertising include promises that the customer will obtain love, money, health, popularity, success, leisure, security, self-confidence, better appearance, self-improvement, pride of accomplishment, prestige, pride of ownership, or comfort; will receive entertainment; will save time; will eliminate worry and fear; will satisfy curiosity, self-expression, or creativity; or will avoid work or risk.

Effective words and phrases to use in your small ads include: *free, new, amazing, now, how to, easy, discover, method, plan, reveals, show, simple, startling, advanced, improved,* and *you.*

In a full-page ad, the advertisement is the only thing the readers see on that ad. So they are not distracted by any other ads on the page.

But when you run a half-page ad, there are many other ads competing for attention. Again, proven effective techniques for attracting your target prospects to your ad include identifying the ideal reader in the headline (e.g., "heart patients") or the problem the prospects want to alleviate (e.g., "memory loss").

WRITING CLASSIFIED AND TINY DISPLAY ADS

I urge you to test some classified and one- or two-inch display ads. Yes, they are small and seem almost insignificant. But they also cost little to run and test. Therefore, they can produce a profitable ROI. And classified ads that make money can be run for long periods and tested in multiple publications.

One of my most successful mail-order ads, which ran continuously for many years in *Writer's Digest*, reads as follows:

> **MAKE $100,000/YEAR** writing ads, brochures, promotional material for local/national client. Free details: CTC, 22 E. Quackenbush, Dept. WD, Dumont, NJ 07628.

Here are some other examples of how to write classified mail-order ads:

> **EXTRA CASH**. 12 ways to make money at home. Free details . . .

> **MAIL-ORDER MILLIONAIRE** reveals moneymaking secrets. FREE 1-hour cassette . . .

> **SELL NEW BOOK** by mail! **400% profit!** Free dealer information . . .

> **GROW** earthworms at home for profit . . .

> **CARNIVOROUS AND WOODLAND** terrarium plants. Send for FREE catalog.

> **ANCESTOR HUNTING?** Trace your family roots the easy way. Details free . . .

The measure of a successful classified ad is the cost per inquiry. Therefore, if you can get your message across in fewer words, you pay less for the ad and, as a result, lower your cost per inquiry.

Make your classifieds as short and pithy as possible. Here are some tips for reducing your word count:

• *Be concise.* Use the minimum number of words needed to communicate your idea. For example, instead of "Earn $500 a Day in Your Own Home-Based Business," write "Work at Home—$500/Day!"

• *Minimize your address.* You pay the publication for every word in your classified, including your address. Therefore, instead of "22 E. Quackenbush Avenue," I write "22 E. Quackenbush." The mail will still be delivered, and I will save one word. This can add up to significant savings for ads run frequently in multiple publications.

• *Use phrases and sentence fragments* rather than full sentences.

• *Remember your objective.* You are asking only for an inquiry, not for an order. You don't need a lot of copy, since all you are asking the reader to do is send for free information.

• *Use combination words, hyphenated words, and slash constructions.* For instance, instead of "GROW EARTH WORMS," which is three words, write "GROW EARTHWORMS," which counts as two words, saving you a word.

In classified ads, the best way to generate a response is to ask for an inquiry rather than an order. This is done by putting a phrase such as "free details," "free information," "free catalog," or similar phrase, followed by a colon and your address (e.g., Free Details: Box 54, Canuga, TN 44566).

Should you charge for your information? Some advertisers ask the prospect to pay for the information either by sending a small amount of money (25¢, 50¢, $1, and $2 are typical) or by sending a self-addressed envelope with the postage already on it.

The theory is that asking for postage or a nominal payment brings you a more qualified lead and therefore results in a higher percentage of leads converted to sales.

My experience is that it doesn't pay to charge for your information kit, because doing so dramatically cuts down on the number of leads you will receive.

Whenever you offer information to generate an inquiry, I believe it's best to make it free. The exception might be if you are offering a very expensive and elaborate catalog, for which you charge $1 or $2 to cover your costs.

In your classified ads, put a key code in the address, so when you get inquiries, you can track which ad generated them. For instance, in my ad "MAKE $100,000/YEAR WRITING," the key code "WD" refers to *Writer's Digest* magazine. Since the ad runs every month, I don't bother adding a code number to track the month. If you wanted to do so, you could. For example, "Dept. WD-10" would mean *Writer's Digest* magazine, October issue (the tenth month of the year). Keep track of the key code on each inquiry, and record the information in a notebook or spreadsheet to measure ad response.

We have already discussed the two key measurements of two-step classified advertising: the cost per inquiry and the percentage of inquiries converted to orders. The bottom line is this: Did the sales the ad generated exceed the cost of the ad space? If they did, it was profitable. If they didn't, the ad isn't working, and a new ad should be tested.

Place your classified ads in publications that have mail-order classified ad sections. Contact the magazines that interest you and ask for their media kits, which include details on circulation, advertising rates, and readership, and a sample issue of the publication. Ask if the publisher will send several sample issues.

Look at the classified ad sections in the publications. Are the ads for products similar to yours? If so, that's a good sign. See if these ads repeat from issue to issue. The advertisers would not repeat them unless the ads were working. If this publication is working for their offers, it can work for yours, too.

Classified ad sections are divided by various headings. Place your ad under the appropriate heading. If you don't see an appropriate heading, call the magazine and ask if it will create one for you.

If you sell information by mail, avoid putting your classified under the heading "Books and Booklets." This will reduce orders. Instead, put the ad under a heading related to the subject matter. For example, if you are selling a book on how to make money cleaning chimneys, place the ad under "Business Opportunities."

You can test a classified or small display ad by running it just one time in a publication. The problem is, most magazines, and even weekly newspapers, have long lead times—several weeks or more—for placing ads. If you place the ad to run one time only and the ad pulls well, you then must wait several weeks or months until you can get it in the publication again.

In a weekly newspaper or magazine, I test a classified ad by running it for one month—four consecutive issues. For a monthly publication, I test it for three months—three consecutive issues. If the first insertion is profitable, I will probably extend the insertion order for several months so the ad runs continuously with no interruption.

With a full-page ad, you usually get the greatest number of orders the first time the ad runs in the magazine. Response declines with each additional insertion; at the point where the ad is not going to be profitable in its next insertion, you pull it and try another ad.

The reason for this response pattern is that the first time the ad runs, it skims the cream of the prospects, getting orders from those most likely to buy. Those who buy from the first insertion of the ad will not buy when it runs again. Therefore, each time the ad runs it reaches a smaller and smaller audience of potential new buyers.

While response to full-page ads declines with each insertion, the response to either a fractional ad or a classified ad can remain steady for many insertions. Indeed, some mail-order operators (and I am one of them) have run the same classified ad monthly in the same magazine for years at a time, with no decline in response.

Response sometimes increases during the first twelve months the ad is run, as people see the ad over and over again and eventually become curious enough to respond. Some people who responded once, received your sales literature, and didn't buy may respond several times, and get your literature several times, before they eventually break down and buy. Also, keep in mind that each issue reaches a number of new subscribers via subscriptions and newsstand circulation, so the total audience for a classified remains fairly constant.

RESPONSE MECHANISMS

You should always tell the interested prospect what the next stop is and give instructions on how to take action along with a reason to do so. Some of the more popular response options include:

- Toll-free number.
- Standard postal mail.
- Business reply mail.
- E-mail.
- Web form.
- Chatbot.
- Quick response code (fig. 6.1).
- Visit to store or showroom.
- Visit from salesperson to consumer's home.
- Text.

Pick the response option that works best for your offer as your primary response mechanism. But also offer one or two alternatives, as different people respond in different ways (e.g., some do not text).

Fig. 6.1: Quick Response Code (QRC). The prospect scans the graphic with her smartphone and is immediately taken to a Web page featuring your offer or whatever else you wish to show her.

7

WRITING DIRECT MAIL

According to the Data and Marketing Association (DMA), the amount of money spent on direct mail in 2018 was $38.5 billion.[1] Today, more than 120 billion pieces of direct mail pass through the post office each year.[2]

There are a number of factors that account for direct mail's popularity as an advertising medium.

First, you can measure the results by counting how many order forms or reply cards come back. With print ads and broadcast commercials you don't always know how effective your efforts have been. But direct-mail advertisers always know whether a mailing is profitable or not.

Second, direct mail frequently generates a higher ROI than other media. The copywriter for a small chain of furniture stores notes that direct mail draws more people to the stores than newspaper ads, TV commercials, even digital marketing. He says: "People walking into the store with the direct-mail piece, along with the burst in sales when they go out, makes it clear that they read direct mail and it works extremely well."

In its loyalty program, when Nordstrom stopped sending

reward notes to customers via postal mail, the retailer saw a reduction in foot traffic in all of its stores.[3]

Third, direct mail can be targeted to select groups of prospects through the careful selection of the proper mailing lists. The copy for each mailing can be tailored to the needs of the various groups of prospects you want to reach. And you can send as few—or as many—mailing pieces as your budget allows. Which makes direct mail cost-effective for both big corporations and smaller advertisers.

Fourth, direct mail gives you great flexibility in your presentation. Print advertising is limited by the size of the page, broadcast by the length of the commercial. Direct-mail writers can use as many words and pictures as it takes to make the sale. (I recently received a direct-mail piece that featured a sixteen-page sales letter!) Your mailing can even include a sample of the product or a gift for the reader.

Because of these advantages, many advertisers use direct mail for a wide variety of applications:

- To sell products by mail
- To generate sales leads
- To answer product inquiries
- To distribute catalogs, newsletters, and other sales literature
- To motivate the sales force
- To keep in touch with former customers
- To get more business from current customers
- To follow up inquiries
- To tie in with other media such as telemarketing, print advertising, and broadcast (Publishers Clearing House, for example, used to run TV commercials alerting consumers to look for the Clearing House sweepstakes offer in the mail)

- To invite prospects to attend seminars, conferences, hospitality suites, and trade show exhibits
- To renew subscriptions, memberships, service contracts, and insurance policies
- To get customers to come to the store
- To distribute information, news, product samples
- To conduct research surveys
- To build goodwill
- To announce a sale

Fifth, contrary to what you might think, direct-mail response rates are on the rise, having increased on average 14 percent since 2008. During that same period, e-mail response rates declined by a hefty 57 percent.[4]

A PERSONAL MEDIUM

The main difference between direct mail and space advertising is that mail is a personal medium. A letter is a one-to-one communication from one human being to another. An ad appearing in a magazine will be seen by thousands or millions of other readers. But a letter is for your eyes only.

Now, it's true that most direct mail is mass-produced and distributed in bulk mailings to thousands of prospects. Still, the reader views mail as more personal than a magazine or newspaper. The trick is to take advantage of this—by creating direct mail that captures the best characteristics of personal mail.

Unlike an ad, a sales letter is signed. So the writer can use the first person—"I" writing to "you," the reader—to personalize the sale message.

The tone of the letter should also be personal. Successful direct-mail writers favor an informal, conversational style.

They use contractions, colloquial language, and short, snappy sentences. Their letters brim with personality, enthusiasm, warmth, and sincerity.

Unlike print advertising, which many newbie copywriters have limited experience with, direct mail should come easy; we all have experience in letter writing. But too many direct-mail letters sound like . . . well, like advertising. When you write direct mail, don't suppress your natural style. Let the words flow in your own voice. Write the direct-mail letter as if you were writing a letter to a friend.

Direct mail is almost always a response-oriented medium. It asks for the order (or at least for some type of action) *now*, not in a day or a week or a month. Direct-mail writers need to generate an immediate response from the reader. This is why most direct-mail packages include an order form, a reply envelope, and copy that tells you to "act now—don't delay—send in your order TODAY!"

As I mentioned, you have great flexibility in the elements you include in your mailing package. As the copywriter, you decide. Should the package contain a letter? A brochure? An order form? A reply card? A sample? A second letter? A second or third brochure?

The "classic" direct-mail package contains an outer envelope, a letter, a brochure, and a reply card. But knowledgeable direct-mail writers vary this format to suit their objectives. Of course, there's always the option of using a completely different format, such as a self-mailer or an invoice stuffer.

The heart of the package is the sales letter. Most of the selling is done in the letter; the brochure is used to highlight sales points, illustrate the product, and provide technical information not appropriate to a letter. There's an old saying among direct-mail writers: "The letter sells; the brochure tells."

SALES LETTER MECHANICS

It's easy to begin an ad, because they all follow the same format: headline first, visual that illustrates the headline, and lead paragraph that expands on the headline.

But the writer has more options with the start of a sales letter.

First, there's the choice of whether to personalize the letter with the individual recipient's name and address, or send out a form letter.

To personalize, you use a computer to generate customized letters for each person on the mailing list, and that can be expensive. Personalized letters generally get a better response, as long as they look personally typed and sound personal in tone. Don't overdo it by repeating the person's name over and over in the letter ("so, MR. RAYMOND, we have reserved this special offer for you and the whole RAYMOND family . . ."). This technique sounds insincere; you wouldn't use the person's name that often if you were speaking face-to-face.

Also, avoid the old-fashioned "ink jet" printing systems that produce letters in which the name is obviously inserted into a form letter. The letter should look as if it were typed by hand; you can achieve this effect with a laser printer.

In many assignments, economy will require that you use preprinted letters. Some advertisers print form letters and then type in each prospect's name and address (this is the "match and fill" technique). But match and fill is time-consuming, and mailing tests show that match-and-fill letters often don't pull any better than form letters with headlines running across the top.

There are exceptions. It pays to personalize sales letters going to existing customers, and also when writing to high-level executives. The bigger the corporation and the higher up the corporate ladder the recipient, the more likely personalization is to pay off.

Set the letter headline in large, bold typeface, such as 16-point Arial Black. You can place the headline above the salutation, and as an option, you can center the headline and put it in a box to call attention to it. Such a box is called a Johnson Box.

In some letters, you may decide against a headline and simply start with the salutation: Dear Friend, Dear Reader, Dear Business Executive, Dear Friend of the Smithsonian Institute.

A salutation that identifies with the reader's special interest—Dear Farmer, Dear Lawyer, Dear Computer Enthusiast, Dear Future Millionaire—is always better than Dear Sir, Dear Madame, or Dear Friend.

Sometimes you will use a salutation only. Sometimes, a salutation and a headline. In some cases, a headline without a salutation may be more appropriate.

15 WAYS TO START YOUR SALES LETTER

The first sentence of your letter is the most important one. This sentence signals whether there is something of interest in your letter or whether it is worthless junk mail to be thrown away without a second glance. The lead must hook the reader's attention, but it must also entice him to read further.

Over the years, letter writers have found that there are certain types of openings that are more effective in direct mail than other types. Here are samples of fifteen of those leads. When you're struggling with your first letters, turn to these examples for possible ideas on how to structure your own opening.

1. State the Offer
The offer consists of the product for sale, its price, the terms of the sale (including discounts), and the guarantee.

If your offer is particularly attractive, you may make the

offer—and not the product or its benefits—the theme of the letter. Here's how the International Preview Society featured a free ten-day trial offer in a sales letter selling Beethoven CDs:

> **Yours FREE for 10 days—**
> **the legendary music of Beethoven—**
> **Nine Symphonies that epitomize the**
> **beauty and harmony denied him in life.**
> **Plus FREE Preview bonus.**
>
> Dear Music Lover,
>
> Beethoven. The name alone calls to mind some of the greatest music of the ages . . .

The letter writer figured that the reader already appreciated Beethoven, so there was no need to sell her on Beethoven's symphonies. And it's hard to sell one set of classical recordings over another based on the orchestra or conductor or the quality of the performance. So the copywriter concentrated on the offer—a free trial plus a free bonus CD—just for accepting the trial offer.

The headline was typed with an ordinary typewriter font and positioned where the reader's name and address would normally appear in a personal letter.

2. Highlight the Free Literature

Letters that seek to generate inquiries from potential customers usually offer the reader a free brochure, booklet, catalog, or other piece of sales literature. You can increase response by stressing the offer of free literature, and by centering the sales pitch on the benefits of the literature rather than those of the product or service.

Here's an example from a letter sent to me by the Mutual Life Insurance Company of New York:

Dear Friend:

We have reserved for you a free copy of Prentice Hall's *TAX-SAVING STRATEGIES*, a helpful book for Corporate Executives and Professionals. It contains practical, timely, and useful ways for you to maximize the value of your deductions and save dollars.

3. Make an Announcement

If you have something new to announce—a special offer, a new product, a new club, a one-of-a-kind event—start your letter with this important news, as in this letter from Calhoun's Collectors Society:

In the world of U.S. stamps, there is only one name older than that of the Federal Bureau of Engraving and Printing itself. The revered house of Scott—known since 1863 as the ultimate authority on American philately.

Now, for the first time ever, Scott's stamp experts have selected the subjects to be commemorated in a limited philatelic edition that is unprecedented in collecting annals.

4. Tell a Story

Copy written in story format has great reader appeal. First, it creates empathy with the reader. By telling a story that relates to the reader's own situation, you build a bridge between the reader's needs and your sales pitch. Second, people are familiar with stories and enjoy reading them. The news they get from newspapers, magazines, and television is related to them in narrative form. Stories hold their interest and get them to read letters they might otherwise put aside.

A subscription letter for *Inc.* magazine begins with the story of a man who quit his job to become an entrepreneur—a move many of us with corporate positions may daydream of now and then.

Dear Executive,

Three years ago this month, a man I know—he was then a
vice president of a big corporation in Illinois—walked into his
boss's office and handed in his resignation.

Two weeks later, he started his own company.

The man had everything going for him. He was smart, he
was energetic, he was dedicated, and he knew his particular
field inside out.

Almost from the start, the new company caught on. It grew
quickly, adding new customers, new employees, new equipment.

But then, about a year ago, the picture began to change.
Orders were still coming in, but the company was stumbling.
Things went steadily from bad to worse until . . .

A week ago Friday, that man—who had started out on
his own with such high hopes just three years before—was
forced to go out of business. His company closed its doors
for good.

What happened? What went wrong? Could it have been
avoided? How? . . .

This story holds our attention because it could happen to
us someday. We want to know what went wrong and how *Inc.*
magazine can help us avoid the same mistakes.

5. *Flatter the Reader*

One reason many people take a negative view toward direct
mail is that they know it isn't really personal. They know they
are just one of thousands of people whose names the advertiser
obtained from a mailing list.

But you can turn this fact to your advantage by using flattery. Tell the reader, "Yes, I got your name from a list. Yes,
you're part of that group. But that group is special; the people
in it have superior characteristics that set them apart from

the crowd. And you're superior, too. That's why I'm writing to you."

There is flattery in the opening of a letter from the Maserati Import Company, a seller of luxury automobiles:

Dear Mr. McCoy:
One of a kind. Is that phrase a little trite?
   I used to think so until I tried to find you.
   Now I know what "one of a kind" really means.
   The process of finding your name and address was the advertising equivalent of panning for gold. . . .

The letter goes on to offer the reader a free bottle of French champagne if he will test-drive a Maserati luxury sedan.

6. Write to the Reader Peer-to-Peer

The logic here is that people in special-interest groups—and most direct mail is aimed at narrow groups of prospects—will be more receptive to a sales pitch from a peer than from an outsider.

So a letter aimed at farmers should be signed by a farmer. And it should be written in the plain, straightforward language of one farmer talking to another.

With this approach, the writer can achieve empathy with the reader by saying, "Look . . . I am like you. I know your problems. I've been through them myself. And I've found a solution. You can trust me."

In a subscription letter for *Writer's Digest*, the pitch is made by one writer talking to other writers:

Dear Writer:
I don't have the great American novel in me.
   I flunked Poetry 102 in college. My first, last, and only short story was rejected by 14 magazines. . . .

7. *A Personal Message from the President*

In direct mail, the owner or manager of a business can talk directly with his or her customers.

Customers like dealing with the person in charge. When the top person in your company signs the letter, it makes the reader feel important. And having the owner's signature on the advertising adds a bit more credibility to the message. (I've often heard people say of such mail, "Well, he wouldn't sign it if it wasn't true.")

FutureSoft begins a mailer on its Quickpro software package with a letter from the company president:

> Personal Message to Microcomputer Owners from Joseph W. Tamargo, President of FUTURESOFT . . .
> I want to tell you why I have chosen to send you an actual condensation of the Operating Instructions of our exciting and unique QUICKPRO, which writes programs for you.

Another example, this one from John L. Blair, president of the New Process Company, a mail-order clothing manufacturer:

> Dear Mr. Bly:
> A memo recently crossed my desk that said I would have to RAISE MY PRICES—NOW—to offset our spiraling operating costs!
> But I said, "NO! NOT YET!"
> I know that customers like you, Mr. Bly, expect the BEST VALUE for their money when they shop at NPC. And that's why I'm going to hold the line on higher prices just as long as I possibly can! . . .

8. Use a Provocative Quote

The quote should contain news or a startling statistic or fact, or say something outrageous. The quote must be like the lead of a news story—it must raise a question or arouse curiosity to make the reader want to read the body of the letter to find out more.

In a letter selling a book on advertising, Prentice Hall began with a quotation taken directly from the book itself:

> Advertising agencies and other consultants score something on the order of a 9 on my Least-Needed scale of 1-to-10. . . .
> This is what Lewis Kornfeld has to say, based on his extraordinary success as Radio Shack's master marketer for over 30 years.

9. Ask a Question

Question leads are effective when the answer to the question is interesting or important to the reader, or when the question arouses genuine curiosity.

Here are a few examples of letters that lead with a question:

> Dear Friend,
> What do you think when you see a letter that starts with "Dear Friend" . . . a letter from someone you've never met?
> WHAT DO JAPANESE MANAGERS HAVE THAT AMERICAN MANAGERS SOMETIMES LACK?

> Dear Mr. Blake:
> Is freelance a dirty word to you? It really shouldn't be . . .

10. Make It Personal

The most personal direct-mail piece I ever received began as follows:

> Dear Friend,
> As you may already know, we have been doing some work for people who have the same last name as you do. Finally, after months of work, THE AMAZING STORY OF THE BLYS IN AMERICA is ready for print and you are in it!

This letter is highly personal for two reasons. First, my name appears several times in the body of the letter. Second, the product is designed especially for me, a Bly. (But the letter is weakened by the stock opening "Dear Friend." A better salutation is the more personal "Dear Friend Bly.")

Personalized mail usually gets more attention than form letters. So whenever possible, make it personal. Insert the reader's name in the copy once or twice (if your budget allows for computer letters). And, more important, make sure the copy speaks to the needs, interests, and ego of the reader (as a book called *The Amazing Story of the Blys in America* has strong appeal to people named Bly).

11. Identify the Reader's Problem

If your product or service solves a problem, you can create a strong sales letter by featuring the problem in the lead, then telling how the product or service solves the problem.

There are two advantages to this technique. First, it selects a specific group of readers for your letter. (Only single people will respond to a letter that begins, "Are You Sick and Tired of Paying Extra Taxes Just Because You Aren't Married?")

Second, the format shows in a clear and direct manner

how the product solves the reader's problem. When you start with the problem, the natural next step is to talk about the solution.

Manhattan dentist Dr. Brian E. Weiss used this technique in a letter inviting me in for an appointment:

> Dear Mr. Bly:
> You know how difficult it is to look your best if dental problems are causing discomfort and pain or if the appearance of your teeth needs improvement.
>   Have you been putting off a dental checkup or consultation on an existing problem? This note may encourage you to take the important step to help yourself feel better by making a dental appointment. . . .

Politician Jim Thompson used the technique in a campaign letter aimed at voters in Chicago:

> Dear Mrs. Vanderbilt:
> If you can't afford higher taxes.
>   If you're afraid to walk the streets at night.
>   If you're sick and tired of corrupt government officials.
>   If your children aren't getting the education they deserve.
>   Then you don't need a Governor appointed by Chicago's City Hall. . . .

12. Stress a Benefit

A straightforward presentation of a benefit can outpull other techniques if the benefit is significant and has strong appeal to the reader.

A sales letter from Prentice Hall offering a new book on advertising began with the headline, "Just published . . . HOW TO MAKE YOUR ADVERTISING MAKE MONEY. A clear, concise guide to effective advertising . . ." The headline is effective because it's safe to assume that all advertising professionals who receive the letter want to create more effective advertising.

To get results, a benefit-oriented headline must appeal to the reader's self-interest. As Cahners Publishing points out in its booklet, "How to Create and Produce Successful Direct Mail," "Don't tell your prospect about your grass seed, tell him about his lawn."

13. Use Human Interest

People enjoy reading about other people, especially about people who have anxieties, fears, problems, and interests similar to their own.

Some of the strongest sales letters center around powerful, dramatic human interest stories. The readers get hooked because the events in the story relate somehow to their own lives. And the letter leaves more of an impression because it deals with human emotions, not just technical product features or abstract sales arguments.

The publisher of *Cardiac Alert* newsletter used an autobiographical approach to add human interest to a sales letter asking for subscriptions to his publication. The headline read:

When I was 16, my father died of a heart attack . . .

You can't help but be interested in the letter that follows.

14. Let the Reader In on Some Inside Information

When a consumer sees your ad in a magazine, he knows he is sharing your message with tens of thousands of other people. But he has no way of knowing whether you've sent the sales letter he received to thousands of prospects, or just a select few.

Direct mail is an excellent medium for appealing to the

reader's need to feel special, important, exclusive. And nothing is more exclusive than revealing some inside information on a sale or product that others don't know about.

Here's exclusive news from a cover letter mailed along with a reprint of a magazine ad:

> Here's a fresh-from-the-printer reprint of our latest *WALL STREET JOURNAL* ad . . .
>
> We'll be running the ad in June because we want potential customers to know more about our latest financial planning services.
>
> But, as someone we've done business with before, we consider YOU even more important than the "new business" out there.
>
> Which is why we're sending you our new ad months before it will break in the press.
>
> You see, we wanted you to be the first to know about our new services which can save you time and build your retirement nest egg.

The message is: we're telling you first because we think you're special.

And what reader of direct mail doesn't think he or she is special?

15. Sweepstakes

A sweepstakes can greatly increase the response to a direct-mail campaign. One sweepstakes mailing I received began:

> American Family Publishers Announces America's First By-Mail GUARANTEED MULTIMILLION-DOLLAR SWEEPSTAKES OFFER: R BLY, A LOCAL NY RESIDENT, MAY HAVE ALREADY WON ONE MILLION DOLLARS.

There are three ways of structuring a sweepstakes:

YOU MAY WIN . . .

YOU MAY HAVE WON . . .

YOU HAVE WON . . .

The "you have won" sweepstakes generates the most entries because the consumer is guaranteed a prize. This sweepstakes is expensive to run because you must award the consolation prize to everyone who claims it.

The "you may have won" is the second most effective sweepstakes. Here the reader is told that the winning entry number has been preselected by computer—and that you just may hold that winning entry number in your hand.

Sweepstakes mailings have declined dramatically over the past few decades. However, I am beginning to notice a slight uptick in sweepstakes promotions again.

These are fifteen common ways of starting your sales letter. There are others. Read the direct mail you receive and keep a file of effective direct-mail leads and letters to use as a reference in your own work.

Marketing tactics are often cyclical. Reason: When too many marketers use a tactic, it becomes less special and more commonplace. So the market is flooded with look-alike promotions using the tactic, and with all the noise it becomes less effective.

When the marketing tactic becomes less effective, marketers abandon it in droves. Soon, it is scarce rather than overused. And when that happens, some smart marketers begin using it again, and find that it is once again working.

SHOULD YOU USE AN ENVELOPE TEASER?

The outer envelope is the first thing the reader sees when receiving your mailing package. It is here that the selling starts. If the outer envelope fails to entice the reader to open the letter or, worse, if it prompts him to throw the letter away, the brilliant copy of your sales letter will be wasted.

There are two basic approaches to outer envelopes. The first is to start your sales pitch right away with headlines and copy printed on the outer envelope. This copy, known as "teaser copy," is designed to entice the reader to open the envelope by arousing curiosity or promising a strong reward for reading the package.

The problem with this strategy is that teasers are labels that instantly identify the package as containing advertising matter. Large headlines and copy lines printed on an envelope shout at the reader, "This is advertising . . . it's worthless . . . throw it away!"

My rule is: use a teaser only if it contains an irresistible message that will compel the reader to open the envelope. But don't feel you must use a teaser; a weak teaser can actually reduce response versus a package with a plain envelope!

We know that people always open their personal mail before they open direct mail. We also know that many people throw away every "teaser" envelope they receive without a second glance.

Teasers are effective only when the message is compelling. For example, I'd have a hard time ignoring an envelope with the teaser, "Inside: The Secret to Living Longer and Feeling Better . . . Without Dieting or Special Exercise."

On the other hand, you'd probably save yourself the trouble of opening an envelope that began, "Sawyer Life Insurance Announces Its 50th Year of Operation . . . Quality Service to the Community for over Half a Century."

Teasers can take many forms. You can have a headline only. Or a headline plus copy.

You can use an envelope with a window so the teaser is copy that shows through the window.

You can mail the package in a clear plastic bag so the whole package shows through to tease the reader.

You can even print illustrations, graphics, and photos on the outer envelope.

However, most teasers seem to follow one of three basic formats:

1. THIS IS THE BEST WIDGET EVER MADE
2. THIS WIDGET MAY SAVE YOU UP TO $500
3. ENCLOSED IS YOUR FREE WIDGET

The third teaser works best because it promises a reward for opening the envelope. (The promise of a prize inside has sold millions of dollars' worth of Cracker Jacks and breakfast cereals.) Even though you know you hold advertising material in your hands, teaser #3 overcomes your resistance to junk mail by making you wonder what's inside.

Teaser #1 is the worst. It's pure boasting, and the reader's reaction to the smug claim will be to throw the mailing away.

Teaser #2, though not as effective as #3, is still an improvement over #1 because it makes the promise of a benefit. This promise says to the reader, "Yes, you hold junk mail in your hands. But it might be worth your while to open the envelope and see what we can do for you."

A "blind" envelope—one with no teaser—is often more effective than one with a teaser. The idea behind the no-teaser approach is to make the direct-mail package resemble personal mail. When the reader sees the envelope, he's not sure whether the envelope contains personal mail or advertising material— and so he opens it, just to be sure. Once the mailer is opened, the battle is half won; if the letter contains a strong, compelling lead, you will hook the prospect and get him to read the body copy.

When using the no-teaser approach, take pains to make the letter look like personal mail. Use a plain white or off-white envelope. Don't let any brightly colored sales literature show through the window, if there is one. And don't embellish the envelope with a company logo; just have the return address set in plain type.

THE LETTER SELLS, THE BROCHURE TELLS

Many direct-mail packages do an effective selling job with a letter and reply form only.

Every direct-mail package should contain a letter; flyers and brochures are optional. As the writer, you must decide whether a flyer is needed.

Here are some helpful suggestions.

Use a flyer when you are selling products that are colorful or visually impressive: subscriptions to colorful magazines, flowers, fruit, fine foods, coins, collectibles, sports equipment, consumer electronics.

Some products are most effectively sold through demonstration. But you usually can't demonstrate by mail. The next best thing is to take step-by-step photos of a demonstration and put them in a flyer to be included in the mailer.

Sometimes the offer is so strong that the writer decides to devote the letter solely to benefits. The features of the product itself can then be covered in an accompanying flyer.

Use a flyer for transmitting technical data or product information that is too detailed to be explained or listed in the letter.

In writing direct mail to sell books, I list a detailed table of contents in a flyer separate from the letter. This way, the small percentage of readers interested in some esoteric topic can scan the contents to see if it is included. And if it is, the flyer will have tipped the odds in favor of a sale.

You are not limited to one flyer or one letter or one order form. You can include whatever you think it will take to make the sale.

HOW TO INCREASE RESPONSE TO YOUR MAILINGS

In direct mail, response is the name of the game. Building brand awareness or getting people to remember your message is not important. The only thing that counts is how many sales or inquiries your mailing generates. The more responses, the more successful the mailer.

Reaching the right audience with the right offer and the right copy is the key to successful direct mail. But a number of response-increasing techniques have little to do with copywriting skill or common sense. Here are a few that you can use:

- Always include a response mechanism. This can be a business reply card, reply envelope, order form, sales page URL, or toll-free number.
- Use self-addressed, postage-paid envelopes and reply cards (known as business reply envelopes and business reply cards). They generate more response than cards or envelopes that require a postage stamp from the prospect.
- Order forms and reply cards with tear-off stubs or receipts generate more response than those without.
- The letter should be the first thing the reader sees when he opens the envelope. The package should have a natural flow from outer envelope to letter to flyer to reply card.
- Offer a premium: a gift to prospects who respond to the mailing. The premium should be something that they want, and it should ideally relate to the product or the offer.

- Offer something of value in return for responding to the letter: a free brochure, booklet, catalog, demonstration, survey, estimate, consultation, or trial offer.
- Allow for a negative response. And turn it into a positive. The reply card for a letter promoting my freelance copywriting services gives the reader the option of checking off a box that reads, "Not interested right now. But try us again in _____." Even if the reader doesn't need my services now, she can still respond to the mailing.
- Use physical objects in the mailing. An envelope that feels bulky almost always gets opened. These objects can include product samples, premiums, 3-D pop-ups, and other gimmicks. (I've received direct-mail packages that contained instant coffee, chili powder, a set of coasters, a calendar, pens, pencils, a flashlight, and a magnifying glass.) Although costly, mailings with objects enclosed can really stand out in a mailbox or in a basket full of flat envelopes containing regular letters and flyers.
- Put a time limit on the offer. Once the reader puts the letter aside, she probably won't come back to it, so you'll get the most response if you urge her to act now . . . by putting a time limit on the offer.
- You can put a real date limit on the offer. ("Remember, Beethoven's Violin Concerto is yours to keep just for taking advantage of this offer within the next 10 days.")
- You can hint that the offer won't last forever ("But hurry—supplies are limited").
- Or you can add a sense of urgency to your call for action ("Remember—the time to buy insurance is before tragedy strikes. Not after").
- Make the outer envelope resemble an invoice or other "official-looking" document. People almost always open such envelopes.

- Use a plain outer envelope with no copy, not even a return address. The mystery of such a mailing is irresistible.
- Use a P.S. in the letter to restate the offer or reemphasize a sales point; 80 percent of readers will read a P.S.
- Guarantee the offer. When you sell by mail, make a money-back guarantee good for 15, 30, 60, or even 90 days.
- When you are generating leads, tell the prospect that he's under no obligation and that no salesperson will call (unless he wants one to).
- Envelopes addressed with labels attached to the reply device and showing through a glassine window on the envelope are often as effective as envelopes individually typed with the recipient's address. Addressing envelopes by hand can reduce response, perhaps because it looks amateurish.
- If your mailing list contains titles but not names, print a description of the person you're trying to reach on the outer envelope ("Attention Buyers of Electronic Components— Important Information Inside").
- An envelope with live stamps or a postage-metered envelope outpulls an envelope with a preprinted indicia.
- An order form printed in color, or designed as an elaborate certificate, or printed with a lot of information outpulls a clean, ordinary-looking order form.
- Letters with indented paragraphs, underlined words, and portions of the text set in a second color outpull plain letters.
- Letters with a lot of "bells and whistles"—arrows, fake handwritten notes in the margins, spot illustrations, highlighting—can increase response when mailed to lower- and middle-class consumer audiences. Avoid these techniques when writing to business executives, professionals, or upper-class consumers.
- A form letter with a headline can often be just as effective as

a form letter with the recipient's name and address typed in by hand.

- A package with a separate letter and brochure does better than a combination letter/brochure.
- Repeat the offer on the reply card.
- Use action words in the first sentence of the reply card and restate the offer in the body copy. ("YES, I'd like to know how I can cut my phone bill in half. Please send a free selection guide on your long-distance services. I understand I'm under no obligation and that no salesperson will call.")
- Avoid intimidating, legal-type wording. State your offer, terms, and guarantee in plain, simple English.
- Make it easy to respond to the mailing. This means having a simple offer and an easy-to-complete order form. And be sure to leave enough space on the form for the reader to fill in the required information (a surprising number of reply cards and coupons don't).
- Keep in mind the buyer's level of interest in your product so you don't oversell or undersell. (Prospects whose names were taken from the *Nintendo Force* magazine mailing list probably have a greater interest in video games than the subscribers of *Field and Stream*.)

Writing direct mail is the best education I can recommend for novice and experienced copywriters alike. Within a few weeks of your mailing, you know whether your copy is successful or not. No other form of copywriting, except for online marketing, yields such immediate or precise feedback on your work.

ALTERNATIVE DM FORMATS

The traditional package described above has long been the workhorse of direct mail. But there are many other direct-mail formats, and they increasingly outperform standard direct-mail packages.

These include bookalogs, magalogs, tabloids, digests, trifold self-mailers, billboard mailers, tear sheets, oversize postcards, impact mailings, video brochures, and shock-and-awe packages. Here are some of the most popular mail formats being used today:

- Brochure-style self-mailer—11 x 17–inch sheet folded once to form four panels.
- Slim-jim—8½ x 11–inch "letter-size" sheet folded twice to form six panels.
- Slim-jim with extra panel—8½ x 14–inch "legal-size" sheet folded three times to form eight panels.
- Broadsides—an oversize sheet of paper printed in color on one or both sides and folded for mailing.
- Faux newsletter—a direct-mail piece designed to look like an informational newsletter.
- Magalogs—a multipage direct-mail piece designed to look like a magazine.
- Digests—similar to magalogs but the pages are half the size, made by folding 8½ x 11–inch sheets of paper once vertically and saddle-stitching them.
- Bookalog—a long-copy direct-mail promotion in the form of a small paperback book enclosed in a 6 x 9–inch or other envelope with a cover letter and reply form.
- Snap Pack Mailers—mailers that are made of multiple plies or pages, and sealed at the edges and at the top. You have to tear off the perforated seals before you can open the snap pack and leaf through the pages.
- Tabloids—similar to magalogs but larger, with the pages approximately the same size as in a newspaper.
- "Shock-and-awe" package—a box filled with multiple components (e.g., cover letter, product brochure, reply form,

DVD or audio CD), plus miscellaneous premiums such as pencils, pens, pads, small toys, posters, candy, and many others.

- Video brochures—an expensive mailer that when opened shows one or more product-related videos.
- Audio mail—a mailer with a built-in sound chip that plays when you open the letter or brochure.
- Structural mailing—a mailer that unfolds and expands into a 3-D structure such as a sphere or miniature building.
- Impact mailing—a mailer sent with an attention-getting enclosure such as a bag of shredded money or a brick silk-screened with the sender's business card.
- Oversize postcards—color promotional postcards measuring 6 by 9 inches or larger.
- And many more . . .

8

WRITING BROCHURES, CATALOGS, AND OTHER PRINTED AND PDF SALES MATERIALS

Promotional literature has been around for a long time. According to *Ripley's Believe It or Not*, the first brochure was written by Hernán Cortés almost five hundred years ago. It was circulated as a broadside to the people of Spain by Charles V, and it advertised a sale on turkeys.

Even in the digital era, many businesses still use printed sales literature: travel agents, supermarkets, banks, residential contractors, department stores, insurance companies, medical practices, colleges, and many other types of organizations distribute brochures, circulars, flyers, catalogs, and other printed advertising matter to help make the sale.

That's convenient when a salesperson calls on prospects at their home or office, or when the prospects visit the marketer's trade show booth. Also, print brochures have a tactile appeal that PDFs don't. And they're easier to file for future reference.

In addition, brochures are also often available as PDF downloads from the marketers' Web sites. Whether print, electronic, or both, advertisers need sales literature for two reasons. First, credibility—people expect a "real" company to have product literature. Anyone can spend $50 on letterhead and business cards and call themselves a corporation. But a brochure, in particular a hard copy, proves you are in business and shows you're more than a fly-by-night operation.

Second, the brochure is a time-saving device. People want printed information they can take home with them and study at their leisure. But it would take too much time to type individual letters of information to every prospect that asked about your product. And while some prospects love to go on Web sites to learn more about products, others prefer information they can hold in their hands.

The solution is to collect your basic information on a particular product in a single, mass-produced brochure. The brochure gives prospects most of the information they need to know; the rest can be filled in by letter, phone, or a visit to the store.

Even consumers who generally conduct business on PCs and mobile devices, and who can find out what they need to know about your product by going to your Web site, will frequently ask to receive sales literature. A brochure saves them the trouble of printing out information from your Web site.

Brochures support advertising and direct-mail programs. They are also used as sales tools by salespeople and distributors. Brochures are a handy way of quickly communicating the essentials of your product to new customers, prospects, employees, and dealers.

Brochures are primarily a medium of information. They tell prospects what the product is and what it can do for them. Your brochure should also explain how the product works, why people should buy it, and how they can order.

But a good sales brochure does more than explain and inform. It also persuades. Remember, the brochure is a sales tool, not an instruction manual. Good brochure copy does more than list facts or product features; it translates these facts and features into customer benefits—reasons why the customer should buy the product.

11 TIPS ON WRITING BETTER SALES BROCHURES

Here are eleven tips on writing brochures that (a) tell readers what they want to know while (b) selling them on buying the product:

1. *Know where the brochure fits into the buying process.*

Unlike packaged goods you buy off a supermarket shelf (soap, shampoo, canned beans, cigarettes), products that require a brochure are seldom sold in a single step. Computers, cars, vacation trips, insurance, telephones, financial services, seminars, club memberships, real estate, and dozens of other products and services require several meetings or contacts between buyer and seller before the sale is closed.

For most of these products and services, a brochure comes in somewhere between initial contact and final sale. But where? Do you write the brochure for the uninformed buyer who shows initial interest in the product? Or is the brochure used to build credibility and answer questions as you get closer to closing the sale?

The answer is: it depends on the product, the market, and the advertiser's individual approach to making the sale. Some advertisers might even use a series of brochures to guide the buyer through the steps of the buying process.

For instance, I make my living as an advertising copywriter. I get sales leads from many sources: ads I run in advertising journals, direct mail, publicity from articles and speeches I give, word of mouth, the Web, and referral from other clients.

When a lead comes in, I chat with the caller to determine his level of interest. By asking a few questions over the phone, I can quickly determine whether the caller is a likely potential customer for my service.

Once I qualify the lead by phone, the next step is to send a comprehensive package of sales literature. It contains seven or eight separate pieces including a biography, client list, four-page sales letter, reprints of articles I've written, samples of my copy, a price list, and a form the prospect can use to order copy by mail. In short, it gives the prospective client everything he needs to know about my freelance copywriting services.

From this material, the prospect should be able to decide whether to hire me. There may be a follow-up call or a mailing of more samples of my work, but the basic literature package allows the client to order the service directly, by mail. No additional information or sales visits are required.

On the other hand, a friend of mine who is a management consultant mails very little information to prospects. He sends a brief cover note along with a slim booklet that presents his services in concise outline form.

The reason he sends incomplete information is that the next step in his sales sequence is a meeting with the prospect. If he sent a package as weighty as mine, there would be little left to follow up with. But by sending less, he whets the reader's appetite with key sales benefits of his service, while raising questions that can only be answered if the reader requests a face-to-face meeting with the consultant.

Keep in mind that we both have Web sites with extensive information about our backgrounds, qualifications, services, and clients. But many prospects who are willing to take the time to visit my Web site also say, "Send me some information in the mail or e-mail."

Here are some of the ways brochures can fit into the buying process:

• *As leave-behinds.* A leave-behind is a brochure you leave behind after a meeting with a potential customer. The leave-behind brochure should summarize your sales pitch and present a fairly complete description of the product and its benefits.

• *As point-of-sale literature.* Point-of-sale literature is displayed at the point of sale. A travel agent's office, for example, typically has racks holding brightly colored pamphlets on trips and tours. The cover of the point-of-sale literature should have a catchy headline and visual that team up to make the passersby stop, pick up, and keep the brochure.

• *To respond to inquiries.* An inquiry is a request for more information about your product. The person making the inquiry became interested in you through your advertising, publicity, Google search, or referral and represents a "hot" sales lead—someone much more likely to buy than a prospect who has not contacted you.

The inquiry fulfillment package should contain enough information to answer the prospect's questions and convince him to take the next step in the buying process. The hot prospect has already expressed interest in your product, so don't hesitate to load your inquiry fulfillment package full of facts and sales points.

• *As direct mail.* As mentioned in chapter 7, brochures and flyers are used to add information to direct-mail packages. The sales letter does the selling; the brochure provides additional sales points, lists technical features, and contains photos and drawings of the product. In the interest of keeping mailing costs down, this type of brochure is usually slim (and is designed to fit in a standard mailing envelope).

• *As a sales support tool.* Many products—hospital supplies, office equipment, life insurance, industrial equipment—are sold by salespeople who visit prospects at their home or office. These salespeople use brochures as selling aids in their sales pitches (and also as leave-behinds). Such brochures have large pages, big illustrations, and bold headlines and subheads that lead the salesperson and prospect through the pitch. Sometimes, a standard product brochure is adapted for use as a sales aid and printed as separate panels in a three-ring binder, self-standing easel that sits on the prospect's desk, or PowerPoint.

Whatever your application—leave-behind, point-of-sale, inquiry fulfillment, direct mail, or sales support—let the advertiser's particular method of selling be your guide in writing and designing the brochure. The best brochures contain just the right amount of product information and sales pitch to lead the prospect from one step of the buying process to the next.

One additional tip on designing sales literature: think about how the reader will use and file the brochure. A small pocket-size brochure may be ideal for direct mail or point-of-sale display, but it will be lost in a file folder or on a bookshelf of full-size literature (8½ x 11 inches, the kind your competition is probably publishing).

In the same way, a brochure of unconventional shape or size may stand out from the crowd but might be thrown away because it won't fit in a standard file cabinet. And a brochure aimed at purchasing agents will probably be punched for a three-hole binder, which means part of your copy will be punched out unless you leave sufficient margins.

2. Know whether the brochure stands alone or is supported by other materials.

In some selling situations, the brochure stands alone. Aside from the salesperson, it is the only sales tool the company has.

Other firms use a brochure to supplement their promotional campaign, which may consist of print advertising, radio and TV commercials, direct mail, publicity, trade shows, and seminars.

Some companies have one product—and one brochure. Others use a series of brochures, each describing one product in their product line, or one segment of the total market they sell to.

The brochure writer must know whether his brochure stands alone or is supported by other material, because the existence of other material determines the content of his brochure.

For example, a company that has detailed product features and specifications on its Web site may elect to simply summarize the high points in an abbreviated brochure, and include the Web site URL as a source of more detailed information.

Some duplication among different promotional pieces may be necessary, but avoid creating too many redundant sales brochures. For instance, I normally devote half a page of an eight-page product brochure to a description of the manufacturer and their capabilities.

But if the manufacturer already had a separate "corporate capabilities brochure," I wouldn't need to do that. Instead, we could mail both brochures—product and company—to prospects requesting more information.

Another example. A client asked me to write a sales brochure on an industrial mixer. He wanted to include detailed calculations on how to determine the energy consumption of the mixer.

Although some engineers might be curious as to how the calculation is done, such an elaborate mathematical treatment is wasted space in a selling piece. The solution was to talk about energy savings without showing the calculation in the sales brochure, and to create a separate "technical information sheet" that showed the detailed calculation.

Find out the environment in which your brochure will be working. Is it a stand-alone brochure or part of a series? Is it supported by print ads, direct mail, publicity?

Has the advertiser also published an annual report, corporate capabilities brochure, catalog, or other general brochure describing the corporation? Are there article reprints, fact sheets, or other pieces of literature that can be mailed along with the main brochure?

Form should follow function. I was asked to write sales literature describing a system of modular software. For this modular product, I wrote a modular brochure. The main piece is a four-page folder. Copy giving the reader an overview of the system is printed on the left inside page; the right page is a pocket containing eight sheets, each describing a different software module.

This approach allows salespeople to use the sheets as separate flyers for presentations and mailings. In addition, the brochure is easy to update. When a new module is added to the package, or an existing module is updated, we just add a flyer to the brochure.

3. Know your audience.

We've already seen that a brochure must fit into the right step in the buying process. Your brochure must also fit the informational needs of your audience. Think about the readers and what they expect to get out of the brochure. Ask yourself, "How can I use the brochure to convince the readers to buy the product?"

Let's say you are writing a brochure selling alfalfa seeds to farmers. The farmer probably isn't interested in the history of alfalfa (or the history of your company). And he doesn't much

care about alfalfa's biological structure or the chemical com-
position of the seed.

The farmer wants to know that your seeds are plump
and healthy . . . that they're free of weeds . . . that they'll
yield a good, healthy crop of alfalfa . . . and that the price is
right.

How do you convince him? One way is to show the results.
Put two photos of alfalfa fields on the cover of your brochure.
The one on the left shows weed-infested, scrawny alfalfa. The
one on the right shows a field of lush, healthy plants. Add a
caption that tells him the field on the right was planted with
your seeds, and how your seeds can increase crop yield by 40
percent.

The brochure can go even further. Why not attach a sample
bag of seed to the brochure and mail it to the farmer? The brochure copy can begin, "Our alfalfa is clean, healthy, practically
weed-free. But don't take our word for it. See for yourself."

Know your reader. Farmers don't want hype or a scientific
treatise; they want straightforward talk that shows them how
to run their farms more profitably. Scientists are most comfortable with charts, graphs, and tables of data, so include plenty
of them in a brochure aimed at scientists.

Engineers are at home with diagrams and blueprints.
Accountants understand tables of financial figures. Human
resource managers will probably be interested in photos of
people.

Also, the length of your copy depends not only on the
amount of information you have, but on whether your customer is someone who will read a lot of copy. A brochure selling a new microfilm system to librarians can be long, because
librarians like to read.

A brochure aimed at busy executives should probably
be shorter, because most executives are pressed for time. A

brochure offering a new cable TV service will probably contain mostly pictures, because people who watch a lot of TV would rather look at pictures than read.

4. Put a strong selling message on the front cover.

The first thing readers see when they pull your brochure out of an envelope or off a display rack is the cover. If the cover promises a strong benefit or reward for reading the copy, the reader will open the brochure and read it (or at least look at the pictures, captions, and headings).

If the selling message on the cover is weak or, worse, if there is no selling message on the cover, the reader has no motivation for opening the brochure. It is just junk mail, something to be thrown away.

A surprising number of brochure covers contain no headline or visual, just the product name and company logo. This is like running an ad without a headline: it wastes a valuable selling opportunity.

For instance, a brochure from the Prudential Insurance Company of America has the headline: "Now . . . you can enroll in this AARP Plan of Group Hospital Insurance—designed to help pay expenses your other insurance does not cover!" The cover is illustrated with a drawing of a retired couple enjoying a life of leisure.

This brochure cover is effective because it offers a strong, solid benefit, simply stated: "Designed to help pay expenses your other insurance does not cover!" What gimmick or clever cover design could do a better selling job than this promise?

Sometimes, the visual communicates the benefit more strongly than the headline. My favorite summer retreat is Montauk, Long Island, and no words can make me long for a weekend on the island as much as a beautiful color photo of the waves rolling in and lapping against the soft sands of the shore.

If you own a hotel on the Montauk beach, put such a photo on the cover, and I'll be sold!

Occasionally, a brochure writer attempts to lure the reader into the brochure with a gimmick that doesn't relate to the product. In front of me is a brochure whose cover features a drawing of a church and a diamond ring and the headline, "Forget about marriage . . . why not just 'get engaged.'"

This caught my eye years ago, when I was engaged. But when I opened the brochure, I was given a sales pitch on why it's better to rent cars instead of buying them. The brochure had nothing at all to do with engagement or marriage. I was more than disappointed: I felt misled. I'm sure other folks felt the same and I doubt that this brochure sold many car rental contracts.

The traditional brochure cover contains a headline and graphic only, with no text; body copy begins inside. But you can get people to start reading your sales pitch by breaking this tradition and beginning your body copy on the front cover. The readers' eyes will automatically go to the lead paragraph, and if it's strong enough, they'll be hooked.

5. Give complete information.

Give as much information as it takes to get the prospect to take the next step in the buying process.

The average brochure contains a lot of words. Certainly more than you read in most ads or hear in TV commercials.

But remember that the brochure is a medium of information. Ads, commercials, and direct mail may be an unwanted interruption in the reader's life. But the reader has asked for the brochure, and he is interested in the information it contains.

Don't be afraid to make the brochure as long as it has to be. Include all the necessary information—prices, product specifications, ordering information, guarantees, descriptions.

The reader who represents a serious potential customer will read the copy as long as it is interesting and engaging. The minute you write boring copy, or copy that doesn't give useful information, you'll turn the reader off.

There is a ridiculous tendency among brochure designers to use a large amount of white space on the page and very little copy. I've seen 8½ x 11–inch brochures where each page had only one or two paragraphs in small type in the upper corner. The rest of the page was mostly blank and decorated by some graphic design: stripes, color patterns, lines, shapes.

This is a waste of space and printing costs. Your customer doesn't send for your brochure to look at fancy designs; she sends for it because she wants information. If you want proof that this myth is untrue, take a look at your daily newspaper: pages and pages of sold text and photos. No white space, no graphic "design elements." Just information that the reader wants and has paid for.

Of course, not every page in your brochure should be solid type to the edges. Margins and space between paragraphs help increase readability. Photos, illustrations, captions, and sub-heads break up the text and help tell the story. But to think your brochure should be largely blank space is folly. Don't be afraid to write and print all the words it takes to make your sales pitch. Give the reader complete information.

6. *Organize your selling points.*

People read brochures in much the same order they read paperback novels. They look at the cover first, maybe take a quick peek at the back cover, and thumb through the book once. Then, if it looks promising, they open to page 1 and start reading.

Your brochure, like a novel, should have a logical structure to it. A good brochure tells a story—a product story—with a beginning, a middle, and an end. The organization of a brochure is dictated both by the product story you want to tell and by the informational needs of the reader.

For example, my in-laws had a business in which they bought books from publishers and resold them to corporations. This is a rather unusual service, one the corporate librarian may not have thought about before, so my in-laws began their brochure with a summary of the service they offered and why corporate librarians would find it useful.

Next, they presented six major benefits of using the service. These benefits were listed in simple 1-2-3 fashion so the reader could quickly see how she could come out ahead by doing business with the book-buying service.

Finally, the brochure told the reader the technical details of how the service worked and gave instructions for placing orders.

Let the organization of your brochure be dictated by what your customer wants to know about your product. If you own a computer store, and you find that customers coming in off the street seem to ask the same questions over and over, you might write a booklet titled "Six Important Questions to Ask Before You Buy a Computer." The booklet would present computer shopping tips in a simple question-and-answer format.

If your company designs and decorates offices, your brochure could be organized as a walking tour of the modern office. At each point of the tour, from the copier to the water cooler, the copy could point out how redesigning that section of the office can make the office a better place to work and improve productivity.

There are many ways to organize a brochure: alphabetical order, chronological order, by size of product, by importance of customer benefit, question and answer, list of customer benefits, by product line, by price, by application, by market, by steps in the ordering process. Choose the approach that best fits your product, your audience, and your sales pitch.

7. Divide the brochure into short, easy-to-read sections.

As you organize your brochure, devise a way to organize your material: an outline that breaks the topic into a number of sections and subsections.

You should keep this organizational scheme in the final copy. Write the brochure as a series of short sections and subsections, each with its own headline or subhead.

There are a number of benefits to this approach. First, the use of headings and subheads allows readers to get the message even if they only scan the brochure. Many people won't read all the copy, but a series of heads and subheads gives them the gist of the sales pitch at a glance.

Be sure to write headings and subheads that tell a story. Avoid headings that are just clever plays on words. Instead of "Hitachi plays it cool," write, "Hitachi chiller-heaters cut cooling costs in half."

Second, breaking the copy into short sections makes the brochure easier to read. People are intimidated and tired by long chunks of text; they prefer to read a short section of copy, stop, take a rest, and absorb the information before going on to the next section. (This is why novels are divided into chapters.)

Third, short sections make the brochure easier to write. You just follow your outline and put the information in your notes under the appropriate section. If you uncover new facts that don't fit anywhere in the outline, you can simply add a new section to the brochure. And, like your reader, you can rest after writing one section before you go on to the next.

When you write your brochure, think about how the sections will appear on the pages of the published brochure. For example, you might like the clean look and feel of having a six-page brochure with four sections (one on each page), a headline on the front cover, and the company logo and address on the back cover.

Some brochure writers design their brochures so that each page contains a complete section or two. Other writers claim that a good way of getting the reader to turn the page is to have the sections run off one page and continue on the next. Both techniques have their merits, and the choice is really a matter of taste. But you should be aware of how organization and layout work together.

If your brochure is folded or designed in an unusual format, make a mock-up out of scrap paper. Use the mock-up (called a "dummy") to show the layout and how the copy flows from page to page. Make sure that the reader will see the various sections of text in the same order you wrote them in the manuscript.

8. *Use hardworking visuals.*

Photos in brochures are not ornaments. They are included to help sell the product by showing what it looks like, how it works, and what it can do for the reader.

The best brochure photos demonstrate the product's usefulness by showing it in action. Putting people in these photos usually adds to the visual's appeal (people like looking at pictures of people).

Photos make the best visuals because they offer proof that a product exists and works. But artwork is also useful for many purposes.

A drawing can illustrate a product or process that is not easily photographed (such as the inner workings of an automobile engine).

A map can show where something is located.

A diagram can show how something works or how it is organized. An organizational diagram, for example, uses arrows and boxes to show how the divisions and branches of a company are organized.

A graph is used to tell how one quantity changes as another quantity changes. In a brochure on air-conditioning, a graph could show how your electric bill goes up as you lower the temperature setting on your air conditioner.

Pie charts show proportions and percentages (for example, the percentage of your company's annual income spent on research and development). Bar charts demonstrate comparisons among quantities (this year's sales versus last year's). And tables are a handy way of listing a body of data too large to include in the text of the brochure.

Use visuals when they can express or illustrate a concept better than words can. If the visual doesn't improve on the written description, don't use it.

Popular brochure visuals include:

- Product photographs
- Pictures of the product photographed next to other objects to give a sense of the size of the product. (A brochure on semiconductors might show a photo of a microchip on a postage stamp to dramatically convey the smallness of the integrated circuit.)
- Photos of actual installations of the product
- Photos of the product in use
- Photos of the product being manufactured
- Tables of product specifications
- Tables summarizing product features and benefits
- Photos of items made with (or from) the product
- Photos of the company headquarters, manufacturing plant, or research laboratories
- Photos of the product packed and ready for shipping
- Photos of the product being tested by company scientists or inspected for quality control
- Photos of people who are enjoying the use of the product
- Photos of people who attest to the product's superiority

- Tables listing the various models and versions of the product
- Graphs presenting scientific proof of the product's performance (heat tests, ability to stand up under pressure, longevity of operation, etc.)
- Photos of available parts and accessories
- A series of photos demonstrating the product's performance or how to use it
- Diagrams explaining how the product works or how it is put together
- Sketches of planned product improvements, forthcoming new products, or more applications

Always use visuals that illustrate your key selling points. In an automobile brochure that extols the benefits of rack-and-pinion steering, it would be helpful to have a diagram that shows how rack-and-pinion steering works. But if rack-and-pinion steering is not a selling point, there would be no reason to include a picture of it.

Label all visuals with captions. Studies show that brochure captions get twice the readership of body copy. Use captions to reinforce the body copy or make an additional sales point not covered in the copy.

Make captions interesting and informative. Instead of labeling a photo "Automatic wiring device," write "A microprocessor-controlled, fully automatic wiring device (above left) makes approximately 1,000 wire-wrap connections an hour, significantly reducing manufacturing costs."

9. Find the next step in the buying process—and tell the reader to take it.

Do you want your reader to buy pasta from your gourmet shop? Enroll for membership in your health spa? Visit your factory? Or test-drive a new luxury sedan?

A brochure moves the customer from one step in the buying process to the next.

To do this successfully, the brochure must identify this next step and tell the reader to take it.

Typically, this "call for action" appears at the end of the brochure. The copy urges the reader to call or go online for more information, or to take some other action. Make it easy for the reader to respond by using such devices as reply cards, self-addressed stamped envelopes, order forms, toll-free numbers, URLs, and listings of local dealerships and distributors.

End the brochure with copy designed to generate an immediate response. Use action words and phrases: "Give us a call today." "For more information, write for our FREE catalog." "Please complete and mail the enclosed reply card." "Visit our store nearest you." "Order today—supplies limited." "Download your free selection guide now."

Here's an effective closing from a brochure for an advertising agency:

THE NEXT STEP
Now that you know something about us, we'd like to know a little bit more about you.

Send us your current ads, sales literature, and press releases for a free, no-obligation evaluation of your marketing communications program.

If you'd like to meet with us, give us a call. We'll be glad to show you some of the work we've done for our clients, and take a look at what we can do for you.

This closing is effective for three reasons: 1) it's personal; 2) it asks for specific action ("Send us your current ads," "Give us a call"); and 3) it offers the reader something for free ("a no-obligation evaluation of your marketing communications program").

Always ask for the order in your brochure. Or at least for action that will lead to an eventual sale.

10. Don't overlook the obvious.

Sometimes you get so wrapped up in the creative aspects of copywriting that you forget to include basic information—phone numbers, directions, street addresses, store hours, zip codes, and guarantees.

When you write a brochure, don't forget the obvious. Often, seemingly minor details can mean the difference between a sale and a no-sale.

For instance, one company forgot to include its second telephone number in a direct-mail brochure. As a result, the phone was frequently busy when prospects called in to order the product, and many sales were lost.

When you're proofreading your brochure copy, be sure you've checked the following items:

- Company logo, name, and address
- Phone numbers
- E-mail address
- Street address in addition to box number
- Directions ("located on the corner of Fifth and Main off I-95")
- Prices, store hours, branch locations
- List of distributors, dealers, or sales reps
- Instructions for placing orders by phone, mail, online, or text
- Credit cards accepted
- Product guarantees and warranties
- Shipping and service information
- Trademarks, registration marks, disclaimers, and other legal information
- Form numbers, dates, codes, copyright lines
- Web site URL

Also, be sure to proofread for errors in spelling, punctuation, and grammar.

These details are important. For instance, mail-order firms know their sales increase when they add a toll-free number and "major credit cards accepted" to their brochures.

11. Make the brochure worth keeping.

When the customer receives your brochure, he can do one of three things:

1. Respond to it by placing an order or asking for more information.
2. File it for future reference.
3. Throw it away.

You want the first two things to happen. You want the customer to respond to your brochure. And you want her to save it for when she needs the product again in the future.

To get someone to save your brochure, you must write a brochure that is worth keeping. Brochures that are worth keeping are valuable because of the information they contain. This information may be directly related to the product. Or it may be service information of a general nature that is indirectly related to the product.

For example, a brochure for a resort hotel in Montauk might print a detailed map of the town on the back cover. Travelers will save the brochure because of the map.

The literature package I mail to potential clients for my freelance copywriting services includes a reprint of an article I wrote ("Ten Tips for Writing More Effective Industrial Copy"). The reprint includes my picture, name, address, and phone number. Even if prospects throw away the promotional part of my package, they are likely to keep the article because it contains information that may be useful to them in their work.

Most people don't have a good idea of how the stock market works. So if a broker published a booklet titled, "A Layperson's Introduction to the Stock Market . . . and How to Play It," people would be likely to save this booklet. Later, when they accumulate enough money to invest in stocks, they would find the brochure in their files and call the broker or open an online account.

So if you want your brochure to keep selling for you, make your brochure worth keeping. Another example: a casino added value to its promotional brochure by printing the rules of blackjack on the back cover.

HOW TO ORGANIZE YOUR BROCHURE COPY

This is an oversimplification, but basically there are only three types of brochures:

1. Brochures about a product
2. Brochures about a service
3. Brochures about a company (known as "corporate" brochures or "capabilities" brochures)

The content and organization of every brochure is unique, because every selling situation and product, service, or company is unique. However, many brochures share common characteristics. Most brochures describing consulting services, for example, include a list of the consultant's clients.

Below are three outlines for "typical" product, service, and company brochures. These will give you a rough idea of what to include in the sales literature you write for your clients.

For a Product Brochure

• Introduction—a capsule description of what the product is and why the reader of the brochure should be interested in it.

• Benefits—a list of reasons why the customer should buy the product.

• Features—highlights of important product features that set the product apart from the competition.

• "How it works"—a description of how the product works and what it can do. This section can include the results of any tests that demonstrate the product's superiority.

• Types of users (markets)—this section describes the special markets the product is designed for. A wastewater plant, for example, might be sold to municipalities, utilities, and industrial plants: three separate and distinct markets, each with its own special set of requirements. This section might also include an actual list of names of well-known people or organizations that use and endorse the product.

• Applications—descriptions of the various applications in which the product can be used.

• Product availability—lists of models, sizes, materials of construction, options, accessories, and all the variations in which you can order the product. This section can also include charts, graphs, formulas, tables, or other guidelines to aid the reader in product selection.

• Pricing—information on what the product costs. Includes prices for accessories, various models and sizes, quantity discounts, and shipping and handling. Often printed on a separate sheet inserted into the brochure so the brochure does not become obsolete when prices change.

• Technical specifications—electrical requirements, power consumption, resistance to moisture, temperature range, operating conditions, cleaning methods, storage conditions, chemical properties, and other characteristics and limitations of the product.

• Questions and answers—answers to frequently asked questions about the product. Includes information not found in the other sections.

• Company description—a brief biography of the manufacturer, designed to show the reader that the product is backed by a solid, reputable organization that won't go out of business.

• Support—information on delivery, installation, training, maintenance, service, and guarantees.

• "The next step"—instructions on how to order the product (or on how to get more information on the product).

For a Brochure Describing a Service

• Introduction—outlines the services offered, types of accounts handled, and reasons why the reader should be interested in the service.

• Services offered—detailed descriptions of each of the various services rendered by the firm.

• Benefits—describes what readers will gain from the service and why they should engage the services of your firm instead of the competition.

• Methodology—outlines the service firm's method of rendering its service.

• Client list—a list of people or organizations who have used and endorse the firm's services.

• Testimonials—statements of endorsements from select clients. Testimonials are usually written in the client's own words, surrounded by quotation marks, and attributed to a specific person or organization.

• Fees and terms—describes the fees for each service and the terms and method of payment required. Also includes whatever guarantee the service firm makes to its clients.

• Biographical information—capsule biographies high-lighting the credentials of the key employees of the service firm.

• "The next step"—instructions on what to do next if you are interested in hiring the firm or learning more about its services.

For a Corporate Brochure

- The business or businesses the company is engaged in
- The corporate structure (parent company, divisions, departments, subsidiaries, branch offices)
- Corporate "philosophy" or mission statement
- Company history
- Plants and branch offices
- Geographical coverage
- Major markets
- Distribution system
- Sales
- Ranking in its field relative to competition
- Extent of stock distribution
- Earnings and dividend records
- Number of employees
- Employee benefits
- Noteworthy employees
- Inventions
- Significant achievements (including industry "firsts")
- Research and development
- Quality-control practices
- Community relations (environmental programs, contributions to public welfare, charitable activities, support of the arts, etc.)
- Awards
- Policies
- Objectives, goals, plans for the future

The above outlines are suggestions only, not mandatory formats. Mold them to suit your needs; let your product, audience, and sales objectives be your primary guide to content and organization of the copy.

Prior to widespread Internet access, brochures tended to be lengthy—eight, twelve, sixteen, even twenty-four pages or longer—because they were the primary vehicle for communicating product information.

In the digital age, Web sites have now taken that role as the repository of all product information. Many brochures today are just four to six pages presenting the highlights, with the detailed and in-depth product data available online.

CATALOGS

Catalogs are similar to brochures but with two important differences:

1. Brochures usually tell an in-depth story about a single product. Catalogs give short descriptions of many products. Because each item is given limited space, descriptions must be terse. Catalog copy is often written in a clipped, telegram-like style, with crisp, short sentences that convey a great deal of information in the fewest possible words.

2. The brochure's mission is usually to provide enough information to take the reader to the next step in the buying process. Many catalogs are mail-order vehicles from which you can order the product directly; salespeople are rarely involved. (The exception is the industrial product catalog.) As a result, a great deal of the copywriter's time is spent designing an order form that is easy to use and encourages the reader to send in an order.

In addition to using the order forms in catalogs, consumers can also place their orders by phone or online. This has resulted in many companies drastically shortening their catalogs and serving to drive prospects to the Web site for product information and ordering.

While they are fewer in number, thick catalogs are still published by some companies, especially those who produce catalogs as product reference guides for purchasing agents. A good example is Uniline, a hefty compendium of shipping supplies.

A popular strategy today is to mail a mixture of short and long catalogs throughout the year. For instance, mail a large full-line product catalog to your customers quarterly—four times a year—and a slimmer catalog monthly for the other eight months. These shorter catalogs contain fewer pages than the full quarterly catalogs and focus on driving customers to the company Web site for more production details.

Catalog writing is a separate art from brochure writing. The basics are the same but the mechanics are different. Here are a few tips to help you write successful catalogs:

Write Snappy Headlines

Even if space requires that your catalog headlines be short, you can still add selling power to them. Don't be content to simply describe the product in the headline; add a fresh phrase, a strong benefit, a descriptive adjective that hints at the product's distinct qualities.

In its order-by-mail book catalogs, Boardroom Books turns mundane book titles into strong, hard-selling catalog headlines. Instead of *The Book of Tax Knowledge*, they write, "3,147 Tax-Saving Ideas." For a book titled *Successful Tax Planning*, the catalog description reads, "Did your tax accountant ever tell you all this?" And a book on how to buy computers is advertised with the provocative headline, "What the computer salespeople don't tell you."

Include a "Letter from the Manufacturer"

Many catalogs include a "personal" letter from the company president, either printed on letterhead and bound into the catalog or printed directly onto one of the pages in the front of the catalog, often the inside front cover.

In the letter, the president talks about the quality of the products in the catalog, the firm's commitment to serving its customers, and the manufacturer's guarantee of customer satisfaction. The letter may also be used as an introduction to the company's product line, or to call attention to a particular product or group of products that is especially noteworthy or attractively priced.

Here's a homey paragraph from a letter in an L.L.Bean catalog:

> "L.L." had a simple business philosophy: "Sell good merchandise at a reasonable profit, treat your customers like human beings and they'll always come back for more." We call this "L.L.'s" golden rule. Today, 72 years later, we still practice it.

You can't help but be won over by the good sense of this honorable business philosophy and the sincerity of its statement. Putting a letter in your catalog adds warmth and a human quality to an otherwise impersonal presentation of product facts, specifications, and prices.

Give All the Key Product Facts

A catalog description must give the reader all the information needed to order the product. This includes sizes, colors, materials, prices, and styles. The copy should also give readers a concise but complete description of the product, so they can make a decision as to whether they want to buy it.

Devote the Most Space to Your Best Sellers

Devote a full page or half page to your best-selling items and list them up front. Less popular items get a quarter page or less and appear toward the back of the catalog. Items that don't sell should be dropped altogether, or appear only on the Web.

Use Techniques That Stimulate Sales

These include toll-free numbers; credit card orders accepted; a gift to the customer for placing an order; two-for-one offers; arrows, stars, bursts, and other graphic devices used to highlight special discounts within the catalog; last-minute items added as a special insert sheet or printed on the order form; volume discount for large orders ("10% off when your order exceeds $50"); discount codes for customers ordering online; gift packaging available for merchandise ordered as gifts; special sale items featured on the order form.

Make the Order Form Simple and Easy to Fill Out

Give the customer sufficient space for writing in his order. Print step-by-step instructions for ordering right on the form. Print the guarantee in large type and set it off with a border. Provide a business reply envelope in which the customer can enclose his check. And, of course, give alternative order options: fax, Web, and toll-free number.

Indicate Discounted Items in the Copy

One way of doing this is to write, "25% Off! Was $11.95—Now $8.95." Another is to cross out the old price and write in the new price—$11.95 "$8.95."

OTHER TYPES OF SALES LITERATURE

Brochures and catalogs account for most of the sales literature published in the world. Still, there are a few other types of sales literature you may be asked to write.

Annual Reports

Annual reports, the number of which seems to diminish with each passing year, are summaries of the company's performance for the past year. They combine the company information found in "capabilities brochures" with financial data on the company's sales, profits, revenues, and dividends. Annual reports are usually lavish affairs, printed on glossy stock and featuring expensive four-color photography, sophisticated graphics, and stylish copy.

Flyers

Flyers are sales literature printed on one or two sides of an unfolded 8½ x 11–inch piece of paper. Visuals, if used, are limited to simple line drawings. Flyers are used as handouts at conventions and trade shows or as bulletins posted around the neighborhood. Many small businesses find flyers an inexpensive way of reaching new customers.

Broadsides

Broadsides are flyers folded for mailing. Companies that maintain mailing lists of customers often send monthly broadsides announcing sales, new products, or other news of interest to their customers.

Invoice Stuffers

Invoice stuffers are small pieces of promotional literature designed to fit in #10 envelopes. They are mailed to customers along with the monthly bill or statement and used to announce a sale or solicit mail-order sales of a special item. The advantage of using invoice stuffers is that they get a "free ride" in the mail because they're sent with routine correspondence rather than in separate mailings.

Circulars

Circulars are printed advertising sheets that are mailed, inserted in packages or newspapers, or distributed by hand or in stores. They are usually four to eight pages long, printed in color, and contain price-off coupons for products sold in local retail outlets.

Pamphlets

Also called booklets, pamphlets are similar to brochures, except they usually contain useful information of a general nature while brochures describe the features and benefits of specific products and services.

White Papers

A white paper is a promotional piece in the guise of an informational article or report. Just as many infomercials convey the look and feel of an informative, unbiased TV program rather than a paid commercial, a white paper attempts to convince readers that they are being educated—about the issue or problem your product addresses (e.g., computer security, improving customer service, managing your sales force, saving for retirement), rather than being sold on a specific product.

The white paper serves the same sales purpose as a brochure—to sell or help sell a product or service—but it reads and looks like an article or other important piece of authoritative, objective information.

Unlike a sales brochure, a white paper must contain useful "how-to" information that helps the reader solve a problem or make or justify a key business decision (e.g., whether to lease or build a new warehouse).

But make no mistake, both the brochure and the white paper have the same ultimate objective: to sell or help sell a company's product or service.

Where white papers and brochures differ is their approach to making the sale: brochures contain a straightforward presentation of product features and benefits, whereas white papers take more of a "soft-sell" approach. Chapter 17 covers the organization, contents, and format of white papers in greater detail.

9

WRITING PUBLIC RELATIONS MATERIALS

When the first edition of this handbook was published in 1985, the primary audience for press releases was newpaper and magazine editors and reporters as well as radio and TV producers.

But in the Internet age, marketers post press releases on their Web sites, where they are read by consumers, who have become the bigger audience for PR materials. Therefore this updated PR chapter will show how to write releases to be read by consumers as well as journalists, and that are optimized for search engines through use of keyword phrases.

HOW PR DIFFERS FROM PAID ADVERTISING

Although public relations is a different discipline than advertising, they overlap, and almost every copywriter is asked to write press releases or other public relations materials at some point.

To the copywriter trained in hard-sell persuasive writing, the soft-sell touch of PR writing takes some getting used to.

Advertising reaches readers directly and makes a blatant, undisguised pitch to part them from their money. Press releases are sent to editors in the hopes that editors will publish them in their magazines or papers.

Once you send out a release, you have no control over when it will appear, in what form it will appear, or even whether it will appear. The editor can publish the release as is, rewrite it or cut it as he or she pleases, use it as the basis for a different story, or ignore it altogether. The editor has total control and, unlike the publication's advertising department, has no interest in helping you promote your firm.

The editor's only concern is publishing a magazine or paper filled with news and information of interest to his readers. If your press release contains such news or information, the editor is likely to use it. If the release is just a warmed-over ad, the editor will recognize it as such and trash it.

Companies new to public relations ask me, "Do editors really use press releases?" The answer is that they do. The *Columbia Journalism Review* surveyed an issue of the *Wall Street Journal* to find out how many of the stories were generated by press releases. The survey revealed that 111 stories on the inside pages were taken from press releases, either word for word or paraphrased. In only 30 percent of these stories did reporters put in additional facts not contained in the original release.

There are no figures on how many press releases are generated each year, but my guess is that it runs into the hundreds of thousands—maybe even the millions.

One reason why press releases are so popular is that they are inexpensive. To print a one-page release and mail it to a hundred editors costs around $100—and less if you send it pasted into the body of an e-mail, which is the way most press releases are distributed today.

If an editor picks up your release and runs it as a short article in the magazine, your firm receives the space free. Running an ad of the same size could cost hundreds or even thousands of dollars.

What's more, publicity is more credible than paid advertising. The public has a built-in skepticism for advertising but is more likely to believe what it reads in the paper or hears on TV. They do not realize that most of the news they read and hear is generated by press releases—releases sent out by the same firms that run ads and commercials.

But there is no guarantee that a press release will be picked up by the media or, once picked up, will generate much interest or new business. Some releases are ignored; others generate spectacular results. When Leisure Time Ice sent out a press kit claiming that packaged ice is clearer and purer than homemade ice, the head of the association was interviewed by at least twenty-five editors and appeared on fifteen radio and TV talk shows.

The *Wall Street Journal*, *New York Times*, *Los Angeles Times*, United Press International, and Associated Press all ran feature stories on Leisure Time Ice. The association's membership increased by 10 percent. And sales of manufactured ice went up. More and more firms are using publicity to promote their products and services.

Even professionals who traditionally look down upon public relations—doctors, lawyers, architects, engineers, management consultants—are now writing releases, placing stories, and appearing on radio and TV talk shows: a survey of 523 members of the American Bar Association revealed that 20 percent of these lawyers use publicity to promote their practices.

DIRECT-TO-CONSUMER PR ON THE WEB

By far the biggest development in public relations in the twenty-first century is "DTC PR"—direct-to-consumer public relations.

In the twentieth century, press releases were sent to and seen by media outlets only: newspaper editors and reporters, magazine editors, program directors and radio stations, and television producers. This is "DTM PR"—direct-to-media public relations—and indeed virtually all PR was DTM PR.

These media professionals either threw the press releases in the trash because the content was not of interest to them or used some of the material in their publication or broadcast. Most commonly, some of the content in the release was used as source material for stories the reporters and editors were working on.

Or sometimes, most notably in trade magazines and newsletters, an excerpt from the press release was published as a short stand-alone item. On occasion, the publication would print the entire release almost word for word as you gave it to them, when the topic was of great interest to readers and all the content was interesting or useful—or it saved the publication's staff writer from having to do the work herself.

Now, press releases are also used in DTC PR. The marketer's Web site typically has a section called "Press Releases," "Press Room," "News," or "Media." All or at least major press releases distributed to the media are also posted in the PR section of the site, typically in HTML, where visitors can read them directly, as they were written, without the vetting or editing by the media.

There is virtually no difference between DTM and DTC press releases save one. When preparing to post your DTC PR on your Web site, make sure to judiciously add relevant keywords to the text. This can help ensure that the press release shows up when prospects are searching that keyword. In addition, having a lot of press releases on your site can raise your search engine rankings, because Google and other search engines give higher ranking to content than to sales copy such as product pages.

WHAT IS A PRESS RELEASE?

A press release is a news story prepared by an organization and distributed to the media for the purpose of publicizing the organization's products, services, or activities.

Here's a sample of an effective release typed in the proper press-release format:

FROM: Kirsch Communications, 226 Seventh Street, Garden City, NY 11530

For more information please call: Len Kirsch, XXX-XXX-XXXX

FOR: Pinwheel Systems, 404 Park Avenue South, New York, NY 10016

Contact: John N. Schaedler, President, XXX-ABC-DEFG

FOR IMMEDIATE RELEASE

INTRODUCTORY KIT FOR NEW "RUFF-PROOFS" COLOR COMPS OFFERED BY PINWHEEL SYSTEMS

A special Introductory Kit of watercolor dyes and other supplies which can be used with its new "Ruff-Proofs" do-it-yourself coloring system has been developed by Pinwheel Systems, New York, it was announced today by John N. Schaedler, president of the company.

Ruff-Proofs are latent-image prints made from black and white artwork. They can be transformed into multicolor art for layout and design comps, packaging, flip charts and other graphics, Schaedler said, merely by applying watercolor dyes or markers. (Patents are pending on the process.)

The prints are delivered in sets of four to give the artist an opportunity to experiment with different colors and explore varying color combinations. They are available from franchised Pinwheel Studios.

The Introductory Kit has a retail value of $45, Schaedler said, and is being offered to artists and designers for $20 with the purchase of Ruff-Proofs. It contains a complete set of coloring materials:

- A 36-bottle assortment of Dr. P. H. Martin's Synchromatic Transparent Watercolor Dyes, with a swatch card of actual color chips.

- A 30-cup palette for mixing colors, squeeze-bottle dispensers for water and cleanup solution, plus absorbent tissues and cotton swabs used in the coloring process.

More information about the kits and the Ruff-Proofs process is available from John Schaedler at Pinwheel Systems, 404 Park Avenue South, New York, NY, telephone XXX-ABC-DEFG.

Here are twelve tips on press-release format and content.

1. What you say is more important than using fancy PR letterheads or layouts. Clarity and accuracy are critical.

2. When an outside public relations firm writes the release for you, its name and your own should appear as the sources for the release. If you wrote the release yourself, you become the sole source for more information. Either way, be sure to include names and phone numbers so the editor can get more information if needed.

3. The release can be dated with a release date or with the phrase "For Immediate Release." Date the release one day in advance of the actual distribution date to make it timely.

4. Place the release date under the headline and underline it.

5. The headline should sum up your story. Maximum length: two to three lines. This tells a busy editor, at a glance, if the story is worth considering.

6. The lead contains the "who, what, when, where, why, and how." If the editor chops everything else, at least you've gotten the guts of your story across.

7. Include a person to be credited if there's something worth quoting or if you make any claims. Editors don't want to take the position they are claiming something—they'd rather hang it on you. The personal credits often get deleted, but it's wise to put them in where needed.

8. The body of the story picks up the additional facts. Lay off the superlatives and complimentary adjectives. Remember, the press releases is content, not advertising.

9. Length: shoot for a single page, no more than two pages. Beyond that, reading becomes a burden for the editor.

10. When the reader might need it, include the name, address, phone number, and e-mail of someone to contact for more information.

11. Photos, visuals, and graphics can be pasted into the body of the e-mail. But add a note to the editor that separate image files of 300 dots per inch (dpi) are available upon request.

12. Keep the release simple, straightforward, newsy. If you need only two paragraphs, don't write ten. Excess verbiage turns editors off, especially now that most releases are distributed via e-mail or online PR distribution services rather than mailed as hard copies.

YES, BUT IS IT NEWS?

Editors look for press releases containing news. Like a good ad, the headline of the press release must instantly transmit the news to the reader.

Editors are flooded with press releases and don't have time to wade through your release and dig for the real story: an editor at a technology magazine said her staff received two thousand press releases a month. Your release must telegraph the news in the first five seconds of reading.

But what makes for a news story? It depends on your industry and your audience. *Forbes* and *Fortune* would not consider publication of your new ball-bearing catalog to be news. But the editors of *Machine Design*, *Design News*, and other trade magazines whose readers use ball bearings might very well run a short news release on the catalog and a picture of its cover.

One thing that is not news is advertising and promotion. Editors will not publish descriptive stories about your product, service, or organization unless the story tells them something new or provides service information useful to the publication's readers.

A press release with the headline, "Ajax Dry Cleaners Provides Top-Quality Cleaning at Reasonable Prices" will not generate any coverage. But if Ajax sent out a release titled "Ajax Dry Cleaners Offers Expert Advice on How to Remove Tough Stains," editors might reprint the advice as a how-to article. Ajax gets publicity by being listed as the source of the expert advice.

Here is a list of possible topics for news releases about your company. They all hold interest because they contain either news or useful information, or both. You can write a press release about:

- A new product
- An old product with a new name or package
- A product improvement
- A new version or model of an old product
- An old product available in new materials, colors, or sizes
- A new application of an old product
- New accessories available for an old product
- The publication of new or revised sales literature—brochures, catalogs, data sheets, surveys, reports, reprints, white papers
- A speech or presentation given by an executive
- An expert opinion on any subject
- A controversial issue
- New employees
- Promotions within the firm
- Awards and honors won by your organization or its employees
- Original discoveries or innovations (such as patents)
- New stores, branch offices, headquarters, facilities
- New sales reps, distributors, agents
- Major contracts awarded to your firm
- Joint ventures
- Management reorganization
- Major achievements, such as number of products sold, increase in sales, quarterly earnings, safety record
- Unusual people, products, ways of doing business
- Case histories of successful applications, installations, projects
- Tips and hints ("how-to" advice)
- Change of company name, slogan, or logo
- Opening of a new business
- Special events such as a sale, party, open house, plant tour, contest, or sweepstakes
- Charitable acts or other community relations

The only type of press release that does not need to contain news is the "background release," or "backgrounder." Backgrounders present a brief overview of your company.

Even though the backgrounder is not, strictly speaking, a news story, you should try to put something new, or at least some little-known fact or startling piece of information, in the backgrounders you write. This will grab an editor's interest more strongly than a bland summary of your organizational chart.

Another special type of press release is the "fact sheet." Fact sheets contain detailed information, usually in list form, too lengthy to be included in the body of the main release.

A press release announcing the opening of a new gourmet food store might be distributed with a fact sheet listing recipes for three or four of the store's specialties. A fact sheet for a consulting firm could contain a list of clients or brief biographies of the firm's principals.

Often copywriters are faced with a client who wants publicity and asks us to write a press release but has nothing new to report. In such instances, a creative publicist or copywriter can "manufacture" a hook or angle strong enough to gain the media's attention.

For instance, when Jericho Communications, a New York City PR firm, was looking for a way to gain publicity for its client Domino's Pizza, someone said, "When we work late at night, we order pizza. Maybe the White House does the same thing. Can we see whether pizza deliveries to the White House increase when there is a national emergency?"

Sure enough, they did. And Jericho created the "Pizza Meter," publicizing the fact that you could judge the state of the nation by the volume of pizza delivery to the White House. The tactic was successful, garnering major media coverage for the pizza maker.

When Giga Pets were the rage, my then seven-year-old son

dropped his into the toilet and was upset that it "died" (the water shorted out the electronics). To make him feel better, we buried the Giga Pet in our backyard and held a mock funeral, which gave me an idea for some PR.

I sent out the press release below, and within a week a major New Jersey newspaper did a large feature article on our "Giga Pet cemetery" (please don't send for the booklet, which I lost track of long ago).

FROM: Microchip Gardens, 174 Holland Avenue, New Milford, NJ 07646

CONTACT: Bob Bly, phone 973-263-0562

For immediate release

MICROCHIP GARDENS, WORLD'S FIRST "GIGAPET CEMETERY," OPENS IN NORTHERN NJ

When 7-year-old Alex Bly's Giga Pet died after he dropped it in the toilet, he couldn't find a place to bury it. So his father, NJ-based entrepreneur Bob Bly, created Microchip Gardens—the world's first Giga Pet cemetery—in the family's suburban backyard.

Now if your child's Giga Pet dies and can't be revived, instead of unceremoniously tossing it in the trash, you can give it a proper burial in a beautiful, tree-lined resting place.

For fees starting at $5, based on plot location and method of interment (burial, mausoleum, cremation), Bly will give your dearly departed Giga Pet an eternal resting place in Microchip Gardens, complete with funeral service and burial certificate.

"Even Giga Pets don't last forever," said Bly. "There are pet cemeteries for dogs and cats; now Giga Pets have one, too."

To help owners get the most pleasure from Giga Pet ownership, Bly—author of 35 published books including *The "I Hate Kathie Lee Gifford" Book* (Kensington) and *The Ultimate Unauthorized Star Trek Quiz Book* (HarperCollins)—has written an informative new booklet, "Raising Your Giga Pet."

The booklet covers such topics as purchasing your first Giga Pet; taking the pet home; care and feeding; and play and discipline. Giga Pet burial rituals and the origins of Microchip Gardens are also covered.

To get your copy of "Raising Your Giga Pet," which includes complete information on the Microchip Gardens Giga Pet cemetery, send $4 to: CTC, 22 E. Quackenbush Avenue, Dumont, NJ 07628.

QUESTIONS AND ANSWERS ABOUT PRESS RELEASES

Here are some questions I'm frequently asked by companies that are just getting into public relations:

Q: *What's the best length for a press release?*
A: For a new product release, one to two pages. If you have a lot to tell, three pages is acceptable. But certainly no longer than that.

Case histories and backgrounders usually run longer; three to five pages is average. If it takes more than five pages to tell your story, make it a feature article, not a press release.

Q: *Is it better if the release comes from a PR firm or straight from the company?*
A: What counts is not who wrote the release, but whether the release contains interesting news clearly presented. Some people have a theory that editors are wary of dealing with public relations people and prefer to go straight to the source. I know a few editors who feel this way. But the majority don't.

Q: *How do I reproduce the release?*

A: Offset printing is best and doesn't cost very much. Photocopies are acceptable if they are crisp, sharp, and free of smudges or streaks. Or you can run off copies on your laser printer. Today, most releases are distributed electronically.

Q: *Do I need to send a photo out with my release?*

A: It's helpful but not mandatory. An interesting photo of a product, person, plant, process, or package will heighten the editor's interest. Remember, most magazines and papers publish pictures as well as words.

Paste a few of your most interesting photos in the body of the e-mail, and also offer to send them as 300 dpi color images in a separate file the editor can request. If the photo files are too large, send in a Dropbox.

Q: *What's the best way to distribute a press release?*

A: The basic methods are postal mail and online, with most marketers using the latter.

Do not send a press release or any other copy as an attached e-mail file to an editor who does not know you and is not expecting it; the editor will delete it without opening it for fear of catching malware or a computer virus. When in doubt, call editors prior to sending your release and ask how they prefer to receive materials.

WRITING A FEATURE ARTICLE

Copywriters also get called upon to "ghostwrite" full-length feature stories for trade and business publications.

Take a look at some trade journals. They contain many articles written by outside contributors: scientists, engineers, managers, and other professionals employed by companies.

These contributors write not for pay (most trade journals pay a small honorarium or nothing at all) but to promote their own careers as well as the companies they work for. Many companies have a regular scheduled program of placing feature articles in magazines. And they hire professional writers to ghostwrite these articles.

Another option is to post the article on your blog. Include a link to a page with more detail on the subject matter. Opinions on optimal blog length vary, but 500 to 1,000 words is common.

Although each article is different, there are four basic types of articles that magazines publish:

1. Case Histories

A case history article is a product "success story." It tells the story of how a product, service, or system was helpful to a specific customer.

Case history reporting derives its effectiveness from the principle that what works for one customer might work for others. Case histories are effective, too, because they're credible. They deal in specifics rather than in claims or generalities. Finally, case histories are an inherently storytelling approach to selling.

Here's how a typical case history article gets started. A telephone manufacturer installs a new office phone system in a customer's sales office. The office manager finds that the new system has increased the productivity of the sales force by 25 percent and cut phone bills in half.

When the telephone manufacturer gets wind of this, he asks the office manager or other company executive if he can write up this success story and place it with an appropriate trade journal. If the manager agrees, the telephone manufacturer hires a writer.

The writer interviews the office manager at the sales firm and writes the story. After it is approved, it is submitted to the magazine and published. The byline may be that of the manufacturer, the manager, the magazine editor, or the writer. It depends on the nature of the article.

2. How-to Articles

These provide useful information that helps the reader do something better ("How to Choose the Right Lighting for Your Small Business," "Seven Ways to Cut Energy Costs," "A Guide to Ball-Bearing Selection"). How-to articles are also known as "tutorials," perhaps because they tutor the reader in a new skill or area of knowledge.

The how-to article is content marketing (see chapter 17). It does not discuss your product directly (your company shouldn't even be mentioned, except in the byline). Instead, it promotes you indirectly by establishing your firm's reputation as a leader in the field. Readers tend to clip and save how-to articles. So, although your article may not generate immediate business, some people will keep it and call on you when the need arises.

3. Issue Articles

In issue articles, industry experts speak out on some topical, controversial, or technical issue of the day. These articles help strengthen your company's image as a leader in its field. Example: "Should Internet Users Be Prosecuted for Illegal Downloading of Movies, Music, and Other Copyrighted Materials?"

4. News

News articles are usually prepared by staff editors and reporters, not outsiders. Occasionally, though, a corporation with big news to report—a merger, an acquisition, a revolutionary new invention—will work with a reporter to develop a feature story. The reporter gets a scoop, while the company gets good press.

QUERY LETTERS

The first step in getting a feature story published in a magazine is to get an editor interested in the article topic. This means first suggesting the topic to the editor, either in a phone conversation or by letter, usually sent today as an e-mail.

Some editors will listen to your pitch over the phone. Most want to see the idea written up in a short proposal known as a "query letter." This is a one- or two-page outline, in letter form, of the article you propose to write.

The query letter explains what the article is about, what your "angle" is, why the magazine's readers will be interested in the article, and what makes you qualified to write it. The letter is also a demonstration of your writing style. Boring query letters rarely result in an article assignment, because the editor assumes your article will be as boring as your letter.

Here is a sample of a query that got me an assignment to write an article for *Amtrak Express*:

Mr. James A. Frank, Editor
AMTRAK EXPRESS
34 East 51st Street
New York, NY 10022

Dear Mr. Frank:
Is this letter a waste of paper?
   Yes—if it fails to get the desired result.
   In business, most letters and memos are written to generate a specific response—close a sale, set up a meeting, get a job interview, make a contact. Many of these letters fail to do their job.
   Part of the problem is that business executives and support staff don't know how to write persuasively. The solution is a formula first discovered by advertising copywriters—a

formula called AIDA. AIDA stands for Attention, Interest, Desire, Action.

First, the letter gets attention . . . with a hard-hitting lead paragraph that goes straight to the point, or offers an element of intrigue.

Then, the letter hooks the reader's interest. The hook is often a clear statement of the reader's problems, her needs, her desires. If you are writing to a customer who received damaged goods, state the problem. And then promise a solution.

Next, create desire. You are offering something—a service, a product, an agreement, a contract, a compromise, a consultation. Tell the reader the benefit he'll receive from your offering. Create a demand for your product.

Finally, call for action. Ask for the order, the signature, the check, the go-ahead.

I'd like to give you a 1,500-word article on "How to Write Letters That Get Results." The piece will illustrate the AIDA formula with a variety of actual letters and memos from insurance companies, banks, manufacturers, and other organizations.

This letter, too, was written to get a specific result—an article assignment from the editor of *Amtrak Express*.

Did it succeed?

Regards,
Bob Bly

P.S. By way of introduction, I'm an advertising consultant and the author of *Technical Writing: Structure, Standards, and Style* (McGraw-Hill).

Editors usually respond to query letters within a month or so. (If a month goes by and you haven't heard, follow up with another letter or a phone call.)

A positive response to a query is, "Your proposed article idea interests us. Send a manuscript." This means the editor wants to see the article. It doesn't mean a promise to publish it. The editor won't make that decision until after reading it. A positive response to a query letter is no guarantee that your article will be printed.

If the editor turns down your proposal, you can send your query letter to other publications. Few article ideas are restricted to one magazine only. Most are appropriate for at least half a dozen publications or more.

In the twenty-first century, most publications want to receive digital queries. They either provide an e-mail address on their site to where you can send your query or else have an online submission form for proposing article ideas. When sent via e-mail, the query letter is pasted into the body of the e-mail, not transmitted as an e-mail attachment.

HOW TO WRITE A SPEECH

Business and association executives don't always communicate by writing articles. Sometimes they make speeches. And, as with article writing, executives often hire ghostwriters to write their speeches for them.

When I got my first speech-writing assignment, I was paralyzed with fear because I had no idea how long—in minutes or words—a speech should be.

Now I do. The average speaker speaks at a rate of 120 words a minute. It follows that a twenty-minute speech should be 2,400 words long.

For lunch and dinner talks, many speeches are brief, about twenty minutes. Less seems insubstantial. More can get boring. No speech, no matter how important, should last more than an hour.

Every speech should have a clear-minded purpose. Most speeches are given to entertain, to teach, to persuade, or to inspire.

Speeches are effective at getting across ideas, opinions, and emotions. They are less effective at transmitting a large body of facts (print is the appropriate medium for that).

Here are some additional tips for writing speeches that accomplish their goals without boring the audience to tears:

1. Find Out What the Speaker Wants to Say

Few writing assignments are as personal or as idiosyncratic as writing someone else's speech. You'll avoid headaches if you take the time to know the speaker's requirements before you sit down to write.

"You have to ask the right questions of your client to prepare a speech that he'll deliver as if he really means it," writes freelancer Nancy Edmonds Hanson. "Sometimes a lengthy discussion of the topic is necessary before the client himself clarifies his position on it. Your job is to probe, to ask him to carry his own thoughts a little further until he's worked the topic through in his own mind."

Interviews with the client reveal the basic thrust of the speech and provide most of the facts. Information gaps can be filled in through library research or by browsing through the client's private files on the subject.

2. Know Your Audience

Learn as much as you can about the group you'll be speaking to. This will help you tailor your talk to their specific interests. For example, a speech on podcasting should be geared toward the professional interests of the audience. Engineers are interested in the technology: how it works. Advertising executives want to know more about podcasting as a marketing medium.

3. Write a Strong Opening

The first sentence uttered by the speaker is like the headline of an advertisement or the lead paragraph of a direct-mail piece. An engaging opening grabs attention and gets the audience enthusiastic about your topic. A sample speech introduction:

> Today, I would like to share with you some of my innermost thoughts and memories, which have been locked away deep in my heart for the longest time. It has been seven years since the passing of my husband, Joseph. This is the first time many of these memories and thoughts will see the light of day. I have agreed to speak with you today in order to impress upon you the importance of Sephardic Bikur Holim (SBH) and what it meant to my children. My story starts with something we all know, yet very rarely face, and that is how vulnerable we all really are.
>
> Joseph was a wonderful husband, a caring father, and a successful businessman. He had such a passion for helping others, and he took the plight of the unfortunate very personally. He was instrumental in making SBH the organization that it is today, and it was always his dream to become a social worker. To me it seemed like a natural progression for Joseph to trade in his business career for college life.

4. Then, There's Humor

Speechwriters are always uncertain when it comes to using humor. They know that humor can quickly warm an audience to the speaker. But a joke that bombs can ruin the whole talk.

My advice is to pepper the speech with little tidbits of warm, gentle, good-natured humor. Not big gags, old jokes, or nightclub-comic routines. Just a few well-chosen, humorous comments that make the speaker seem a bit more human. Audiences respond well to self-effacing humor.

Leading off with a prepared joke is risky. Often jokes fall flat, because what is funny to some people is not to others. Worse, some audience members may think you are there to clown and have nothing important to say.

5. Don't Try to Cover Too Much

Remember, a twenty-minute speech has only 2,400 words. Also, the spoken word is often not quite as compact as written English. Therefore, there's only so much information you can put in your talk.

Don't try to cover your whole subject. Just break off a little piece of it and tell your story with warmth, wit, humor, and authority. Delete trivial information and limit your talk to the important key points.

For example, "Your Career" is too broad a topic for a speech. "How to Start Your Own Digital Agency" is a more manageable subject for an after-dinner talk.

6. Write in a Conversational Tone

Speeches are to be heard, not read. A speech is one person talking, and it should sound like talking, not like an academic thesis or a corporate memorandum.

Write in a conversational tone. That means short words. Short sentences. Plenty of contractions. Even a colloquial expression every now and then.

The best test of a speech is to read the draft aloud. If it doesn't sound natural, rewrite it until it does.

Use bullets, headings, and numbers to divide the speech into sections. The speaker can catch her breath during the pauses between sections.

If the copy can't be broken up this way, then indicate places where the speaker can pause between paragraphs. These stops give nervous speakers a chance to slow down.

7. *Keep It Simple*

A speech is not the appropriate medium for delivering complex ideas and sophisticated theories.

For one thing, a speech is limited in the amount of information it can contain. For another, the listener can't stop to ponder a point or go back to information presented earlier (as he can when reading an article, ad, or brochure).

Ideally, your speech should be centered around one main point or theme. If a fact or observation doesn't tie in with this point, throw it out.

Give the listener easy-to-grasp tidbits of information and advice. Don't try to get the audience to follow a rigorous mathematical proof, a complex argument, or a complicated process. They won't.

8. *What About Visuals?*

When I worked in the corporate world in the 1970s, slides were the rage. No speaker would think of giving a presentation without a carousel full of brightly colored slides to back him up. Today, PowerPoint presentations run on laptops and are projected onto screens large enough for everyone in the audience to see.

In some cases, visuals can be useful. If you want to introduce the new corporate logo, you must show a visual of it; words alone can't adequately describe a graphic concept.

Avoid making text slides too wordy, as the more text on the slide, the smaller the words will appear on the screen. A good rule of thumb is to have a maximum of five bullets per slide with no more than five words per bullet.

9. *Handouts*

At conferences, attendees often get a thick binder containing the PowerPoint presentations from all of the speakers. When speaking to local groups, a reprint of an article you wrote makes a good handout. Or you can distribute a sheet summarizing your key points.

10. Pick a Catchy Title for Your Speech

When you speak, you'll lead off with the first sentence, not the title. But the title will be used in mailings, flyers, and other promotions aimed at attracting an audience for your talk. The name of your speech can make the difference between an empty house and an attentive crowd.

"Effective Management of Overseas Trade Show Exhibits" is a boring title. "How to Set Up a Booth at a Japanese Electronics Show—And Live to Tell About It" is much more enticing.

WRITING PROMOTIONAL NEWSLETTERS

Many organizations publish newsletters that they distribute free to customers, clients, prospects, employees, journal editors, and decision makers in their industries.

Most companies today use e-newsletters distributed as e-mails. They work. But a minority of marketers mail traditional paper newsletters (fig. 9.1). Because of their rarity, they stand out more than the electronic kind.

Whether you use print or digital, the stories in these newsletters are similar in tone and content to the press releases and feature stories I've discussed—only the articles are usually shorter. Newsletters are designed to promote, either directly or indirectly, the organization and its activities, services, or products.

The newsletter has less credibility than a story appearing in a magazine or on major media Web sites, because readers know it is self-published by the firm. On the other hand, a company can use the newsletter to say whatever it wants without fear of being censored, rewritten, or misquoted by an editor.

Newsletters build your image and reputation with a select group of prospects (those who receive the newsletter) over a period of time.

Fig. 9.1: Copywriter's rough layout of a two-sided, 8½ x 11–inch newsletter.

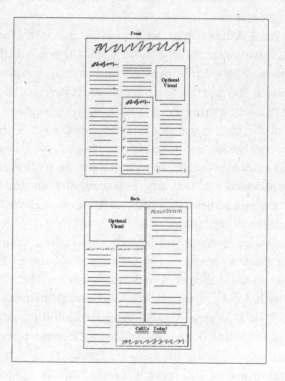

Many clients start out with ambitious plans to publish the newsletter on a regular basis—every quarter, every other month, every month. But when media costs run over budget for the new Facebook ad campaign, the marketing manager may make up the difference by skipping an issue or two of his newsletter.

Companies try to lure freelancers and agencies to do their newsletters for a low price with the logic, "It's not as key as advertising or online videos, so we can't afford to spend a lot. But we'll make up the difference with volume, since it's a steady thing."

Writers and agencies should approach newsletters with caution. Often a promised assignment of six newsletters turns into two.

The typical print promotional newsletter is four pages long. Text is set in two or three columns, and there is little or no white space. There are three or four major feature stories (about 200 to 500 words each), a few short items (two to three paragraphs), and a number of photos with captions.

Most of the stories are not written especially for the newsletter but come from other sources: press releases, condensed feature articles, speeches, case histories, sales literature, ad campaigns, social media posts, and webinars. In this way, the newsletter gives additional exposure to messages you're communicating in other media.

For instance, a bank published a newsletter called "As a Matter of Fact: A Consumer Newsletter with Money Facts for You." It was available from a rack display at local branches and filled with helpful information on personal finance. Articles included "The Mortgage Maze," "The 10% Factor . . . the Facts Behind Withholding Taxes on Interest," "Recovering from the Recession," and "The Pathway to Investing."

The relationship between a bank and its customers is based on trust. By providing investment counseling at no cost through its newsletter, the bank was helping to cement that relationship.

A local supermarket published a four-page newsletter on food, available at the checkout counter. It contained tips on nutrition, exercise, food shopping, and cooking. Each issue also featured a number of recipes.

By helping me exercise and eat right, the supermarket gained my goodwill. By giving me recipes, it got me to come into the store to buy more food.

A CHECKLIST OF NEWSLETTER STORY IDEAS

The above examples give you an idea of the types of stories published in promotional newsletters. The checklist below can serve as a source of ideas for putting together your own newsletter:

❑ News
❑ Explanatory articles ("how it works")
❑ Product stories
❑ Case histories
❑ Background information
❑ How to solve a problem
❑ Technical tips for using the product
❑ General how-to information and advice
❑ Do's and don'ts
❑ Industry updates
❑ Employee news
❑ Employee profiles
❑ Community relations news
❑ Financial news
❑ Roundup of recent sales activities
❑ Interviews and profiles
❑ Letters column
❑ Announcements or write-ups of conferences, seminars, trade shows, meetings
❑ Photos with captions
❑ Product selection guides
❑ Checklists

As mentioned, today, many companies are distributing their promotional newsletters online, either in addition to or as a replacement for a printed customer newsletter. For specific guidelines on writing and publishing online newsletters, see chapter 13.

10

WRITING TV AND RADIO COMMERCIALS

Today, with hundreds of TV and streaming video channels, more commercials are competing for our attention than ever before. The challenge is to make your commercial stand out from the rest and attract the consumer's attention. But advertisers are unsure as to how to do this.

One school believes that the "creative" approach is the solution to TV's clutter. Dramatic stories, fast-paced action, surreal fantasy landscapes, animation, humor, computer graphics, the "new wave" look, and other techniques are used to give commercials distinct graphic appeal—often, in my opinion, at the expense of the sales pitch. These commercials stand out, but they don't sell, because they tend to ignore the product and its appeal to the consumer.

A second school embraces old-fashioned values. Its adherents believe that simple commercials, with honest and straightforward presentations of the product and its benefits, are what convince consumers to write checks and open wallets. One example is the spots for OxiClean Stain Remover. They are persuasive because they demonstrate the product, which catches your attention. Also effective are the TV commercials for My

Pillow, where the company owner and inventor of the pillow enthusiastically explains and demonstrates the product's superiority to ordinary store-bought pillows.

Many advertising experts are rising to defend the straightforward approach to TV commercials. Faith Popcorn, futurist and founder of BrainReserve, says we're moving into an age of product intelligence, in which consumers will demand real information, "real sell." She predicted this decades ago, and the rise of content marketing seems to have proven her right.

In the content marketing era, many people take things in through information. Browse the shelves of your local bookstore; you'll find that "how-to" and straight informational-type books dominate the publishing industry. What's more, the authors of these books don't resort to trickery, grandstanding, or gimmicks—they tell their story through a straightforward presentation of the facts. They know that the real customer for their book is someone who wants and needs the information it contains.

And so it is with products. The serious prospect is an information seeker; she wants to be well informed before she spends her hard-earned dollars. Too many commercials waste their effort pitching to the nonprospect, someone who is unlikely to turn into a paying customer.

Advertisers emulate the showmanship and production values of Hollywood feature films in their efforts to get these nonprospects to watch their commercials. They forget that the goal is not to get people to watch, but to get people to buy or to prefer one brand to another. Long ago, David Ogilvy and other advertising pioneers proved there is no correlation between a person liking a commercial and being sold by it.

"I have wondered often if 'creativity' doesn't sometimes get in the way of believability," *Advertising Age* columnist Sid Bernstein once wrote in a column on TV commercials. "I have a feeling that what we really need is more simplicity. More

simple, honest selling. More dignity, more clarity. Less confusion . . . less emphasis on sensational entertainment and more
emphasis on making a sensible buy."

On the other hand, Ogilvy famously said, "You can't bore
people into buying your product." What seems to be working
today is "edutainment," a term so named because it combines
education (information) with entertainment.

THE 12 TYPES OF COMMERCIALS

I've always thought writing fiction was an original act, one that
didn't fit into a formula.

But in a class on screenwriting, the instructor surprised us
by saying, "I know you think what you've written is very special. But people who write and produce films have documented
just thirty-six dramatic situations. All screenplays can be put in
one of these categories." She listed some of the categories as
revolution, madness, crimes of love, ambition, remorse, disaster, and adultery.

Although TV commercials seemingly offer infinite variety,
there are fewer TV commercial formats than there are screen-
play situations. Twelve of these are described below.

1. Demonstrations

Demonstrations show how a product works. If you are selling
a food processor, you show how quickly and easily it slices,
dices, blends, and mixes.

Demonstrations are effective for comparing two products.
On the left of the screen, you show how sticky and dull most
car waxes are. On the right, you show how easily your wax
goes on, how brightly it shines, and how it repels water like
a duck.

A commercial for a pool chlorinator showed a woman sitting
by a pool as the voice-over told how crystal clear the chlorinator

makes pool water. Suddenly, the woman shoots up through the water. We find out she was actually in the pool and that the commercial was shot underwater, dramatically demonstrating the clarity of water treated with the product being advertised.

2. Testimonials

Testimonials are used to add credibility to a claim. People more readily believe praise for a product when it comes from a customer or a third party rather than the manufacturer.

Some of the most effective testimonials are those featuring real people who use and like the product. Real people are more believable than paid actors or "staged" interviews. To get genuine testimonials from real product users, commercial producers use hidden cameras to film reactions to product use and answers to questions.

Many advertisers pay celebrities to endorse their products, reasoning that celebrities draw attention and that people hang on their every word.

Commercial makers do agree that a celebrity must be right for the product. Britney Spears generated excitement for Pepsi but would be less appropriate for investment banking commercials. Marie Osmond does Weight Watchers. Peyton Manning is featured on Nationwide Insurance TV spots.

3. Stand-up Presenter

In this type of commercial, an actor stands before the camera and delivers a straightforward sales pitch on the virtues of the product.

The stand-up presenter, also known as a "talking head" or "pitchman," can be especially effective when the sales pitch you have is so strong that it doesn't need to be gussied up. Alex Trebek is a stand-up presenter for Colonial Life and also reverse mortgages. Because it is a direct response commercial, the results can be measured. And it must be working. Otherwise, these expensive spots would not have run so often.

4. Slice of Life

The slice of life is a miniature play centering around two or more people and a story involving the product. In one toothpaste commercial, a little boy in pajamas is teary-eyed. He is sad because Mom scolded him for not brushing his teeth. Dad explains that Mom is not mad but concerned for his health: brushing will give him a mouth full of pearly white, cavity-free teeth. The little boy smiles and laughs; Mom loves him after all.

5. Lifestyle Advertising

A lifestyle commercial focuses on the user and how the product fits into his lifestyle. Corona beer features young, fit teens on the beach having fun with good friends, portraying a relaxed, easygoing lifestyle. Commercials for assisted living facilities for the elderly, as well as active adult communities you can buy in to as early as age fifty, portray them as pleasant living environments offering both companionship and activities.

Note: If you are going to use still photos or videos showing actors depicting your target market, use actors or models who are about ten years younger and weigh ten pounds less than real people in your demographic. Reason: people like to think of themselves as younger-looking and slimmer than they really are or else aspire to be like the guy or gal in the picture.

6. Animation

Animation—cartoons—is effective in selling to children, especially when featuring popular cartoon characters. Animation aimed at adults ditches the cartoon characters for the most part, simply showing the actions that would normally be portrayed by live actors as animation.

7. Jingles

A jingle is an advertising slogan set to music. Famous jingles of the past include McDonald's "You Deserve a Break Today," Pepsi's "Catch That Pepsi Spirit," and Diet Coke's "You're Gonna Drink It Just for the Taste of It." The best jingles implant slogans in people's minds by setting the slogans to catchy, memorable tunes that people just can't stop humming or singing. Farmers Insurance has a signature semi-jingle that goes like this: "We are Farmers; dum-de-dum-dum-dum-dum-DUM."

8. Visual as Hero

Some advertisers treat commercial making as filmmaking, not as selling. They produce mini-feature films with color and visual quality that surpasses most television shows and motion pictures. An example of this was the auto commercial for the Turbo Z. The action took place in a steamy, dark "city of the future" reminiscent of the science-fiction film *Blade Runner*.

Unusual graphic treatments can glue viewers to the set. But do these far-out entertainments sell products? I haven't read any articles or case studies that say they do.

9. Humor

Funny commercials are in (e.g., "No can left behind" for Pepsi Max). We know many people enjoy funny commercials. Whether they are sold by them is another story. In fact, a common problem with funny and other entertaining commercials is that immediately after viewing them, often the consumers can't name the product being advertising—because the commercial, not the product, was made the center of attention.

Very few copywriters are able to write humorous copy. And when a funny commercial falls flat, it becomes a sales disaster. Unless you are 99.9 percent sure that you are funny (and that your audience will think so, too), avoid the funny commercial. What is funny to one viewer is foolish to another.

10. Continuing Characters

The use of a continuing character—a fictional person who appears in a series of commercials and print ads—is extremely effective in building recognition of a brand. Successful fictional characters include Mr. Whipple, the Jolly Green Giant, Aunt Bluebell, Mr. Goodwrench, the Maytag Repairman, the Keebler Elves, and the Pillsbury Doughboy. If you create a fictional character that captures the public's fancy, use him continuously and heavily until research or sales show that your customers are tiring of him. In recent years, this style seems to have declined in usage.

Sometimes the recurring character is the company owner, such as Jimmy Dean for his sausages and the Purdue family for their chickens. Others can be actors such as the woman for Popeye's or Patrick Warburton for National Car Rentals or Peyton Manning for Nationwide Insurance.

11. Reason-Why Copy

Reason-why copy lists the reasons why people should buy the product. A commercial for Hebrew National Franks showed people eating and enjoying hot dogs while the voice-over narration listed the reasons why people like to eat the franks. Reason-why commercials can be effective, although reason-why copy seems to work better in print than on the air.

12. Emotion

Commercials that use nostalgia, charm, or sentimentality to tug at your heartstrings (and your wallet) can be both memorable and persuasive. In a Budweiser commercial created for the Super Bowl, the spot shows the affection between a horse trainer and a horse he raised from a foal, which he sells to

Budweiser. At a parade, where the trainer is in a crowd as a spectator, the horse, now one of the Budweiser horses, sees the trainer. He breaks away from the parade, runs in the opposite direction to where the trainer is standing, and they have what is clearly an emotional reunion.

Like humor, genuine emotional copy can be difficult to write. If you can do it, more power to you. Most copywriters have a better shot sticking to demonstrations, pitchmen, testimonials, and other "straight-sell" formats.

TIPS ON WRITING TV SPOTS

Here are some tips on writing TV commercials that are arresting, memorable, and persuasive:

• TV is primarily a medium of pictures, not words. Be sure your pictures deliver a selling message. If you can't figure out what is being sold when the sound is turned off, the commercial is not as strong as it could be.

• However, sight and sound must work together. Words should explain what the pictures are showing.

• Viewers can take in a limited amount of sight and sound in 30 or 60 seconds; direct response commercials (DRTV) often run 120 seconds, or thirty minutes for infomercials. So, if your sales pitch requires a barrage of words, keep the pictures simple. On the other hand, if you use complex graphics, keep the words to a minimum. Viewers can't handle a dazzling visual display and a fast-talking announcer at the same time.

• Think about your customer—the guy or gal in front of the television. Is your commercial interesting and important enough to stop your customer from getting up and going to the refrigerator or the bathroom?

• Plan your commercial within existing budgetary limitations. Special effects, jingles, actors, animation, computer graphics, and shooting on location make the cost of commercials skyrocket. Only the stand-up presenter and straightforward, in-the-studio product demonstration are relatively inexpensive to produce.

• Make sure the lead of your commercial is a real grabber. The first four seconds of a commercial are like the headline of a print ad; they decide whether the viewer will sit through your presentation or fix a snack. Open with something irresistible: snappy music, an arresting visual, a dramatic situation, a real-life problem.

• If you are selling a product that can be purchased off the supermarket shelf, show the label. Use close-ups to draw attention to the package. People will buy the product later if they remember the package from your commercial.

• Use motion. Video, unlike slide shows, is a medium of motion. Show cars driving, maple syrup pouring, airplanes flying, popcorn popping, club soda fizzing. Avoid stagnant commercials. Keep it moving.

• Also, don't forget that television offers sound as well as pictures. Let the viewer hear the car engine roaring, the pancakes frying, the airplane whooshing, the popcorn popping, the club soda fizzing, the ice cubes plopping into a cold, tall drink. Many people find the sound of sizzling bacon more appetizing than the look. (Smell may be even more appetizing, but television with smell is not yet a reality. Nor do I know of any manufacturers who are developing such a device.)

• Use "supers." These are titles, in white type, superimposed over the picture. The super reinforces a sales point made in the commercial or makes an additional point not covered in the spoken narration. If you are selling vitamins by mail, put up a super that says, "NOT AVAILABLE IN STORES." People will not buy from a mail-order commercial if they think they can get the product in a store.

• Repeat the product name and the main selling point at least twice. There are two reasons why you should do this. First, repetition aids the viewer in remembering the product. Second, many viewers may not have been paying attention during the beginning of your commercial, so you want to make sure they know who you are and what you are selling.

• Don't neglect the product. Show people eating it, wearing it, riding it, using it, enjoying it. Demonstrate the product. Have people talk about how good the product is. Apply proven techniques of print advertising to television, and you will be delighted with the results.

• If you want viewers to call or write in to order a product or request more information, announce this at the beginning of the commercial ("Get paper and pencil ready to take advantage of this special TV offer . . ."). Few people keep a notepad handy while they watch TV. So use phone numbers and URLs that are easy to remember.

• If you use celebrities (either on camera or in voice-over), identify the celebrity with a voice-over introduction or superimposed title. A large number of people will not recognize celebrities unless you identify them. And they will not be impressed or swayed by the celebrities unless they are well known.

• In local retail commercials, give the address and clear directions to the store.

• The four basic commercial lengths are 10, 30, 60, and 120 seconds. Ten-second commercials are usually "ID" or identification spots. ID spots just drive home a product name and support the campaign's 30- or 60-second spots.

• Because time is limited, a commercial should stick to one main thought or sales point: flame broiling beats frying; Midas installs more mufflers than anyone else; Verizon's network is more reliable than Sprint's; Apple makes the sleekest and most advanced smartphones.

FORMATTING THE SCRIPT

The manuscript format for TV commercials is simple: video (pictures) is typed on the left, audio (words and sound effects) is typed on the right.

What's important is writing a good commercial. Don't worry about the technical terms. You'll learn them when you need to, but they are not essential. All that counts is that your commercial is arresting, memorable, and persuasive.

Here are just a few of the basic terms to help get you started:

ANNCR—Announcer. The narrator of the commercial.

CU—Close-up. An extremely tight shot in which a single object, such as a package label, dominates the screen.

LS—Long shot. A shot of a distant subject.

MS—Medium shot. A shot of the subject in the foreground, showing a substantial amount of the scenery behind it.

SFX—Sound effects. Background sound other than human voice or musical instruments.

TS—Tight shot. A shot leaving little or no space around the subject.

VO—Voice-over. The voice of an off-camera narrator.

The commercial below is typed in proper commercial manuscript format. It's also a good example of straightforward copy packed with product benefits.

Writer: Amy Bly
Product: Galantine Chicken (30 seconds)

VIDEO:	AUDIO:
1. MS to CU: Golden brown Galantine chicken on platter.	1. ANNCR: (VO): You're looking at a plump, juicy Galantine chicken. But this is no ordinary chicken. Because we've taken out the bones.
2. MS: Man slicing chicken. One-quarter to one-third of meat is already sliced on platter.	2. You can slice right through it . . .
3. CU: Array of chicken dishes on buffet table.	3. Prepare any number of delicious chicken dishes, from chicken scampi to chicken salad, quickly and easily, without having to cut around bones.
4. MS: Smiling family eating chicken.	4. A Galantine chicken costs a bit more than an ordinary chicken.
5. CU: Fully sliced chicken on platter.	5. But then there's no waste. You get one hundred percent meat.
6. CU: Packaged chicken, showing Galantine name and logo.	6. So if you have a bone to pick with ordinary chicken, try Galantine instead. At your butcher's and at fine grocers everywhere.

There are a number of things I like about this commercial:

1. It's simple—easy to take in—and inexpensive to produce.

2. The visuals show the product, a demonstration of the

product (easy slicing of boneless chicken), people enjoying the product, and the package—all in thirty seconds.

3. The narration tells us the unique selling feature of the chicken (no bones), the benefits of this feature (slice right through it, no waste, quick and easy), and shows what you can do with the product (prepare any number of dishes).

4. The ending ("if you have a bone to pick with ordinary chicken") is a clever play on words that leaves a smile on your face. And it tells you where you can buy the product.

Here's another effective thirty-second spot from the same writer:

Writer: Amy Bly
Product: YOURS beer for women (30 seconds)

VIDEO:	AUDIO:
1. MS: Well-dressed couple sitting in fancy restaurant. Man reaches for bottle of beer on table. Woman slaps his hand away playfully.	1. WOMAN: Hey, that's YOURS!
2. MS: Man's face. He looks over at her, puzzled, grinning.	2. MAN: If it's mine, why can't I have it?
3. TS: Woman's finger pointing at label on bottle.	3. WOMAN: Because YOURS is the beer that's made for women only.
4. MS: Woman pouring beer.	4. SFX: Beer being poured into glass. ANNCR: YOURS is bubbly, light, and has fewer calories than ordinary beer.

5. MS: Woman finishes pouring beer and picks up glass.	5. ANNCR: And, it comes in convenient ten-ounce bottles that pour one perfect glass of beer . . . enough to quench your thirst without filling you up.
6. MS: Man reaching for glass of beer.	6. MAN: Why can't I have YOURS?
7. MS: Woman pulls glass away, smiling.	7. WOMAN: 'Cause it's mine . . .
8. TS: Bottle of YOURS against black background.	8. ANNCR: (VO): YOURS . . . the first beer for women only.

This is basically a lifestyle commercial combined with a presentation of product benefits. YOURS is a beer for women who eat in fancy restaurants, dress well, and have attractive, personable dinner companions. You can picture Cameron Diaz and Dylan McDermott playing the upscale duo.

Other things I like about the script:

1. It is fun, humorous, and playful. But all the playfulness is relevant to the product!
2. The product has a strong position: "The first beer for women only."
3. The commercial highlights product features that would appeal to women: light, few calories, small servings per bottle.
4. The name is repeated five times and the label shown twice.

HOW TO WRITE RADIO COMMERCIALS

Radio is different from TV and print. And the difference is threefold. First, the radio spot may be prerecorded by professional voice-over actors with music and sound effects, or it may be read on the air by the radio personality.

Second, buying radio time is usually far less costly than buying TV time. Third, much of your audience is driving while listening to your commercial, which makes writing down a phone number or URL more difficult.

The radio copywriter works with words and sounds. Words and sounds must create a picture of the product in the reader's mind.

A radio commercial for "Aunt Lucy's Luscious Blueberry Pie" can't show the family eating and enjoying the pie. So you must use sound to paint the picture of the pie being sliced, of a fork cutting into crust, of chewing, of people "mmm"-ing in delight and praising their hostess.

Suppose the blueberry pies are sold in local supermarkets in a distinctive blue foil wrapper. You can't show the package on radio. You must have the announcer say, "Look for the home-made pie in the blue foil wrapper at your local supermarket and bake shop."

A mini-industry has developed around independent radio production houses that write and produce radio commercials for ad agencies and their clients. Many ad agency writers and creative directors look down their noses at radio (perhaps because the money involved is insignificant compared with television) and are happy to pass on radio commercials to outsiders.

There are trends and stars in radio advertising. For years, Stan Freberg was the rage with humorous radio commercials for Chung King and others. Then, Dick Orkin and Bert Berdis were the reigning kings. Then John Cleese of Monty Python fame became a hit with his spots for Callard & Bowser candies and Kronenbourg beer. And Jerry Seinfeld has featured in American Express ads.

In an article published in *Writer's Digest*, copywriter David Campiti offered these tips to radio novices.

• Lock on to a salesperson's "keys." This is "inside information" a company's salespeople get from talking with customers.

• Feedback from customers can reveal key selling points. For instance, a copywriter interviewed farmers to find out why his radio commercial was not selling rat poison by mail. He discovered that farmers with rat problems were embarrassed about it and didn't want the postman or neighbors to see them receive rat poison packages in the mail. The copywriter added a line to the commercial about how the poison was mailed in a plain brown wrapper, and sales soared.

• Talk about benefits. Tell the audience what the client's goods will do for them.

• Be concise. Use short sentences.

• Repeat key information. Minimum: list store names twice; the URL toward the end once or twice. Include phone numbers at least twice, more in a sixty-second commercial. A recent development is encouraging response online or via texting.

• Know what you're writing about. Research the product.

• Know what resources are available to the producers of radio commercials. Learn to use production facilities. Know the extent of their music and sound effects libraries, the quality and capability of recording equipment, and the abilities of actors who will read your copy over the air.

Here are two radio commercials I like and the reasons why. First, a sixty-second spot from the Masonry Institute of St. Louis:

MAN: Uh, today we're speaking with the Three Little Pigs, is that . . . ?

PIGS: Yes, that's right. You got it, buddy.

MAN: Yeah, well, tell me, ever since you guys opted to build with brick, have you had any further difficulties with uh . . .

PIG #1: Big, bad, and breathless?

MAN: Right.

PIG #2: No, he never comes around anymore.

MAN: That's good.

PIG #3: He knows better than to try and blow this pad down, boy!

MAN: Yes, well, besides solving your security problems, there must have been other reasons for your choosing brick.

PIG #1: Listen, when you're spending eighty big ones on a house these days you want something that'll last, right guys?

PIG #2: Oh yeah.

PIG #3: You said it.

MAN: Well, brick certainly does that, all right.

PIG #1: With little or no maintenance.

MAN: Right.

PIG #2: Not only keeps the wolf from the door but withstands fire, hail . . .

PIG #3: Aluminum-siding salesmen.

MAN: Yes, well, I notice you also have a solid brick fireplace as well.

PIG #1: Yes, we do.

MAN: Very attractive.

PIG #2: We think it adds a nice little touch.

PIG #3: Especially when the girls come over.

MAN: Safe, too, I'll bet.

PIG #1: It is. They aren't. (Man and Pigs laugh.)

MAN: Is there anything else we should know about building with brick?

PIG #1: If there is, don't ask us.

MAN: Oh?

PIG #2: Ask the folks at the Masonry Institute.

MAN: The Masonry Institute?

PIG #3: They'll be happy to send you complete information.

MAN: On brick.

PIG #1: No, on paper.

MAN: What?!

PIG #1: They couldn't get a brick in the envelope . . .
(MUSIC)
ANNCR: If you'd like to know more about building with brick, call the Masonry Institute of St. Louis at 555-550-5888. That's 555-550-5888.

The commercial caught and kept my attention because it is both fast-paced and genuinely funny. The banter between the three pigs and the interviewer keeps things lively. Yet this clever little dialogue manages to pack a great deal of product information into sixty seconds. We learn that:

1. Brick stands up to the environment—hail, wind, storms.
2. Brick lasts a long time and requires little or no maintenance.
3. It is fireproof.
4. If your house is made of brick, you won't need aluminum siding.
5. You can use brick to build a safe, attractive fireplace.
6. The Masonry Institute will send free information on building with brick to anyone who asks for it.

The second radio spot that caught my ear is this classic sixty-second commercial for the California Milk Advisory Board, produced and performed by Dick Orkin and Bert Berdis:

MILK EXECUTIVE: Hello.
SIDNEY: California Milk Advisory Board?
EXECUTIVE: Yes.
SIDNEY: May I make a small suggestion about your jingle?
EXECUTIVE: "Any time is the right time for milk"?
SIDNEY: Yes, it's real catchy, but maybe you ought to change it to, "Any time is the right time for milk except at a bullfight."

EXECUTIVE (laughs): Sounded almost like you said, "Any time is the right time for milk except at a bullfight."

SIDNEY: That's what I said.

EXECUTIVE: What . . . ?

SIDNEY: Allow me to introduce myself. I'm Sidney Feltzer, freelance matador.

EXECUTIVE: Uh-huh.

SIDNEY: I love your milk.

EXECUTIVE: Uh-huh.

SIDNEY: Drink it all the time. It's cold and refreshing . . .

EXECUTIVE: Go on, Sidney.

SIDNEY: But trying to drink milk with one hand and wave my cape with the other is just so . . .

EXECUTIVE: Sidney, you didn't try to, uh . . . ?

SIDNEY: Just today I went through six cartons.

EXECUTIVE: Of milk?

SIDNEY: Pants.

EXECUTIVE: Pants?

SIDNEY: See, when you turn and run, the bull is right there . . .

EXECUTIVE: Sidney, why not have your milk afterward?

SIDNEY: In the hospital?

EXECUTIVE: No, no, I meant after you exercise, milk is terrific, or with snacks, or just sitting down watching television.

SIDNEY: Oh, I can't do that.

EXECUTIVE: Watch television?

SIDNEY: No, sit.

EXECUTIVE: Oh.

SIDNEY: See, when you turn and run, the bull is right there.

EXECUTIVE: I see, I get it all right, Sidney.

JINGLE: Yeah! Any time at all . . . is the time for milk!

SIDNEY: Except during a bullfight.

EXECUTIVE: Hang it up, Sidney.

SIDNEY: My cape?

EXECUTIVE: The phone.

SIDNEY: Oh, right. (Music fades.)

ANNCR: This phone call brought to you by the California Milk Advisory Board.

Again, a fast-paced, humorous commercial with a persuasive message. Note the use of very short (one- and two-word) sentences to set the pace.

NONBROADCAST AV

Radio and TV commercials are the most visible part of the copywriter's work, because we hear them every day. But each year, there are thousands of scripts written and produced that we never get to hear or see.

This area of copywriting is known as *nonbroadcast audiovisual (AV)*. These are audiovisual presentations created by a company and used to reach select, small audiences. Instead of being aired over radio or TV, these presentations are shown at meetings, at trade shows, at seminars, at presentations, and in one-on-one sales pitches where the salesperson is sitting down with a customer. They are also posted today as videos on YouTube and Web sites.

Many different media are available for nonbroadcast AV. These include:

- PowerPoint
- Online video content
- DVD
- Videotext
- Software

And these presentations are used in many different applications:

- Employee communications
- Trade show exhibits
- Seminars and conferences
- Recruitment
- Community relations
- Public relations
- Sales support
- Advertising inquiry fulfillment (free DVDs sent to select prospects who respond to commercials for your ab machine or Caribbean cruise ship)
- Presentations to top management
- Training
- Product introduction
- Product demonstration
- Case histories
- Meetings
- Sales aids for company salespeople and sales reps
- Point-of-purchase display in retail locations
- Executive summaries of annual reports, sales presentations, and other printed literature
- Records of historic events

The script format for slide shows and films is the same as for TV commercials: visuals on the left, audio on the right.

But nonbroadcast AV is not limited to thirty or sixty seconds. You can make it as long or as short as you like. Eight to ten minutes is the best length for a slide show or film. Twenty minutes is the maximum. Beyond that, your audience will begin to fade.

Nonbroadcast AV is much less expensive to produce than TV commercials. A one-minute commercial could cost $40,000 or more. A ten-minute nonbroadcast videotape can be produced for as little as $500 to $1,000.

Here are a few tips for writing nonbroadcast AV:

- Write words for the ear, not for the eye. A script is not simply words on a page, but words that are spoken aloud.
- The spoken words should be precise, coherent, and full of vivid images.
- Be crystal clear. The listener doesn't have the luxury of referring back to the text. Your writing must be readily understood the first time it is heard.
- Research. Find out all you can about the topic, the product, the purpose, the audience.
- The script should repeat the key selling points several times.
- The beginning is critical and must "hook" the audience, locking their attention.
- Be lively, catching, precise. Use active verbs, colorful words and phrases.
- Spoon-feed the audience. Don't assault them with fact after fact. Be selective about the facts you choose. An AV presentation doesn't tell the whole story but should leave the viewer hungry for more information.
- Use words to paint pictures that complement the actual visuals on the screen.
- Be as concise and direct as possible. Avoid complicated sentences.

WRITING FOR POWERPOINT

Okay. Let's say you are putting together a presentation and PowerPoint is required. What can you do to make it more effective?

First, you don't have to show slides all the time. Use Power-Point selectively, not throughout the entire presentation.

When there's a valuable picture to show, show it. When you're through with it, use a blue or black blank slide.

Second, use visuals only when they communicate more effectively than words. If you are talking about quality, having the word *Quality* on-screen adds little to your point. On the other hand, if you want to explain what an aardvark looks like, there are no words that can do it as effectively as simply showing a picture.

Third, don't overcrowd your slides. Have no more than one major visual per slide, and keep it simple; avoid, for example, process diagrams with too many lines and connections.

Fourth, consider adding other media as supplements or even alternatives to PowerPoint. When I taught telephone selling, the sound of a ringing telephone and a prop—a toy telephone—engaged the trainees in a way computer slides could not.

Fifth, design your presentation so that, if there is a problem with the computer equipment, you can go on without it. There's nothing more embarrassing than watching a speaker fall apart because he can't find the right slide. Use visuals as an enhancement, not a crutch.

Graphic design consultant Roger C. Parker offers the following tips for preparing your PowerPoint presentations:

- Keep visuals simple. Avoid decorative clip art. These often project a cartoon-like image. Add graphics only when they support your arguments.
- Use keywords, not sentences. Visuals should provide a framework, not a script, for your presentation. Limiting text to keywords permits you to use a large, easy-to-read type size.
- Avoid complex backgrounds. When in doubt, choose black type against a white background.
- Personalize your visuals. Add your logo to each visual, along with the presentation title and date.

To Roger's suggestions I would add these of my own, based on my experience of creating dozens of PowerPoint presentations over the years:

- Do not make charts, graphs, and diagrams too cluttered, complex, or small. The slides should be easy to see and read for all attendees, even those sitting in the back row.
- If you in fact have a lot of information or data to communicate using bullet lists or visuals, remember the 5 x 5 rule for word slides: no more than 5 bullets per slide and no more than 5 words per bullet.
- Mix word slides with image slides (e.g., if you are selling corn seed, show a farmer planting the seeds and then tall, healthy corn stalks). Ideally have one image per slide and no more than three.

11 ✒

WRITING WEB SITES

Twenty years ago, 100 percent of my copywriting was print and zero percent was on the Internet. Today, 30 percent of my copywriting is print and 70 percent is online.

The conclusion? A working copywriter today is going to be doing a lot of writing for the Internet. Some of your assignments will focus on driving traffic to an existing Web site. Others will focus on creating Web copy, either adding pages to existing sites or creating brand-new sites.

WHAT'S WORKING IN ONLINE MARKETING TODAY

There are many different business modes for e-commerce companies.

Here is one online marketing methodology that has been proven effective for many different types of businesses: online marketing works best when you e-mail to people who already know you.

Therefore, successful online marketers build their "house file" or "e-list" (lists of prospects and their e-mail addresses) using the process outlined below, and then sell to those people via e-mail marketing. This is called the "Organic Model" or "Agora Model," (fig. 11.1).

Fig. 11.1: The Agora Model of online marketing.

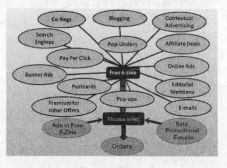

First, the marketer builds a Web site that positions his company as an expert resource in a specific niche or industry. This is the client's "base of operations" for his online marketing campaign.

This Web site should include a home page with a banner at top (fig. 11.2), an "About the Company" page, and a menu with links to a series of pages, each with a brief description of the client's products and services (each product or service description can link to a longer document giving more details on the item).

The home page should also have one or more calls to action (CTAs). In figure 11.2, this is a sign-up box to subscribe to a free e-newsletter, indicated by call-out C on the diagram. Also recommended: another CTA where interested potential buyers can inquire about your products or services.

Fig. 11.2: Copywriter's rough layout for home page.

(A) **Banner**	
(B) **Top Row**	
(C) ── E-Zine Sign-up Box (Optional)	
(D) *Left Column*	(F) ── **Main Panel**
(E) **Bottom Row**	

You should also have an "Articles Page" where you post articles you have written on your area of specialty, and where visitors can read and download these articles for free.

WHY YOU SHOULD *NOT* USE A ROTATING BANNER

Rotating banners consist of a series of slides or images running on a loop at the top of your home page.

The banners display, in a quick-moving, auto-rotating loop, four to eight promotional messages, which can include still images, videos, or text.

Despite rotating banners being a hot trend on Web sites, you should not use them on your site because:

1—Only about 1 to 2 percent of your Web site visitors will ever click on a rotating banner.

2—Banners are perceived to be advertising, and are therefore ignored by the vast majority of your visitors, 86 percent of whom won't even recall reading them.

3—Image banners are large files that can slow Web site load

speed, and even a one-second delay causes 7 percent of visitors to abandon the site.

4—Rotating banners do not display well on mobile devices.

5—Visitors have to wait to view all of the banners. And the banners change so rapidly, they often don't have time to read the messages.

Write a short special report or white paper on your area of expertise, and make this available to people who visit your site. They can download it for free, but in exchange, they have to register and give you their e-mail address (and any other information you want to capture).

Consider also offering a monthly or weekly online newsletter, or "e-zine." People who visit your site can subscribe for free if they register and give you their e-mail address. You may want to give visitors the option of checking a box that reads: "I give you and other companies you select permission to send me e-mail about products, services, news, and offers that may be of interest to me."

The more "content" (useful information) on your site, the better. More people will be attracted to your site, and they will spend more time on it. They will also tell others about your site.

The model is to drive traffic to your site, shown in fig 11.1, where you get them to sign up for either your free report or your free e-zine. Once they register, you have their e-mail address and can now market to them via e-mail as often as you like at no extra cost.

The bulk of your online leads, sales, and profits often comes from repeat e-mail marketing to this "house e-list" of prospects. Therefore your goal is to build a large e-list of qualified prospects as quickly and inexpensively as you can.

There are a number of online marketing options that can drive traffic to your site. These include free publicity, e-mail marketing, banner advertising, co-registrations, affiliate marketing, search engine optimization, direct mail, and e-zine advertising (see fig. 11.1).

The key to success is to try a lot of different tactics in small and inexpensive tests, throw out the ones that don't work, and do more of the ones that are effective.

COMMON ONLINE COPYWRITING ASSIGNMENTS

There is often confusion as to what the particular "deliverables" are in online copywriting, what the terms mean, and how much copy is involved.

For instance, what exactly do we mean by a "microsite"? How long is it? When should you use it?

Here are the most common online copywriting assignments I write for my clients, and the definition and scope of each:

• A *microsite*, also known as a *long-copy landing page*, is a Web site designed to sell a product—such as a newsletter, e-book, vitamin, ab machine, or conference—directly. Copy length is equivalent to a four- to eight-page sales letter.

• A *name squeeze page* is a simple landing page for a product or offer. Often used for white papers, software demos, and other inquiry fulfillment. Copy length is about the same as a magazine ad and often briefer, with a headline, a few paragraphs of descriptive product copy, and an online reply form.

• A *transaction page* is similar to a short-copy landing page, but with even less descriptive product copy. It is basically an online form the visitor can use to either order the product or request more information.

• A *long-copy e-mail* is designed to sell a product directly by driving the recipient to a short-copy landing page or transaction page. Number of words is roughly the same as a two- or three-page sales letter. (E-mails are covered in the next chapter.)

• A *teaser e-mail* is a short e-mail designed to drive the readers to a microsite or long-copy landing page where they can order the product. It's the online equivalent of a half-page sales letter.

• A *lead-generation e-mail* is similar to the teaser e-mail, but the purpose is to drive readers to a landing page or transaction page where they can request a free white paper or other information.

• An *online e-mail conversion series* is a series of follow-up e-mail messages, sent via autoresponder, designed to convert an inquiry into a sale.

• An *online text ad* is typically a 50- to 100-word classified ad to run in an e-zine and drive readers to a microsite or landing page.

• A *banner ad* is an HTML ad on a Web site. It hyperlinks to a landing page or other page.

• A *pop-under* is a window that appears on a Web site when the visitor takes a certain action (typically trying to leave the site without ordering). It makes a special offer—usually free, in exchange for the visitor giving his e-mail address.

WRITING AN E-COMMERCE WEB SITE

An *e-commerce Web site* sells many different items, and in a way that is the online equivalent of a catalog. Examples include Amazon, Alibaba, Target, Walmart, and Blue Nile.

Many successful e-commerce Web sites have the following characteristics:

• A large, searchable database of product photos and descriptions.
• A shopping cart that enables you to buy products online.

The biggest e-commerce Web site is Amazon.com, which originally sold books only and has branched into numerous other products including videos, music, tools, and electronics.

Another example of a successful e-commerce Web site is www.bluenile.com, an online marketer of jewelry. It's a great example of how to set up an attractive Web site that sells merchandise online.

There, the home page has pictures of jewelry and product descriptions that are hyperlinked to pages showing and describing those products. Simple and basic, but sensible; I wouldn't do it any other way.

Value-added links at the bottom of the home page provide consumers with offers of free guides and education on diamonds (which periodically change).

- Choosing a Diamond
- Know the 4Cs Video
- Astor by Blue Nile
- Precious Metals
- Gemstone Guide
- Birthstone Guide
- Pearl Guide
- Engagement Rings
- Wedding Rings
- Find Your Ring Size

The mission of the Web site—to help the consumer shop for and buy a diamond or other jewelry online—is crystal clear. The entire site is designed to make the transaction as easy and painless as possible.

Most of the hyperlinks on the home page go to specific products, so you can see what stones and jewelry are available. These pages are augmented by a useful but not overwhelming choice of helpful hints on buying diamonds, product searches, and interactive jewelry design.

It's fun and easy to shop for jewelry on Blue Nile. You can easily find what you are looking for, the shopping cart works well, and there are links that let you drill down for more product detail and consumer information, whether it's a close-up photograph of a ring or a schematic diagram showing how a certain setting holds the stone in place. All told, Blue Nile is a case in point that functional, useful copy and design can help create an accessible and successful Web site.

THE TROUBLE WITH SINGLE-PAGE WEB SITES

A big fad in designing company Web sites today is "single-page" sites. On these one-page sites, rather than create separate Web pages for each major topic (e.g., testimonials, client list, about the company, products), where you reach each page by selecting the topic from a menu, all the topics are on one long home page, and you reach them by scrolling down that long home page.

Usually there is also a menu. But when you click the topic button on a one-page Web site, instead of taking you to a separate page, it just takes you immediately to where that information appears on the home page—eliminating the need to scroll.

Single-page sites are popular today, even "all the rage." But I don't like them, and I recommend that most businesses not use them for four reasons:

• First, Link-Assistant.com and others note that one-page Web sites are not good for search engine optimization. With a one-pager, you usually can't drive a lot of organic search traffic via search engine optimization (SEO). This is because you won't have enough content to target a wide range of keywords and topics.

• According to a study by insurance company NN Group, 76

percent of users surveyed said the most important factor to them when on a Web site is ease of finding what they want. Traditional multipage sites make it easy for visitors to go to the content they seek quickly.

• Only 10 percent of users said that the design is first in importance to them when visiting Web sites. And single-page Web sites were innovated for their cool look, not their SEO or usability.

• Users prefer to consume content in small chunks rather than big gulps. Traditional multipage sites accommodate the visitor's natural preference for modular content. Single-page sites violate it, presenting all the content on one enormous page that is intimidating to search and to read.

WRITING A CLICKFUNNEL WEB SITE

A "sales funnel" (fig. 11.3) is the sequence of steps that take a consumer from being a stranger to either making an inquiry for more information about your products or service or becoming a customer and making a purchase.

Fig. 11.3: A typical online sales funnel for converting clicks to customers and sales.

ClickFunnels is a platform designed to put your entire sales funnel online on a single Web page or site. To see how these funnel sites are written and designed, visit www.clickfunnels .com.

A ClickFunnels site is laid out in a vertical format. The first section is the top of your sales funnel. Middle sections follow the steps of your sales funnel. And the last section is the call to action. In consumer ClickFunnels, the CTA is to buy the product.

From top to bottom, the sections of the ClickFunnels site are typically organized using the Motivating Sequence presented in chapter 4. As a reminder, the steps in the Motivating Sequence are (a) get attention, (b) state the problem, concern, or need the potential customer for your product has, (c) show him that your product is the solution to his problem or need, (d) prove that your product is superior to other products addressing the same needs and problems your does, and (e) ask for the order with your call to action.

Each step is presented in a separate level in the funnel. Because the layout has limited space, ClickFunnel copy is relatively brief and frequently presented in bullet form.

The "proof" step of the sales funnel may be spread over several descending levels, each covering just a single proof element. One panel might be customer testimonials. The next panel could be a description of the product; e.g., how it works, how it is made, the materials it is made of. The panel after that could highlight awards the product has won or press coverage it has garnered. Then, you might have a panel presenting more scientific evidence of product superiority, such as clinical studies or test results.

Although there are similarities, the ClickFunnel is a dedicated sales page whose only purpose is to get a lead or an order. By comparison, the single-page Web sites we discussed earlier are used as a format in full company Web sites, not sales pages.

MORE TIPS ON WRITING WEB SITE COPY

Since putting up my Web site, www.bly.com, in April 1998, I've received a ton of unsolicited e-mails, faxes, and phone calls—from casual Internet surfers as well as Web professionals—with all sorts of advice on how to make my Web site better. Unfortunately, more than 90 percent of their suggestions are totally off the mark—and would be a complete waste of my time and money.

Why is this the case? It's not that site visitors don't have valid opinions on graphics or content, or that Web professionals also don't have good ideas. They often do.

The problem is, all the advice is given with no thought to the business objective of the site. For example, a Web consultant called and said, "You're not getting nearly as much traffic as you should. I can help you get much more." He would advise me, he promised, on how to help my Web site get more hits than the New York Yankees. I politely explained that I had absolutely no desire to increase hits to my Web site and was not interested in what he was selling.

Frankly, he was baffled. Maybe you are, too. Who doesn't want more hits on their Web site? Plenty of folks do. Before you can meaningfully enhance a Web site, you need to understand the business of the person or company sponsoring that site, as well as the business objectives they want the site to achieve.

In the case of www.bly.com, I'm a freelance writer specializing in direct marketing. I serve a higher-end clientele—major direct marketers, Fortune 500 companies, and substantial technology firms—and charge accordingly.

This makes me different from many entrepreneurs who have Web sites—in two important ways.

First, 99.99 percent of people cruising the Internet are not my prospects. I'm highly selective, and I infrequently work with small firms, start-ups, mom-and-pop operations, home-based businesses, and wannabe entrepreneurs—precisely the mass market that's cruising the Internet looking for free marketing information and advice.

Second, with more business than we can handle, our office (I have two assistants) can't waste time responding to low-level leads. Handling inquiries from casual Internet surfers takes time and effort, and we need to devote those to the needs of our many ongoing clients.

Then why do I have a Web site? That's the key relevant question, and it's one almost no one who seeks to advise me asks.

My Web site exists primarily for instant inquiry fulfillment to qualified prospects.

What does that mean? Before the Internet, when a serious prospect called, we'd send him an information package describing my services. That meant a lot of priority mail and overnight courier bills. And even with overnight shipping, the prospect often waited up to twenty-four hours to get his hands on the material.

Having a Web site eliminates that cost and wait. When prospects want a package, we can send it, but first we tell them that all the information they need to make a decision about using my services is online.

What should that information be? In his book *Roger C. Parker's Guide to Web Content and Design*, my friend Roger Parker says that content on your Web site should consist of two components:

1. Information your prospects need to know in order to buy from you
2. Information that will convince prospects to buy from you

My Web site covers both these areas. The "need to know" stuff includes:

- An overview of my services (our home page)
- An online portfolio of my copywriting samples
- Pages on each major service (copywriting, consulting, copy critiquing)
- My credentials (on an "About Bob Bly" page)
- Client list

The stuff that helps convince prospects that I'm the person they should hire to write their copy includes:

- Client testimonials
- Case studies highlighting my success stories
- Descriptions of the marketing books I've written
- A library of how-to articles I've written on marketing
- A list of recommended vendors that shows I have the connections to help potential clients get whatever they need done

As you can see, my Web site is totally oriented toward the needs of my potential clients, not to someone who happened upon it online. But does this mean I don't want you to visit www.bly.com? Not at all.

On the contrary, I invite you to stop by. You may enjoy reading and downloading the free articles I've posted. And I'd be pleased and happy if you bought any of my books there (though you would not be buying them directly from me—our publication page links to Amazon.com, from which we get a 15 percent commission on every book it sells through our site).

And what if you're a small entrepreneur and need professional marketing help? Just click on "Vendors." You'll find a list of folks who can help you with everything from Web design to mailing lists. But do me a favor. When you call them, tell them Bob Bly sent you. They're busy, too, and it helps if they know you're a qualified referral.

Another problem with offers of unsolicited advice on how to improve your Web site is that the caller has little or no idea of your metrics: the factors by which you measure results and the numbers you are currently getting. This is like an interior decorator giving clients advice on how to decorate their homes without having even seen the house. Absurd, right?

SEO COPYWRITING

The growing usage of Google has given rise to a new discipline: *SEO (search engine optimization) copywriting.*

When writing online copy, you have to consider not only how the reader will react to the copy, but also whether the words you use will attract search engines to your site and increase your rankings within these search engines and directories.

Google ranks traditional Web sites, in which the content is broken up into many individual pages, higher than landing pages and single-page Web sites. Traditional sites typically have a separate page on each of the products and services the company offers. Each page is optimized for keywords related to the subject matter of the page. For instance, if one page of an exercise equipment manufacturer's site advertises its ab machine, what keywords do you think prospects for ab machines would use to search the Web for the product? Possibilities might include abs, ab machines, ab exercisers, and six-pack.

There are many online tools to help you search for the most relevant keywords for your Web pages. They include Soovle, Jaaxy, Ahrefs Keywords Explorer, SEOCockpit, and the Google Search Console.

Each page of your site should be optimized for two or three keyword phrases. Use the most important keyword in the page headline, preferably as the first word in the headline, and then jucidiously within the page's body copy. When possible, link these keywords to other pages on your site that contain additional content on that topic.

Using keywords in meta tags also helps optimize your pages for search engines. Meta tags are not visible in the Web site copy your visitors see. Rather, the meta tags are embedded in the HTML code supporting each page.

When people Google your pages' keywords, meta tags help the search engine find your page. The two most important meta tags are the meta descriptions and the title tags. The *meta description* helps Google find the Web page.

When you search a keyword and find the page, the meta description text from that page is usually displayed on the Google Search Engine Results Page (SERP). It gives a concise description of the page contents, not to exceed 158 characters. The keyword should appear at the beginning of the meta description.

. The *title* tag is an HTML title for the page, no longer than sixty characters. Again, the keywords should be at the beginning of the meta tag. The main title is given the designation H1 in the HTML coding for the Web page.

You may think that cramming the keywords into Web page copy and meta tags as many times as possible would improve SEO. But using too many keywords in your Web copy and tags, a practice known as "keyword stuffing," can backfire. Keyword stuffing can result in your page being ignored by the search engine algorithms or, in some cases, your page and site will be penalized. Worse still, keyword stuffing can makes pages read strangely and awkwardly to human visitors.

Using keywords too often on a page and in the meta-tags is worse than not using them at all. The frequency of keywords on a page has nothing to do with whether a spider will find the page. And if a spider finds the page, it doesn't need a keyword repeated frequently in order to find it.

The more the keywords reflect what the user is searching for, the better the SEO results will be. Use descriptive keyword phrases of two to four words, not a single word; i.e. "Boston cosmetic dentists" instead of just "dentists."

Work the keyword phrases naturally into the body copy, so the writing sounds smooth and not stilted. Instead of "modern technologies," for instance, use "modern cosmetic dentistry technologies."

12

WRITING LANDING PAGES

A "landing page" is a dedicated Web page that allows site visitors to proactively contact you online. The landing page is designed to capture some information about the visitor such as e-mail address and name.

"Conversion" means taking that click and moving it forward to the next step in the sales funnel. Some of the many objectives for which you can use landing pages include:

- Opt-in to your e-list.
- Subscribe to your newsletter.
- Download a white paper or other content.
- Fill out online forms.
- Purchase products online using PayPal or credit cards.

A "call to action" (CTA) tells visitors to take a specific action (e.g., register for a webinar) and includes the instructions needed to take that action (e.g., filling out and submitting a form on a webinar registration to sign up for the event).

There's lots of buzz about blogging, viral marketing, social networking, and other new methods of generating eyeballs (people viewing your pages) and traffic online. But all that traffic won't make you any money unless you can convert those unique visitors to leads or customers.

That's where your landing pages come in. Landing page performance is measured as conversion. Specifically, of the people who click onto the page, how many take the action you want them to take? If a hundred people click onto your page and five buy your widget, the conversion rate is 5 percent.

According to an article in PR Daily, businesses with ten to fifteen landing pages increase leads by 55 percent, and those with more than forty landing pages get twelve times as many leads as companies with five or fewer landing pages.[1]

10 TIPS FOR INCREASING LANDING PAGE CONVERSION RATES

Depending on whether you are selling a product directly from your landing page, asking visitors to download a free white paper, or promoting a webinar or demonstration, conversion rates can range from as low as 1 percent or less to as much as 50 percent or more. Here are ten keys to writing landing pages that maximize online conversion rates:

1—Build credibility early. People have always been skeptical of advertising, and with the proliferation of spam and shady operators, they are even more skeptical of what they read online. Therefore, your landing page copy must immediately overcome that skepticism. One way to do that is to make sure one or more "credibility builders" is clearly displayed on the first screen the visitor sees. In the banner at the top of the page, use your logo and company name if you are well known; universities, associations, and other institutions can place their official seal in the upper left of the screen. Within or immediately under the banner, above the headline, put a strong testimonial or three. Consider adding a pre-head or subhead that summarizes the company's mission statement or credentials.

2—Capture the e-mail addresses of non-buyers. There are a number of mechanisms available for capturing the e-mail addresses of visitors who click on your landing page but do not buy the product.

One is to use a window with copy offering a free report or e-course in exchange for submitting an e-mail address. This window can be served to the visitor as a pop-up (it appears when the visitor arrives at the landing page) or a pop-under (a window that appears when the visitor attempts to leave the landing page without making an inquiry or purchase). The negative is that both the pop-up and the pop-under are often blocked.

A "floater" is a window that slides onto the screen from the side or top. Unlike the pop-up and pop-under, the floater is part of the Web site HTML code, so it is not stopped by the pop-up blocker.

3—Use lots of testimonials. Testimonials build credibility and overcome skepticism, as do case studies and white papers posted on the Web site. If you invite customers to a live event, ask if they would be willing to give you a brief testimonial recorded on video.

Have a professional videographer tape it, get a signed release from the customer, and post the testimonial on your Web site as streaming video. Require the customer to click a button to hear the testimonial, rather than have the video play automatically when the visitor clicks on the page.

For written testimonials, customers may suggest that you write what you want them to say and just run it by them for approval. Politely ask that they give you their opinion of your product in their own words instead of having you do it. What they come up with will likely be more specific, believable, and detailed than your version, which might smack of puffery and promotion.

4—Use lots of bullets. Highlight key features and benefits in a list of short, easy-to-read, bulleted items. I often use a format where the first part of the bullet is the feature, and after a dash comes the benefit (e.g., **"Quick-release adhesive system**—your vehicle graphics stay clean and don't stick together").

Online buyers like to think they are getting a lot for their money, so when selling a product directly from your landing page, be sure all major features and important benefits are covered in a comprehensive bullet list appearing on your landing page.

When generating leads by giving away white papers, you don't need a huge list of bulleted features and benefits. But using bullets to describe the contents of the paper and the benefits that information delivers can raise conversion rates for download requests.

5—Arouse curiosity in the headline. The headline should either arouse curiosity, make a powerful promise, or otherwise grab the reader's attention so he has no choice but to keep reading. The headline for a landing page selling a training program on how to become a professional property locator makes a big promise: "Become a Property Locator Today—and Make $100,000 a Year in the Greatest Real Estate Career That Only a Few Insiders Know About."

6—Use a conversational copy style. Most corporate Web sites are unemotional and sterile: just "information." But a landing page is a letter from one human being to another. Make it sound that way. Even if your product is highly technical and you are selling it to techies, remember that they are still human beings, and you cannot sell something by boring people to death.

7—Incorporate an emotional hook in the headline and lead paragraph. Logical selling can work, but tapping in to the prospect's emotions is much stronger—especially when you correctly assess how the prospect is feeling about your product or the problem it solves right now.

Another effective tactic for lead-generation landing pages is to stress your free offer in the headline and lead. Example: Kaydon's landing page shows a picture of its catalog with the bold heading above it reading, "FREE Ceramic Bearings Product Selection Guide."

8—Solve the reader's problem. Once you hook the reader with emotional copy dramatizing her problem or a powerful free offer, show how your product—or your free information—can help solve her problem.

For example: "Now there is a better, easier, and more effective solution to wobbly restaurant tables that can irritate customers and ruin their dining experience: Table Shox, the world's smallest shock absorber."

To maximize landing page conversion rates, you have to convince the visitor that the quickest route to solving his problem is taking the action indicated on the landing page, and not—as you might be tempted to let him do—surfing your site.

That's why landing pages should have no navigation, so the reader's only choice is to respond or not respond; there's no menu of click buttons and hyperlinks to other interesting pages to distract him.

9—Make it timely and current. The more your online copy ties in with current events and news, the higher your response rates. This is especially critical when selling financial and investment information, as well as regulatory compliance products in fields where laws and rules change frequently. Periodically update your landing page copy to reflect current business and economic conditions, challenges, and trends. This shows your visitor that your company is current with and on top of what's happening in your industry today.

10—Stress the money-back guarantee or lack of obligation on the part of the user who performs your call to action. If you allow customers to order products directly from the landing page, make sure you have a money-back guarantee clearly stated on that page.

If you are generating leads, stress that your offer—which might be a white paper, online demonstration, or webinar—is free. Say that there is no obligation to buy something.

ADDITIONAL GUIDELINES FOR EFFECTIVE LANDING PAGES[2]

- In your landing page headline, engage the target prospect by promising a big and compelling benefit.
- The marketer in whose voice the sales copy has been written should be clearly identified and her credentials as an expert in the topic presented.
- The sales letter should tell an engaging story that moves the user to buy.
- Prove all sales claims with specifics (e.g., facts, figures, diagrams, testimonials).
- The page layout is uncluttered and easy to follow.
- The primary response mechanism is for the visitor to click a "call to action" button that links to your shopping cart or other transactional page (e.g., a form for downloading a free e-book).
- CTA buttons should be big, bold, and colorful. You can also enable readers to click through to the order or download page by hyperlinking a keyword or phrase in the sales letter copy to that transaction page; the hyperlinked word or phrase is typically blue and underlined.
- In addition to the CTA buttons and hyperlinked keywords and phrases, you can add a toll-free number for phone response.
- The copy, content, and references must be accurate and up to date. Having outdated content on the page causes you to lose credibility with many of your visitors.
- The graphics make the sales copy easy to read.

- Conversely, avoid graphics that make copy difficult to read, as much as your Web designer might like it (e.g., lack of color contrast between the type and background screen).

SEVEN WAYS TO DRIVE TRAFFIC TO YOUR LANDING PAGES

1. Search Engines

Google, the world's largest search engine, facilitates 5.5 billion Web searches per day for its users. As an advertiser, you can buy preference in Google's search engine, based on keyword, on a cost-per-click basis.

It could cost you as little as a dime a click or more than a dollar a click, depending on the popularity of the keyword you want to buy. If the cost of the keyword is 30 cents per click, and 100 people click on your site that day as a result of a Google search on the keyword you bought, Google charges you $30. Google lets you put a limit on how much you spend per day, so the cost can fit any budget.

2. Affiliate Marketing

Find Web sites that cater to the same market you do. Arrange for them to feature your products on their site and in their e-mails. Online ads, e-mail blurbs, and Web pages talking about your product link to your site where the user can purchase the product under discussion. The affiliate receives a percentage of the sale ranging from 15 to 50 percent. To recruit affiliates or make money being an affiliate for other marketers, visit www .affiliatesdirectory.com.

Amazon.com runs one of the largest affiliate programs, enabling you to feature books on your site that are related to your topic and of interest to your audience; when users click on the book page, they are automatically linked to www.amazon.com, where they can buy the book online. It's a service for your visitors, and you earn a small commission on each sale.

3. Co-registration

In co-registration marketing, the user who visits a Web site is served a pop-up window containing a number of special offers; most frequently these are subscriptions to free e-zines. By arranging to have your e-zine or another offer featured in these co-registration pop-ups, you can capture many new names for your online database at a relatively low cost compared to traditional e-mail marketing.

There are a number of companies that can find such co-registration deals for you. One of these is Tiburon Media Group, http://www.tiburonmedia.com/coreg. Another is Opt Intelligence, http://www.opt-intelligence.com/.

4. Banner Ads

Banner ads can work but should be tested conservatively and cautiously, and don't get your hopes of a breakthrough up too high. Banner ads usually supplement other traffic generation methods, and are only occasionally a primary source of unique visits. Exceptions? Of course.

5. E-mail Marketing

Sending solo promotional e-mails to a rented list of opt-in names is an expensive way to acquire new names. Say you rent a list of a thousand e-mail names for $200, get a 2 percent click-through, and 10 percent of those sign up for your e-zine. Your acquisition cost to acquire those two new subscribers is a whopping $100 per name. Business-to-consumer marketers have a better chance of success with careful testing of e-mail marketing, since consumer lists are more reasonably priced than business-to-business names.

6. *Online Ads*

While sending a solo e-mail to a company's e-list can run $100 to $400 per thousand names, a less expensive option is to run a small online ad in its e-zine. Cost can be as little as $20 to $40 per thousand names. The e-zine publisher specifies the format and length of your ad, which are typically a hundred words of text with one URL link. The higher up (earlier) your ad appears in the e-zine, the higher the response.

7. *Viral Marketing*

At its simplest, viral marketing entails adding a line to your outgoing e-mail marketing messages that says, "Please feel free to forward this e-mail to your friends so they can enjoy this special offer." To work, the e-mail you want the recipient to forward must contain a special offer, either a free offer (typically free content) or a discount on merchandise.

13 ✎

WRITING E-MAIL MARKETING

There are two basic types of e-mails you will be writing as a copywriter. The first is the "solo e-mail." This is an e-mail promoting a single product or offer sent to a distribution list. The second is the "e-zine." This is an online newsletter, written and distributed for marketing purposes. A typical strategy is to build an e-list of prospects by offering a free subscription to your online newsletter. Then, once you own those names, you can send them both e-zines—which can contain ads for your products—and solo e-mails promoting your products.

15 TIPS FOR WRITING EFFECTIVE E-MAIL MARKETING CAMPAIGNS

The copy in your e-mail plays a big role in whether your e-marketing message gets opened and read or trashed without a second glance. Here are fifteen proven techniques for maximizing the number of e-mail recipients who open your e-mail and click through to your Web site or other response mechanism:

1. At the beginning of the e-mail, put a "FROM" line and a "SUBJECT" line. The SUBJECT line should be constructed like a short, attention-grabbing, curiosity-arousing outer envelope teaser, compelling recipients to read further—without being so blatantly promotional that it turns them off. Example: "Come on back to Idea Forum!"

2. The e-mail FROM line identifies you as the sender if you're e-mailing to your house file. If you're e-mailing to a rented list, the FROM line might identify the list owner as the sender. This is especially effective with opt-in lists where the list owner (e.g., a Web site) has a good relationship with its users.

3. Some e-marketers think the FROM line is trivial and unimportant; others think it's critical. Internet copywriter Ivan Levison says, "I often use the word 'Team' in the FROM line. It makes it sound as if there's a group of bright, energetic, enthusiastic people standing behind the product."

For instance, if you are sending an e-mail to a rented list of computer people to promote a new software product, your SUBJECT and FROM lines might read as follows: "FROM: The Adobe PageMill Team/SUBJECT: Adobe PageMill 3.0 limited-time offer!"

Here are e-mail FROM line options:

From:	*When to use:*
List Owner	• List owner requires it
	• Community of interest
	• E-zine
	• Popular quality site
	• Frequent visitors

Your Company	• Well-known company or brand
	• Market leader
	• Recipients may think they are your customers (e.g., Microsoft)
You	• Personal message
	• Your company is not well known to recipients
Team (e.g., The Adobe Team)	• Collaborative effort

4. Despite the fact that the word *free* is a proven, powerful response booster in traditional direct marketing, and that the Internet culture has a bias in favor of free offers rather than paid offers, some e-marketers avoid "FREE" in the subject line.

The reason is the "spam filter" software some Internet users have installed to screen their e-mail. These filters eliminate incoming e-mail, and many identify any message with "FREE" in the subject line as promotional.

According to Mailchimp, one out of five legitimate e-mails end up in junk folders. However, my experience is that, despite spam filters, "FREE" typically lifts response.

5. Lead off the message copy with a killer headline or lead-in sentence. You need to get a terrific benefit right up front. Pretend you're writing envelope teaser copy or are writing a headline for a sales letter. Example:

From: Richard Stanton's Stock Speculator

Subject: 6 shocking financial forecasts

Dear [NAME],
What's in store for the U.S. economy?

A new special report from stock analyst Richard Stanton warns of 6 new economic threats to unfold within the next 6 to 12 months. Click here for a free copy: [URL]

"I personally expect this to be the most volatile market of any sort I have ever seen," says Richard, "and with a looming recession and fears of climate change, some of the biggest returns are now being made in solar, wind, and other renewable energy stocks."

Among Richard's observations and predictions . . .

6. In the first paragraph, deliver a mini-version of your complete message. State the offer and provide an immediate response mechanism, such as the option of clicking on a link connected to a Web page. This appeals to Internet prospects with short attention spans.

7. After the first paragraph, present expanded copy that covers the features, benefits, proof, and other information the buyer needs to make a decision. This appeals to the prospect who needs more details than a short paragraph can provide.

8. The offer and response mechanism should be repeated in the close of the e-mail, as in a traditional direct-mail letter. But they should almost always appear at the very beginning, too. That way, busy Internet users who don't have time to read each e-mail and give it only a second or two get the whole story.

9. Experience shows that if you put multiple response links within your e-mail message, the majority of your click-through responses will come from the first two. Therefore, you should probably limit the number of click-through links in your e-mail to three. An exception might be an e-newsletter or e-zine broken into five or six short items, where each item addresses a different subject and therefore has its own link.

10. Use wide margins. You don't want to have weird wraps or breaks. Limit yourself to about 55 to 60 characters per line. If you think a line is going to be too long, insert a character

return. Internet copywriter Joe Vitale sets his margins at 20 and 80, keeping line length to 60 characters and ensuring the whole line gets displayed on the screen without odd text breaks.

11. Take it easy on the all-caps. You can use WORDS IN ALL CAPS but do so carefully. They can be a little hard to read—and in the world of e-mail, all caps gives the impression that you're shouting.

12. In general, short is better. This is not the case in classic mail-order selling where as a general principle "the more you tell, the more you sell." E-mail is a unique environment. Readers are quickly sorting through a bunch of messages and aren't disposed to stick with you for a long time.

13. Regardless of length, get the important points across quickly. People who need more information can always click on a link to your landing page. The key benefits and deal should be communicated on the first screen, or very soon afterward.

14. The tone should be helpful, friendly, informative, and educational, not promotional or hard-sell. "Information is the gold in cyberspace," says Joe Vitale. Trying to sell readers with a traditional hyped-up sales letter won't work. People online want information and lots of it. You'll have to add solid material to your puffed-up sales letter to make it work online.

Refrain from saying your service is "the best" or that you offer "quality." Those are empty, meaningless phrases. Be specific. How are you the best? What exactly do you mean by quality? And who says it besides you? And even though information is the gold, readers don't want to be bored. They seek, like all of us, relevance. Give it to them.

15. Include an opt-out statement that prevents flaming from recipients who feel they have been spammed. State that your intention is to respect their privacy, and make it easy for them to prevent further promotional e-mails from being sent to them. All they have to do is click on Reply and type "UNSUBSCRIBE"

or "REMOVE" in the subject line. Example: "We respect your online time and privacy, and pledge not to abuse this medium. If you prefer not to receive further e-mails from us of this type, please reply to this e-mail and type 'Remove' in the subject line."

GETTING PAST THE ISPS AND SPAM FILTERS

Everyone seems to agree that e-mail marketing is one of the most effective and powerful forms of Internet marketing today. After all, it is quick to deploy, provides immediate measurable results, and delivers a high return on investment.

But there is a downside. Successful e-mail marketing requires experience, expertise, and knowledge of the constantly changing e-mail filtering, spam-eradicating, firewall-building software industry. It has been said that more than one out of five e-mails have problems with delivery—which significantly erode response rates and program effectiveness.

It's not enough to build a list of interested customers or clients, send them informative, engaging e-mails once a week or once a month, and market products or services to them in the process. You've got to know how to get the messages *delivered*, and then *read* by the recipient. In other words, creating wonderful e-mail messages is only *part* of the process—the messages are absolutely worthless to you if never received by list members.

As a result of corporate and Internet Service Provider (ISP) filters, blacklists, and constant e-mail address flux, permission-based marketers often face obstacles in their attempt to deliver solicited, confirmed-consent messages to the inboxes of customers and subscribers with whom they've established relationships.

Deliverability is key. With e-mail, it's simply the ability to complete delivery of a message to a recipient's inbox. We're not talking about readability—those factors that increase the open/read rate—but the process of getting the message into the inbox of the intended recipient.

Simply put, what can you do to ensure receipt of your messages? Let's agree on one thing: delivery *begins* when a recipient grants permission to receive your messages. If your e-mail marketing strategy is based on this premise, delivery challenges are significantly minimized. With permission, the customer or recipient can provide recourse if an ISP, spam filter, or blacklist blocks your messages.

Several factors hinder or prevent solicited e-mail delivery:

• *ISP-blocked incoming mail.* The most common version of ISP blocking. Many ISPs, especially large ones, maintain internal blacklists of IP addresses that are denied any incoming connections. Frequent customer complaints about traffic from particular sources are the most common cause of this kind of blocking. ISPs tend to block IPs without any notification, as they routinely handle complaints about numerous individual e-mail sources.

• *ISP-blocked outgoing mail.* Your ISP blocks outgoing traffic to another ISP. This is rare, as most ISPs block incoming traffic, but it has been known to happen.

• *Distributed content filters.* Several antispam companies help ISPs and corporate Internet users cope with the influx of unsolicited e-mail. These blocking systems employ complex content analysis processes that scan message content and create message "signatures" that are disseminated among the filtering company's client base.

• *Public list.* Publicly accessible blacklists and whitelists, maintained by volunteers, are often used by smaller ISPs and companies without dedicated e-mail administrators. Listing criteria can be reliable or nearly arbitrary, depending on the list owner's preferences. Administrators select the lists that most closely match their company's policy. Whitelists are lists of approved sources from which the user will accept e-mail messages. Blacklists are lists of malicious, untrustworthy, or unsafe sources from which users should not accept e-mails.

• *ISP content filters.* Similar to distributed content filters, ISPs often employ content filters created internally or adapted from others. Content filters scan for a variety of red flags and they can even learn new patterns in spam e-mail, such as inserting periods in words that would normally trigger a block.

• *User lists.* Recent upgrades to e-mail applications, including AOL, MSN, Yahoo!, and Outlook, allow users to compile their own blacklists and whitelists of individual and domain addresses. There are also "challenge/response systems," which extend this process by requiring non-whitelisted senders to respond with a code or other confirmation before their messages are delivered.

• *Message bounces.* A "soft" bounce is a temporary failure where the e-mail wasn't delivered but may be retried in the future. It could be because the mailbox was full, or the receiving mail server didn't respond to the delivery attempt. A "hard" bounce means the message is permanently undeliverable. Maybe the address is invalid, or a remote server is blocking your server.

Naturally, you want to minimize the number of "hard" bounces, those permanently fatal messages that mean loss of contact and "no sale." There are a number of ways to ensure greater delivery rates. The first requires cooperation from the recipients, as you want them to add your e-mail address to their "accepted" messages list.

HOW TO GET INTO THE RECIPIENT'S ADDRESS BOOK OR WHITELIST

Getting your "FROM" address added to your recipient's address book or personal whitelist is, more and more, a crucial step in getting your e-mails into the inbox, rather than into the spam or, worse yet, the trash folder. More and more people, both business and consumer e-mail users, are adopting the use of spam filters, or upgrading their e-mail programs to include some form of spam filtering/whitelist feature.

You need to remind people to take the step of adding your FROM address to their address book/whitelist. Consider adding a single sentence at the top of your e-mail. Here are three examples of effective reminder statements:

> To ensure our e-mail is delivered to your inbox, please add the e-mail address delightfulmessages@ourcompany.com to your Address Book or junk filter settings.

> To ensure regular delivery of our e-mails, please add us (youwantthis@thiscompany.net) to your Address Book. Thank you!

> To guarantee delivery of this newsletter, please add ournews letters@mycompany.com to your e-mail Address Book.

You may wish to go so far as to explain to your recipients how to set their junk filter settings in a special section of an e-mail message, or devote an entire mailing to this issue. Review the process for the major e-mail applications and Internet Service Providers, and write up a step-by-step instructional e-mail message. I've had a number of clients offer phone customer support assistance to any reader who may need a "walkthrough"!

TRIGGERING SPAM FILTERS

The means that the various ISP and e-mail server programs use to identify unwanted or inappropriate e-mail messages change fairly often and it is necessary to be aware of new implementations. But some important essentials can be reviewed.

Be careful with terms and characters used in your promotional e-mail campaigns. Microsoft's Outlook Express junk e-mail filter will send your e-mails straight to the "Deleted Items" folder if it finds things such as "advertisement," "order now," or "for free" in your e-mails. However, the list is under constant revision, and you should regularly update your in-house list of unwelcome words. Visit this URL to view a current list of words and terms that Outlook will filter: https://blog .sendblaster.com/2010/02/25/microsoft-outlook-spam-words -to-avoid-in-your-emails/.

Establish procedures for proofing e-mail campaigns. Your proofing checklist should include HTML validation. Popular HTML editing software already offers effective validation tools and will highlight any errors on the fly, as your message is being created.

For a complete reference specification of HTML formatting, visit the World Wide Web Consortium documentation pages (http://www.w3.org/MarkUp/). Also, you can use the HTML validator in your e-mail application or a third-party validator such as the W3C Markup Validation Service (http://validator .w3.org/).

Here are ten ways to help increase the likelihood that your e-mail messages will be accepted by the receiving ISP and avoid future deliverability problems.

1. **Create a reverse DNS.** Make sure your outgoing mailing IPs (Internet protocols) have valid RDNS (reverse domain name system) entries set up. RDNS resolves IP addresses to domain names. This ensures that when a receiving e-mail server checks who owns the IP trying to connect to it, you'll come up as the result, passing one of the many basic checks ISPs do to deter spammers.

2. **Set up an SPF.** A Sender Policy Framework (SPF) is an

additional step to verify an e-mail sender's identity. SPF uses DNS records that specify the mail servers and IP addresses that are authorized to send e-mail messages from a certain domain. The protocol is fairly easy to set up; your network administrator should be able to do it in less than five minutes. SPF adds another layer of authentication to your outgoing e-mail and protects against "phishing" attacks on your brand. You should know that some ISPs, such as AOL, *require* SPF to be implemented to be considered for their whitelists.

3. **Make only one connection.** When connecting to an e-mail server, send only one message per connection. Some systems still try to shovel as many messages through one connection as possible, which can be likened to throwing five hundred e-mail addresses into the "BCC" field. ISPs frown on this technique, as spammers who want to get as many messages in before being blocked typically use this approach.

4. **Limit sending rate.** Though the ideal send volume depends on the list's nature, a good rule is to limit your transmission to 100,000 or so messages per hour. Keep in mind that you will also need to accept feedback in the form of bounced messages—your outgoing speed shouldn't affect your ability to receive bounces.

5. **Accept bounces.** Some e-mail systems, especially older ones, have a nasty habit of rejecting bounce messages. These "bounced bounces" arrive at the receiving ISP and can raise red flags. Nothing irks an ISP more than sending a response that a recipient doesn't exist, only to have the notification rejected and the mailings continue.

6. **Validate HTML content.** One of the dirtiest tricks in a spammer's arsenal is invalid, broken, and malicious HTML code. If you use HTML in your messages, make sure your code is error-free and follows W3C HTML guidelines, as discussed earlier.

7. **Avoid scripting.** Security risks due to script vulnerabilities in e-mail browsers have increased over the years. The

result is that most scripts are stripped out of messages. Some e-mail systems reject messages outright if scripting is detected. For greatest delivery success, avoid using any scripts in messages. Instead, direct your readers to your Web site, where use of dynamic scripting can be fully implemented.

8. **Understand content filtering basics.** Ignorance of filtering approaches is no excuse for not getting messages delivered. Read bounce messages, track which messages had high bounce rates and low open rates, and see if you can reverse-engineer offending content.

9. **Monitor delivery and bounce rates by ISP/domain.** After every delivery, run reports by major domain and ISP on your messages. Look for unusual bounce, unsubscribe, spam complaint, and open rates at specific domains.

10. **Monitor spam complaints.** Even the best permission marketers with world-class practices receive spam complaints. Monitor the number of spam complaints for each mailing and establish a benchmark average. Look for mailings with spam complaint percentages that vary from the norm. See if you can determine what may have caused the problem. Was it the subject line? Too many messages in too short a time? Remember, a high number of spam complaints may result in an ISP blocking current, or even future, messages.

Some resources you can use to monitor complaints are:

SpamCop: http://www.spamcop.net/fom-serve/cache/94.html
Abuse.net: http://www.abuse.net/addnew.html

Diagnosing the root causes of deliverability problems will help you prevent them. You must monitor your delivery rates religiously because the rules around delivery change every day! Don't make the mistake of understaffing or underfunding around this issue, as it undermines the overall effectiveness of your e-mail marketing program (and your company image at the same time).

Remember, to reach full delivery you must:

• *Monitor*: Use a seed list–based monitoring system that tracks your true delivery rates across all major ISPs. Know when a problem occurs, and don't rely on your bounce-backs to give you all the information you need. Some mail just never gets delivered, or is put directly into "junk" folders or trash bins—and you'll never know without such a system in place.

• *Analyze*: When you're at less than 100 percent delivery, it's high time to find out why. You should look closely at the individual e-mail, as well as the e-mail program as a whole. There are lots of reasons for failed delivery—and early detection ensures smooth future deliveries.

• *Resolve*: Create strong relationships with ISP tech-support people to have a valuable resource to troubleshoot alongside your staff members. ISP relations should be a high priority.

• *Optimize*: Use information from all sources to solve your e-mail delivery problems. Small changes in creative copy, list, or server configuration can make a world of difference in your delivery rates.

Make sure you are tracking your deliveries, testing for ISP blocking and spam filtering before a large mailing, and reacting *quickly* to problems when they arise. Although complicated, it's imperative in the creation and maintenance of a truly successful e-mail marketing program.

LONG VS. SHORT E-MAIL COPY

"What works best in e-mail marketing?" I am often asked. "Long copy or short copy?"

It's a quandary for direct marketers much more so than for general marketers. Here's why. There's a widely held viewpoint that, on the Internet, the less copy the better. Web marketing experts tell us that the Internet is faster paced than the "snail mail" world, that attention spans are shorter, and long messages get zapped into oblivion with the click of the mouse. "Keep it short!" they extol in countless advisory e-zines.

General advertisers, for the most part, also believe that when it comes to copy the shorter the better. Often their print ads have large pictures and only a handful of words. So they have no trouble embracing the "people don't read" mentality that the Web marketing gurus say works best.

But traditional direct marketers whose products are typically sold with long-copy direct-mail packages and self-mailers— newsletter publishers, seminar promoters, magazines, book clubs, insurance, audiocassettes, nutritional supplements—have a problem. It goes something like this:

"In print, I have to use long copy to make the sale . . . or I just don't get the order. We've tested short copy many times—who *doesn't* want a cheaper mailing piece with less ink and paper? But it has never worked for our product. Now my Web marketing consultant says the e-mail should be just a few paragraphs. If a few paragraphs won't convince people to buy offline, why should things be any different online?"

And they are right. Just because a person buys online doesn't change the persuasion process. If she needs the facts to make a decision, she needs them regardless of whether she is ordering from a paper mailing or from a Web site.

Yet we also have a sense that the Web marketing gurus have at least a clue as to what they are talking about. We sense that our four-page sales letter, if sent word for word as a lengthy e-mail, wouldn't work. People would click away long before they got to the end.

I think I have some sensible guidelines to answer this puzzle. First, we need to quantify what we mean by "short" versus "long."

When a Web marketing guru talks about "short" e-mail, he probably means only three or four paragraphs. So when he says that long copy doesn't work, by "long" he means e-mails of more than a few paragraphs.

If I say "long copy *does* work," I mean long compared to the typical e-mail—not compared to the typical direct-mail letter on paper. A "long" e-mail, which may fill several screens, is closer in length to a one-page letter—short by direct-mail standards—than to a four-page letter. And it doesn't even come close to an eight-page letter.

Second, we need to quantify how much shorter online copy is than offline. Should you translate your entire package, word for word? Should you compress it to half its length? Less?

Kathy Henning, who writes extensively about online communication, says, "In general, online text should be half as long as printed text, maybe even shorter." Not a precise formula, but a good starting point for estimation.

Third, and most important, we need to remember that the copy for e-mail marketing campaigns is not wholly contained within the e-mail itself. It is really in two parts.

The first half of the message is in the actual e-mail. The e-mail contains a link to a page on a Web site or server. When you click on that link, you jump to the page, where the remainder of the message is presented, along with the online order mechanism.

In a traditional direct-mail package, the message is unevenly split. Consistently, 98 percent of the copy is in the letter and brochure, with the remaining 2 percent on the order form. In e-mail marketing campaigns, the division is less balanced and more varied.

The diagram of an e-mail marketing mode on the next page shows the various ways the total copy can be divided between the e-mail and the response page. There are four options, as shown in fig. 13.1.

1. *Short e-mail, landing page* (left upper quadrant)—Many marketers with simple lead-generating offers use short e-mails (the traditional three or four paragraphs) with a link to a "landing page." A lead-generating landing page is a Web-based form, usually with a headline, a couple of paragraphs explaining the offer, and a mechanism for the recipient to fill in his information and submit his response. This format is similar in length and style to the traditional one-page sales letter and business reply card used in lead-generating paper direct mail.

Fig. 13.1: E-mail length guidelines.

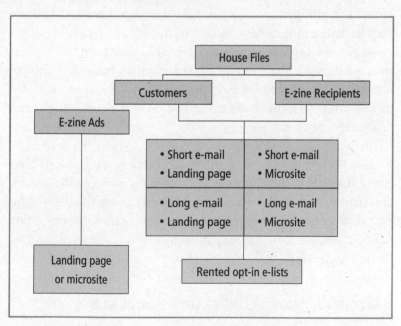

2. *Long e-mail, landing page* (lower left quadrant)—This is similar except the e-mail, by Internet marketing standards, is

"long." For convenience, define a short e-mail as any e-mail that, when printed out, takes half a page or less. By comparison, any e-mail that takes more than a page when printed out is "long." This format is similar in length and style to a one- to two-page letter.

3. *Long e-mail, microsite* (lower right quadrant)—This format has a long e-mail and a long landing page. The microsite is a custom URL designed specifically for the offer. Unlike a landing page, which is usually a single screen, the microsite's lengthier copy requires many screens. The microsite can be broken into distinct pages or it can be one continuous document through which the reader must scroll (see www.surefire customerservicetechniques.com). This long e-mail/microsite format allows for maximum copy and is ideal for translating lengthy mailings, such as magalogs (long-copy self-mailers that look like magazines), to the Web.

4. *Short e-mail, microsite* (upper right quadrant)—This format combines a short e-mail up front with a long-copy microsite on the back end. It is ideal for offers that require a lot of copy but are being transmitted to prospects who might not read a lengthy e-mail.

The bottom line: e-mail marketing can work without having e-mails competing with *War and Peace* in word count. By strategically splitting your copy between the front-end e-mail and back-end response page, you can get your message across without having time-pressured e-mail recipients fleeing in terror.

WRITING AN ONLINE CONVERSION E-MAIL SERIES

"Online conversion" is a proven model for building an e-list of prospects and profitably marketing products on the Internet. Here's an oversimplified version of how online conversion works:

1. You create some free content.
2. You offer people the free content online.
3. When they accept, you then sell them products and services they have to pay for—again, online.

Let's break down each step, starting with the creation of free content. This is the easiest step. Just repackage some of your content as an information premium. The content does not have to be long. Repurposing existing articles works fine for this purpose. So do special reports specifically written for the online conversion campaign. Or the same reports you offer as premiums in postal direct marketing.

The premium is typically offered as a "free special report." It is usually available as a downloadable PDF file. Some marketers prefer to post the report as a multipage HTML document on the Web.

The second step is to collect e-mail addresses of prospects by offering them the free content online. There are many ways to attract potential customers to a Web page where they can download your free content. One way is to send e-mails to lists of prospects. The e-mail offers the content as a "free special report." To get the free report, the recipient clicks on an embedded URL in the message text.

If the content is a downloadable PDF file, the recipient is brought to a short transaction page. She enters her e-mail address, and is then allowed to download and print the PDF file.

If the content is a series of sequential HTML pages, the recipient is again brought to a short transaction page. She enters her e-mail address, clicks SUBMIT, and is brought to the first page of the microsite where the report is available to read as a posted HTML document.

Within the HTML report, put a number of links to a landing page or transaction page for your paid product. Many readers may click on these links and order your paid product while they are in the middle of reading your free bonus report online.

Either way, the reader must give us her e-mail address to read the free report, which is the key to the online conversion method.

There are many other methods you can use to generate leads for your online conversion campaign. Some marketers have had great success with postcards. Others have used banners or online ads in e-zines.

Finally, you need to convert the leads to paid customers. So far, two things have happened. First, we have captured the prospect's e-mail address, so we can market to her as often as we like at virtually no cost. And second, we know that the prospect is interested in the topic of our content, because she at least requested a free article or report on it.

Since the content was free, we do not know at this point whether she will pay for products related to this topic. But she is a qualified lead in the sense that she is (a) interested in the topic and (b) responds to online marketing.

The next step is to send her a series of e-mails, known as the online conversion series, with the objective of converting her from a requester of free content to a buyer of our paid product.

Experience so far shows that our online conversion series works best with between three and seven efforts.

Some marketers want every e-mail in the series to attempt to make a sale. That is, they all have a URL the reader can click to reach a page from which the product may be ordered.

Others like the first two e-mails to be simply goodwill, promoting the value of the information and encouraging the reader to actually read the free content—and in some cases even giving her more free content. These are called "free touch" e-mails, because they touch the reader without asking her to purchase.

Subsequent e-mails in the series ask for the order; these are called "conversion e-mails." In a seven-effort series, the first one or two e-mails might be free touch; the remainder, conversion e-mails.

When the reader clicks on the URL link in your e-mail, she may go to either a landing page or a transaction page. A landing page has a fair amount of descriptive copy about the product you are selling and your offer. It does a strong job of selling the reader on the value of the product. A transaction page has minimal description of the product. It is basically an online order form.

Some marketers always send the e-mail recipient who clicks on the link in the e-mail to the landing page, on the theory that the more sales copy, the more sales made. Other marketers believe that if the conversion e-mail is long and has a lot of sales copy, there is no need to repeat this in a landing page, and so they just send the prospect to a short transaction page.

The best offer for an online conversion effort is a free 30-day trial of the product. If you can set up your site so that the recipient's credit card is not billed until after the 30-day trial period, that's the best choice. Then you are truly offering a free trial.

By comparison, if you charge recipients' credit cards as soon as they submit their orders, it is not really a free 30-day trial; it is a risk-free 30-day trial. The recipients are paying, but if they cancel within 30 days they get a refund.

You can experiment with timing, number of efforts, and mix of efforts (free touch and online conversion) in your online conversion series. A typical series might go like this:

Day 1—e-mail #1, free touch. Thank the prospect for requesting your free content and reinforce its value.

Day 2—e-mail #2, free touch. Encourage the prospect to read the free content and highlight its value. Point out some especially good ideas, tips, or strategies it contains.

Day 4—e-mail #3, online conversion. Tell the prospect he can get of a free 30-day trial of your product. Sell him on the product and its value.

Day 7—e-mail #4. Remind the prospect that he can still solve his problem by getting your product and accepting your free trial offer.

Day 14—e-mail #5. Tell the prospect the free 30-day trial is expiring, resell him on the product you are offering, and urge him to act today. Tell him after that, it's too late.

Write your online conversion series e-mails the same as you would write other online and offline promotions to sell your products. Use the same copy, content, and organization. Get attention in the lead, generate interest, create desire for your product, and ask for the order.

One key difference: in your lead, always acknowledge that they are hearing from you as a follow-up to the free report or article *they asked you* to send them. This has two benefits.

First, they may feel slightly more obligated to read your message; after all, you did give them a gift. And second, if they liked the free content, it automatically puts them in a receptive mood for more of the same.

Should you try online conversion? Every marketer who wants to market products and services online could probably benefit from testing an online conversion series.

Just renting an e-list of opt-in names and asking them to subscribe won't work; people who are online tend not to buy from strangers. But send those same names an offer of a free article or report, and they will take you up on it. After all, what's to lose?

If you have targeted the right audience, and the free content you provide is of high quality and value, then enough of the readers will want more of the same and be willing to accept a free 30-day trial of products related to the same topic.

And if your product is of high quality and value, a large percentage of the readers will not send it back and request a refund. You will have successfully converted free content requesters to paid buyers—your goal in online conversion.

WRITING A MARKETING E-ZINE

For many marketers, the fastest way to build a house list of opt-in e-mail names and addresses—an important asset for online marketing—is with the offer of a free subscription to an online newsletter or "e-zine."

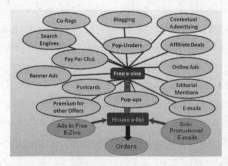

The free e-zine is the online equivalent of a company newsletter, except it is distributed electronically instead of printed and mailed. The cost and time savings are tremendous—an e-zine can be distributed at virtually no cost, almost instantaneously, to thousands of prospects and customers at the click of a mouse.

When you build a large subscription list for your e-zine, you can then send promotions to potential customers via the Internet whenever you want, generating thousands of extra dollars in incremental sales you might not otherwise have made. And you save thousands of dollars on printing and postage.

Many online marketing tools are used to drive potential customers to a Web page where they can sign up for a free subscription to your e-zine in exchange for giving you their e-mail address. You can also ask for their name, which allows you to personalize future e-mails you send to them.

These traffic-building methods include such things as banner ads, online ads in e-zines reaching similar audiences, e-mail marketing, pay-per-click advertising, and search engine optimization of the e-zine sign-up Web site. The acquisition cost per subscriber can range from $1 to $5 a name, depending on the method used and the market targeted.

Generally, the larger and more targeted your subscriber list, the more profitable your online marketing will be. After all, a click-through rate (CTR) of 1 percent to one thousand e-zine subscribers will bring just ten visitors to your landing page; but if you have a million online subscribers, a 1 percent CTR will generate ten thousand visits.

But for your e-zine to work as an online marketing tool, subscribers must not only sign up; they must also open and read your e-newsletters. If they don't open the current issue, they can't respond to any of the ads or offers you make in it. And if they don't read it on an ongoing basis, they will eventually unsubscribe, and you will lose them as an online prospect.

In my experience, the best e-zines—those with the highest open, read, and click-through rates—are those that present useful how-to tips in short, bite-size chunks, the more practical and actionable, the better.

Your e-zine is not the place to pontificate on business philosophy or explain complex technology; you can send your subscribers to Web pages and downloadable white papers or special reports that cover those topics. E-zine readers love practical articles that tell them how to do something useful— and do so in just a few concise paragraphs.

News also can serve as effective e-zine content but, by itself, is not as potent as advice. The best way to use news is to link a tip or other advice to it. For instance, if you are a financial publisher talking about crude oil, tell the reader which oil stocks he should own to profit from volatility in oil prices.

You don't need a news angle to make advice an effective content strategy for your free e-zine. However, if you can relate your tips to current events or news, do so; experience shows that it can potentially double your readership and response.

That being said, you never know which article is going to strike your e-zine reader's fancy. And it's often not the article you'd think. For instance, a manager for a company that sells information on safety to HR managers publishes a regular e-zine on safety and other HR issues. He reports that his best-read article of all time was "10 Ways to Reduce Eye Strain at Your PC."

The eye-strain article generated much more response than more specialized articles targeted to his HR audience. Go figure.

Here's what I've found makes the ideal e-zine article (many of these ideas are borrowed from my colleague Ilise Benun, of www.artofselfpromotion.com):

1. Think of yourself as a conduit. Your job is to pass useful information along to those who can use it.

2. Pay close attention to questions, problems, and ideas that

come up when you're doing your work or interacting with customers.

3. Distill the lesson (or lessons) into a tip that you can share with your network, via e-mail or snail mail or even in simple conversation.

4. State the problem or situation as an introduction to your tip. Distill it down to its essence.

5. Give the solution. Tips are action-oriented. So make sure you give a couple of action steps to take. Readers especially love something they can use right away, like the ten tips on how to reduce eye strain while working at a PC.

6. Describe the result or benefit of using these tips to provide some incentive to take the action. If there are tools readers can use to measure the results of your tip once they put it into practice, give them a link to Web sites offering these tools.

7. Include tips the reader can use without doing any work, phrases they can use verbatim, boilerplate clauses, checklists, forms, and so on.

8. List Web sites and other resources where readers can go for more info.

9. Put your best tip first, in case people don't read the whole thing—because sometimes even really short tips are too much.

Be aware that most e-zines have a dual audience consisting of: (1) prospects who get the free e-zine but are not your customers, and (2) subscribers who have bought products from you and get your free e-zine because they are on your customer list.

For reasons of economy of scale and simplicity of management, most publishers use one e-zine to serve both audiences. But you have to keep the different needs and perspectives of both groups in mind for your e-zine to be effective.

The first group of e-zine subscribers consists of people who have signed up for your free online newsletter. They have not yet bought products from you, and in fact may not even be aware of your products or even who you are.

Your goal with these subscribers is to (a) delight them with the free e-zine they are receiving; and (b) upgrade them to the next step—purchase of one of your products or services.

To accomplish these goals:

• Pack the e-zine with solid content. Nothing beats useful, practical, how-to tips.

• Put a 50- to 100-word ad in each issue of your e-zine offering a free 30-day trial for one of your products, with a link to a landing page where the reader can accept such an offer.

• Send at least one solo e-mail to subscribers between e-zine issues giving them a compelling reason to accept your 30-day free trial offer; this could be the offer of premium, such as a free gift or free content (e.g., a special report). If you offer free content, let them get the report as a downloadable PDF after they order your product on the landing page.

The second group of e-zine subscribers are customers: people who have already purchased one or more of your products. Your e-zine can do any or all of the following for your customers:

• Give them news updates, recommendations, and fresh ideas for using your products
• Highlight product upgrades, new accessories, or other product-related items of interest
• Bring them special discount offers on your other products and services

Can you stray from my formula of how-to advice and tips? Of course. My e-zine, *The Direct Response Letter* (available at www.bly.com), uses many different types of articles including book reviews, quotations, news items, and new product announcements.

But take a tip from me. When you're putting together your next e-zine issue, remember that nothing gains the reader's interest and attention like solid how-to tips.

14

WRITING ONLINE ADS

Many small and medium-size businesses use Internet advertising as a direct response sales tool, meaning the Web surfer sees their ad, clicks on it, and is sent to the Web site or landing page, and buys their product.

The problem with this sales model when it comes to banner advertising is that it relies on interruption. The person who sees their banner presumably is on a Web page they want to be on, and to click the banner interrupts them from what they were doing.

Therefore, banner advertising, though still viable as a direct response tool, may be better suited for image advertising or branding. Because of its broad reach and high frequency, a banner can be very effective for increasing brand awareness. Unfortunately, it is not easy to measure that effect. Branding is a long-term tactic that slowly builds results over time.

Like with a television commercial, viewers may not take immediate action when they see your banner, but they will remember your name when they are ready to buy. But unlike with a television commercial, users still have the ability to take immediate action.

Because banner advertising has become less expensive, and can both build awareness of your product and get an immediate response, it may well be a very cost effective form of advertising as long as you understand that building awareness is part of its purpose.

BANNER SIZE

When you talk about banner ad size, you can be referring to one of two different things: file weight or ad dimensions. File weight is measured in bytes. With broadband Internet, file weight is not nearly as important as it once was. It still is best, however, to keep your banner file size below 25 KB.

An ad's dimensions can be any size that the host page will accept. The Interactive Advertising Bureau (IAB) has defined twenty standard sizes (see below). The IAB is a nonprofit trade association for the interactive advertising industry; it has created these guidelines to reduce the number of ad sizes and simplify the ad creation process.

These dimensions are measured in pixels, which are basic units from which a video or computer picture is made.

RECTANGLES AND POP-UPS

Medium Rectangle	300 x 250
Square Pop-Up	250 x 250
Vertical Rectangle	240 x 400
Large Rectangle	336 x 280
Rectangle	180 x 150
3:1 Rectangle	300 x 100
Pop-Under	720 x 300

BANNERS AND BUTTONS

Full Banner	468 x 60
Half Banner	234 x 60
Micro Bar	88 x 31
Button 1	120 x 90
Button 2	120 x 60
Vertical Banner	120 x 240
Square Banner	125 x 125
Leaderboard	728 x 90

SKYSCRAPERS (VERTICAL BANNERS)

Wide Skyscraper	160 x 600
Skyscraper	120 x 600
Half Page Ad	300 x 600

For the longest time, the 468 x 200 banner was the most common, but with competition for quality advertisers, publishers have begun to give more space for advertising.

Generally speaking, the larger the ad, the more memorable it will be and the more click-throughs it will get, but that doesn't mean that smaller ads won't work; page position, content and relevancy, and design will also play an important role. Advertising.com examined the click-through and conversion rates on banners. It found that the medium rectangle (300 x 250) had the highest click-through rates, and the wide skyscraper (160 x 600) had the second-highest.

PAGE POSITION

Page position plays nearly as great a role in the effectiveness of the ad as its size. For image advertising, a top-of-the-page position is best because it is seen and remembered, but not necessarily clicked upon, whereas an ad further into the page and along the side may be more targeted and therefore more likely to get clicked.

Ads appearing near the scroll bar can generate a high click-through rate. The theory is that users click on the ad because their pointer is already poised near it.

BANNER DESIGN AND CONTENT

Banners have come a long way in recent years. With higher bandwidth and better technologies, animations and graphics are much better. Rather than simply link to a new page, banners and ads can have some mouse-over interactivity. Some things work better than others. Following are generalizations about what works best.

Text: The amount of text on your banner must be kept to a minimum, so a small amount of text must have a large impact. Techniques you can use include offering a benefit for clicking on your ad, like "Get More Traffic." Ask a question, the answer to which is on your site. Create a sense of urgency by using phrases like "For a Limited Time." Use the word "Free." Having a good call to action by using phrases such as "Click Here" or "Learn More" can increase the number of clicks.

Your ad should also be relevant. The closer your ad matches the content of the page you are on, the more effective it will be. Keep the message short. People will not take time to read a lot of text. Simple banners have a higher click-through ratio.

Color and Graphics: Ideally, your ad would complement the page on which it appears, but because a single ad usually is displayed on many different Web sites, it is often impractical to design an ad for each site or page on which the ad appears. Studies have shown that bright colors like blue, yellow, and green get the highest click-through rate. Graphics should be eye-catching, but kept to a minimum. For purposes of branding or recognition advertising, you can use your company logo.

Animation and Interactivity: Animation and interactivity play three important roles in banner and display advertising. First, an ad with motion will gain attention so your ad is less likely to be ignored. Second, when you engage the viewer with interactivity, such as mouse-over effects or drop-down menus, you increase click-throughs. And third, these ads are more memorable, so even if they don't generate a click they do more for image building.

SEARCH ENGINE PAY-PER-CLICK (PPC) ADS

The first step in starting a pay-per-click campaign is to decide how much you are willing to spend and for what purpose. Do you want to capture a lead for future follow-up or do you need your traffic to generate instant sales?

Figure out how much each click is worth to determine the maximum amount you are willing to pay—that will be your maximum cost per click (CPC). If you're selling a single low-cost item, your CPC will need to be pretty low.

On the other hand, when selling an item with a higher profit margin, you can afford a higher CPC. Likewise, if by capturing a lead you can sell to the same person over and over again, though you may not recoup your cost on the first sale, having the ability to sell to that customer over and over again will allow you to afford a higher CPC.

Here is a simple example. If it takes twenty clicks to get one sale, and each click costs you $1, each order costs you $20. Is the profit on your product over that amount? If not, you need to make sure your clicks cost less or that you have a higher conversion rate or price point.

Some people use PPC not to sell products but to build their list. The amount you can spend per click is based on the average value of names on your list. If you have $200,000 a year in online sales and twenty thousand names on your list, your average name is worth ten bucks a year.

To find the best keywords for your product, first brainstorm them yourself. No one knows your product better than you. Think about what a person looking for your product might type into the search engine.

Be specific. Don't just come up with generic terms. Get as specific as you can. If you are a jeweler, it's better to advertise for "gold loop earrings" than to use the more generic keyword "jewelry."

Another set of keywords that may gain high conversions are those that establish your product or service as an alternative to something else. For example, you may use the keyword "diamond" to advertise for cubic zirconium. Your ad would then give reasons why your product is a better deal than the word they searched on to begin with.

Gain holiday and special occasion traffic. Use holidays or special occasions as your keywords, especially when you have a retail item that lends itself to gift giving. "Holidays," "birthdays," "weddings," and "graduations"—all are great search terms. You may come up with phrases like "Mother's Day gift," "engagement ring," or "anniversary present."

After coming up with your obvious keywords, start thinking of less obvious searches or related searches. You may think of "wedding vows" because someone interested in vows may also need a wedding ring or bridesmaid's gifts. Be creative in coming up with your words. When using them, make sure you incorporate them in your title and body copy, such as "The Perfect Mother's Day Gift."

If you can figure out a way to make them relevant, current events, popular celebrities, and hot topics all make good search terms. But make sure you can relate these terms to your landing page and offer; if you don't, you'll just get a lot of traffic but very few conversions.

After you have selected your keywords, use Google's keyword planner tool to see what kind of volume they get in number of searches and how crowded the competition is. Your best case is to see lots of searches and few bidders.

But having competition isn't all bad. When you have competition, you know it is a viable product that people are searching on and buying; otherwise no one would be advertising. This tool will also give you suggestions for similar words. Pull out the ones that you think are best.

You'll find an abundance of other keyword tools that can help you find the most cost-effective and productive keywords. Some are free; some cost a small fee.

Now that you have identified your core keywords, you are going to write several ads for each group of keywords that you have made. Here's how to structure your ad:

Headline: The first line is your headline. Always use keywords in your headline.

Your headline can be two lines of up to 30 characters long. That is not a lot, especially when so much of it is taken up with a keyword or two. Make your headline attention grabbing.

- Ask a Question: "Find Your Engagement Ring Yet?"
- State Superiority: "World's Finest Diamond Engagement Rings"
- Appeal to Basic Emotions (love, greed, fear): "A Diamond That'll Make Her Love You More"

Body: The body is a descriptive line with a maximum of 80 characters.

Display URL with Hyperlink: Your domain is the last line of the ad and is automatically extracted by Google from your final

URL to ensure accuracy. The worst thing you can do is drive tons of traffic to your site at a high cost-per-click without converting that traffic into a sale or lead. Consider adding a qualifying word or phrase to your ad. For example, suppose you're selling a fly-fishing guide for $19.99. By placing the price of the guide in your ad, you'll discourage "tire kickers"—anyone who is looking for free information and is not willing to pay your price.

If at all possible, use a Web address that includes your keywords, even if you have to create it. The best method is to buy a dedicated domain name specifically for each landing page.

ADVERTISING IN E-NEWSLETTERS

All types of e-zine ads can be valuable to you. This section will explain the three different types of e-zine ads and how they can work for you.

Solo Ad: A solo ad is when an e-zine sends your content to its mailing list all by itself. In other words, the e-mail is solely your content and not part of the regular newsletter.

Sponsorship Ad: E-zines can feature any number of sponsorship ads and often break down their pricing by the position the ad is given within the body of the newsletter. A Top Sponsor ad is positioned at the beginning of the e-mail and is usually the most expensive ad.

Whenever an ad is placed anywhere after the first article, it is referred to as a Middle Sponsor. A newsletter can have any number of Middle Sponsor ads. The most effective Middle Sponsor ads are those that appear next to articles on topics related to the product being advertised, e.g., a Middle Sponsor ad selling grass seed positioned next to an article on lawn care.

A Bottom Sponsor ad is the last ad in the e-zine. It appears after all the regular content but before the classified ads. These ads are generally the least expensive sponsorship ads.

Text ad: A text ad is usually between three and five lines long and 60 to 65 characters per line. In the e-zines with the largest readership, these ads are fairly cheap, anywhere from/ $5 to $25 per issue.

Some newsletters allow you to place FREE ads with them in exchange for being placed on their e-mailing list. This is one way they grow their lists. But because it doesn't cost you anything (except your time and a cluttered e-mail box), any response you get is good.

Don't forget that because e-zines are often archived, you will have a permanent link pointing to your Web site. Even if customers aren't accessing your site, the search engine spiders are.

The design of your ad will depend greatly on the newsletter it will be placed in and what type of ad you are running. Check the newsletter's specifications. Many are strictly text with no graphics so they are low in bandwidth and can easily pass spam filters. You may also ask the e-zine publisher what works best. After all, they know their audience better than anyone.

When running a solo ad, your content should be similar to the publisher's regular newsletter. Make your ad seem like the kind of information normally seen in the e-zine. In other words, make it appear to be newsworthy and avoid hype. Solo ads allow you the opportunity to educate your consumer and expand upon the benefits of your product.

Here a killer headline is imperative to attract attention. The headline's job is to get the reader's attention and then draw him into the ad copy. It will do that if it contains the words your prospect has on his mind, so be sure to include one of your keywords if possible. The following is an example of a solo online ad (it ran before 9/11 and the war in Iraq):

BOMBS FALL IN BAGHDAD AND YOU MAKE MONEY!

Little-known defense contractor poised to return 100 percent profit even if Bush never declares war on Iraq, and 500 percent profits if he does. FREE research report gives details on this pure defense play and 4 other "stealth stocks" that have managed to fly under Wall Street's radar. Best part: Our "stealth stocks" system keeps you safely in cash when market sentiment turns negative. Safest way to make money in today's market. We've already earned gains of 58, 108, even 241% . . . generated consistent positive gains—and handily beaten the S&P using this method. FIND OUT MORE.

For sponsorship and classified ads, you don't have the luxury of space and you don't have the reader's undivided attention. You are limited to a half dozen lines or less with fewer than 70 characters per line. Because of this your ad must carry a greater impact.

When push comes to shove, when creating an effective e-zine advertisement, the same rules for all advertising apply: have a strong headline, state a need, show how your product can fulfill that need, and provide a strong call to action.

FACEBOOK ADS

Currently Facebook has well over 2 billion users; LinkedIn, the network for professionals, boasts a user base of 630 million. Again, you want to put your attention where your audience is congregating, so one of the other social sites—Reddit, Tumblr, Instagram, Pinterest, and Twitter—may have advertising potential for your business.

Facebook's Advertising Guide (https://www.facebook.com /business/ads-guide) describes the specifications for three ad formats: video, image, and collection formats. As image ads are a reasonable starting point in Facebook advertising, this section focuses on this format. Due to the popularity of videos online, video ad specifications will follow.

Basically pay-per-click advertising, the average cost of a click, is about $1.25. If you're going this route, you'll quickly find that there are many design and content options. Here are the basic requirements for *single image ads*: run in the right-hand column (as opposed to single-image ads running in the Facebook feed). The specifications below date from March 2019.

Image Specifications
- Recommended image dimensions are 1200 x 628 pixels.
- Minimum width and height of 600 pixels.
- Recommended aspect ratio is between 9:16 and 16:9, but crops to 1.91:1 with link.
- Recommended image formats are JPG and PNG.
- Images with 20% text or more could increase chances of failed delivery.
- Size: 1,200 x 628 pixels.
- Ratio: 1.91:1 (the proportional relationship between its width and its height; it is commonly expressed as two numbers separated by a colon, as in 16:9).
- Facebook suggests you use minimal or no text on the image.

Copy Limitations:
- Text: 125 characters.
- Headline: 25 characters.
- Link description: 30 characters.

WRITING FACEBOOK IMAGE ADS

What makes an effective Facebook image ad? Two things: bright, eye-catching images and compelling, persuasive content. But, according to the ad experts at Facebook, it's the image that does the "heavy work." Research found images are so important that they're responsible for some 75 to 90 percent of an ad's performance. It's smart, they say, to test ten to fifteen images (keeping the ad copy the same across all variations).

Facebook actually recommends de-prioritizing copy; copywriters know better. Always give the words the attention they deserve. Here's an ad with an offer directed at Facebook marketers. Picture this: a distressed, frustrated writer sitting in front of a blank computer screen. Top-level ad content reads:

Let me show you how easy it is to write a Facebook ad. You see the tricks, tips, and gotcha you need to know. Great for the newer marketer!

Get the checklist for writing Facebook ads

This downloadable checklist takes away all the frustrating mystery of "figuring out" how to write a great Facebook ad.

In writing Facebook ads, success is more about capturing attention and inspiring viewers not only to respond to the call to action, but also to "like" and share what they've seen. Since the image is what draws their eyes, it's suggested you put key messages within the image. However, Facebook won't allow you to use an image where copy takes up more than 20 percent of it. "Text" includes copy you've overlaid on an image as well as text-based logos, watermarks, and even text in your video's thumbnail images.

Facebook ads with photos, first and foremost, are usually small. And given that they have an image, copy must be kept to a minimum.

WordStream has a simplified formula for writing Facebook ads that I think is right on the money. The ad has to tell the reader these three basic things:

- What you're offering
- How it benefits them
- What to do next

And AdEspresso offers these eight sensible guidelines specifically for Facebook ad headlines:

1. Use numbers. There's plenty of copywriting research that all points to one conclusion: headlines that start with numbers are often winners.
2. Create a sense of urgency.
3. Be clear and precise.
4. Keep your headlines short.
5. Emphasize the benefits.
6. Include a call to action.
7. Ask a question.
8. Use powerful words.

Specifics on these points are covered earlier in the book; see chapters 1, 2, 3, and 4.

FACEBOOK VIDEO ADS

In November 2018, Hootsuite noted that 71 percent of people had increased their online video viewing during that year. And 60 percent expect to watch more social video in the coming year. Another point of interest: Facebook users look at ads five times longer when they're consuming video. People gaze five times longer at video than at static posts on Facebook.

The Facebook ad specs of single videos ads are:

- Format—.MOV or .MP4.
- Aspect Ratio—16:9.
- Resolution—720p at minimum.
- File Size—2.3 GB maximum.
- Length—120 minutes (Facebook), sixty seconds (Instagram)
- Thumbnail Image—1,200 x 675 pixels, 16.9 ratio.
- Caption—2,200 characters maximum.

Facebook offers a few simple suggestions for making engaging videos, including:

- Create Facebook Video Ads with mobile in mind.
- Create for mobile by using a vertical or square video format.
- Capture viewer attention. Mobile users move quickly, so it's imperative that the video engages them immediately.
- Include your brand or product early.
- Design for silent viewing. Many people silence their phones as a point of courtesy when in public.

Other suggestions from marketers skilled in creating successful Facebook video ad campaigns include:

- Adding text to your videos
- Using imagery that makes sense without sound
- Upload subtitles with your videos

- The most effective length for Facebook ad titles is four words, with fifteen-word link descriptions. Here's an example:
  - **Create Instant e-Books**
  - (thumbnail)

  Watch Me Create an e-Book in 2 Minutes

  Create Stunning e-Books, Reports, Lead Magnets

  and Whitepapers from Your Blog, Word, Google . . .

FACEBOOK VIDEO VS. YOUTUBE: WHICH IS BETTER?

According to a recent survey, 47 percent of consumers state that they now get most of their video content on Facebook, versus 41 percent who say they usually watch YouTube. And 71 percent of those who watch marketing videos on Facebook state that the ads they view are relevant. Even more important to brands is that between 60 and 70 percent of those who view a company's Facebook video then proceed to visit that company's Web site.

ADDITIONAL FACEBOOK ADVERTISING FORMATS

There are other Facebook ad formats, including slideshow carousel and canvas ad formats. The carousel format allows you to use a combination of all other ad types, running up to ten images, slideshows, or videos in one single campaign. Each element can even be linked out to different landing pages.

The slideshow format is as it sounds: it creates a looping video ad out of up to ten different images. The Facebook ads let you create a full-screen interactive experience for the viewer. As there are separate specs for each individual element you'll choose, you'll need to consult the Facebook

Advertising Center (https://www.facebook.com/business) for detailed specifications.

BOOSTED POSTS AND PROMOTED POSTS

A boosted post is the most basic advertising you can do on Facebook. It is created by allocating advertising budget to a post already on the businesses' page. By clicking the button in the top right corner of the post, you have the option to choose pushing the post to either "People who like your page and their friends" or "People you choose through targeting." You'll also be able to set your budget.

Promoted Posts is an advertising option from Facebook that enables you to make sure the posts you want to market get seen in the News Feeds of more people. The advertising value of boosting your posts has been debated. Some argue it's smarter to go with Promoted Posts instead. What that does is push your post into the news feed. The benefit of this strategy is that you have more targeting, pricing, and bidding options.

HOW MUCH DOES FACEBOOK ADVERTISING COST?

Your ad cost depends on many factors: time of year, time of day, audience gender, and ad position. Truthfully, Facebook ads cost anywhere from less than a dollar to over $5, depending on such factors as ad quality and competition. Fortunately, you can get started for as little as $10 to $20.

LINKEDIN ADVERTISING

According to the LinkedIn advertising team, this site for global professional networking currently boasts a membership of well over six hundred million. In their opinion, LinkedIn is the #1 social platform for business-to-business lead generation and networking for jobs (although indeed.com is the #1 job acquisition site).

That said, let's explore the advertising options available via LinkedIn: the common text-based ad, which we'll explore later; then there are dynamic and display ads, Sponsored InMail ads, and Sponsored Content. Knowing what a text-based ad is, let's define those unfamiliar ad formats.

- **Dynamic ads:** Right-column (also called "right rail") personalized ads tailored to each member based on their profile data, such as company name or job title. There are currently three types of dynamic ad formats to choose from: spotlight, follower, and job posting ads (irrelevant to this discussion).

  1. **Spotlight Ads:** Here's your chance to share thought leadership, best practices, insights, and valuable content with your target audience. When members click on your ad, they're directed to your Web site or landing page, where you can record actions like leads, sign-ups, and visits. You can use spotlight ads to drive conversions and to build brand awareness.

  2. **Follower Ads:** This format allows advertisers to promote their LinkedIn page and drive members to follow their LinkedIn page with a single click. This format is recommended for advertisers whose objectives are to generate brand awareness, increase engagement with the LinkedIn page, or convert LinkedIn members into engaged followers. These ads feature the member's profile photo next to your company's logo. They also feature the member's first name and your company name in the ad copy.

- **Display Advertising:** Sometimes called banner advertising, a display ad includes an image and text content.

- **Sponsored InMail ads:** InMail messages are sent directly to another LinkedIn member you're not connected to. If you have a Basic (free) account, you must upgrade to a

Premium account to use InMail. You receive a specific number of InMail credits based on your subscription type. Sponsored InMail allows you to drive more leads and engage your target audience by delivering personalized, private messages right to their LinkedIn inboxes. Sponsored InMail messages consist of a custom greeting, call-to-action button, body text, custom banner image, and ability to add a link to the message body.

- **Sponsored Content:** There are two types of sponsored content, simple sponsored and direct sponsored content.

  * **Simple Sponsored Content** is a LinkedIn page update created by Page admins, which advertisers can choose to sponsor to gain greater distribution.

  * **Direct Sponsored Content** is Sponsored Content that does not appear on the LinkedIn page or Showcase Page. It allows advertisers to create content to sponsor on behalf of the company without cluttering the LinkedIn page or Showcase Page and without first posting a LinkedIn page update.

Note: Showcase Pages are second-level pages accessible off of a company page. They allow a company to promote specific products or market to a specific buyer persona. LinkedIn users can follow singular Showcase Pages without following the business or its other Showcase Pages.

Because LinkedIn offers many advertising options, it's suggested you consult the LinkedIn Marketing Solutions specifications page (https://www.linkedin.com/help/lms/topics/8154/8155/ad-specs-guidelines). When it comes to costs, depending on the format you choose, you'll pay on the pay-per-click (PPC) or cost-per-impressions (CPM) or cost-per-send (CPS) for InMail advertising.

WRITING A LINKEDIN TEXT AD

It's much the same as with Facebook text-based ads. Your creativity will be bounded by character and ad size limitations. Currently the specifications are as follows:

- Available in a variety of sizes: 300 x 250 pixels, 17 x 700 pixels, 160 x 600 pixels, 72 x 90 pixels, and 496 x 80 pixels.
- Image size (if you use one): 50 x 50 pixels.
- Headline: 25 character limit (including spaces).
- Description: 75 character limit (including spaces).

Here's an example of a text-based ad seen on LinkedIn. It's small, features an image of a satisfied professional woman, and reads:

VIP OF LEARNING?
Train your team to Speak to Senior-Level Decision Makers.

Free Webinar

The presentation of this next text ad is slightly different, in that it clearly presents the Web address in question (as opposed to having it embedded in the code of the advertisement) and is *branded*.

FILL YOUR FUNNEL
Generate leads from LinkedIn with HubSpot's free guide. From Hubspot go to URL: http://www.namethislandingpage .com.

15 ✒

WRITING FOR SOCIAL MEDIA

WHAT YOU SHOULD KNOW ABOUT SOCIAL MEDIA PLATFORMS

One aspect of the many social media platforms available that you should be aware of is that you write and post differently for each one. What you post on Facebook will be different from what you post on Twitter or LinkedIn, even if the posts are about the same topic. The main rules of good content writing for any platform are:

1. Concise writing—avoid extra words; social media posts should be short and direct, starting with an interesting title or lead.
2. Write to engage your readers and give lots of interesting information within two to three sentences or paragraphs, depending on your platform.
3. Encourage readers to leave comments on your post by asking "Do you agree?" or "What do you think?"

CREATE BUSINESS ACCOUNTS

Create a business page account rather than using a personal page account to market your products or services. This is a more professional way to brand your company and keep the brand uppermost in readers' minds when they view your content. Using a personal page account to support your business brand makes you look unprofessional and amateurish, unless your name is the brand.

One woman recently sponsored one of her business posts with 500 words of content, which took up the whole length of the page, once opened. There were five or six sentences per paragraph, making it difficult to read through quickly.

Save long content for blogs. Most social media readers prefer to read a few small paragraphs and move on after "liking" the post.

Have the following information available for readers on your business page, such as:

1. The business name and logo.
2. A way to contact you, such as an e-mail address, or phone number if you want calls.
3. Information about your business and what the business offers to clients.

USING A FUNNEL APPROACH

Use a different title for each piece of content you post, based on the platform you use. Each title must still relate to your same subject matter that you are sending all readers to, if that is your post's intent. If you write a blog located on your business Web site, you can funnel readers from each of your social media platform posts, with a link to that blog placed at the end of the post. Here are examples of changing content and titles across platforms, leading to the same blog.

Facebook content post title: "Put Together Winning Google Ads Better and Faster!"

If you want to know more about how to create Google
Ads, then check out our latest blog where we show you,
step by step, how to create your ad. You will also learn about
how to select the right keywords to use with your ad. Check
it out!
https://bestSEOpractices.com/blog/google-ads-creation

Twitter content post title: "Quickly Design Your Google Ads!"

Check out our latest process for quickly creating Google
Ads so you will get found! Click below on the link to find out
more!
https://bestSEOpractices.com/blog/google-ads-creation

LinkedIn content post title: "Create Google Ads in Five Minutes and Succeed!"

Learn about our latest processes for designing Google Ads
in record time. We also show you the best way to select your
keywords to get you noticed in search results.
https://bestSEOpractices.com/blog/google-ads-creation

You can find out more about avoiding duplicate content
at Google's support page here: https://support.google.com
/webmasters/answer/66359?hl=en.

Your strategy for each of your social media accounts
becomes part of your overall multichannel marketing strategy of getting your product or services noticed everywhere
on the Internet. To do that, you must write short, interesting,
informative posts, like the samples shown above that grab
the readers' attention so that they continue down the funnel to your blog or landing page. They may also sign up to
receive your newsletters or e-mails, once they have read your
blog.

A diagram of how your basic funnel works for using social media and blogging to drive traffic to your opt-in e-list sign-up page is shown in fig.15.1.

Fig. 15.1: Social media funnel.

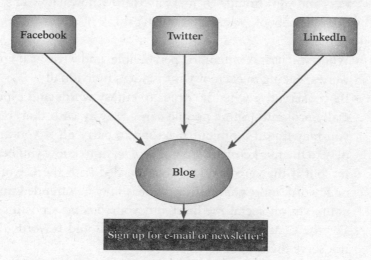

TIPS FOR WRITING SOCIAL MEDIA POSTS

Posts are where you can express your opinion, share content, and have conversations. You pretty much have free reign to say or show whatever you want, with a few possible exceptions—but not many. Among the social media networks that allow comments are YouTube, LinkedIn, Twitter, Facebook, and of course blogs. Your posts are most likely to be seen by your Facebook friends, though they are viewable by many other FB users as well. Your tweets will be seen by your Twitter followers, your LinkedIn posts and articles by your LinkedIn connections.

Here are some guidelines for writing on social media:

- Have an objective. Do you want to express an opinion or your feelings? Speak out on major issues of the day? Share advice, information, tips, or instruction? Make an offer such as a free e-book download? Start or participate in interesting conversation threads? Promote your business and your brand? Or just have fun? Know why you are doing Facebook posts. If you can't think of a reason, why bother?
- When you write content, be personable, and write as if you were speaking to each of your readers individually.
- Be conservative when it comes to cutesy words and especially profanity. Some people can get away with that, but you may find it a difficult persona to carry off if you are new to the marketplace. People will want to know you better, but if they are regularly bombarded with the C word or F word, more than a few readers may be offended and complain on social media about your business postings. For the vast majority of FB users, the C and F words do not serve them well.
- Participate in threads and respond when appropriate to comments left on your posts. Social media is an interactive two-way medium. So it can generate involvement and engagement as well as build relationships.
- If posting on Facebook for business, avoid controversial topics such as anything concerned with politics, religion, race, or gender issues. Facebook may suspend your account if you are sharing negative news about world events or people and making derogatory, coarse comments that are slanted.
- In your posts, end the post with a phrase that openly encourages and asks for feedback and comments. Some of the ones that work well include:

    "What say you?"

"What do you think?"

"Do you agree or disagree?"

"How does this sound to you—good, fair, bad, or terrible?"

KEEP YOUR READERS ENGAGED THROUGH REGULAR POSTING SCHEDULES

You can design a schedule for posting your content on a regular basis, such as every Tuesday and Friday. You can even create a themed post that your readers can expect to see on those days. Keep your posts interesting and focused on a topic that your readers look forward to reading.

For example, you can create original content posts about search engine optimization (SEO) tactics to use, which you post on Mondays and Thursday. On Wednesday and Friday, you post content about multichannel marketing tactics. At the end of each post, ask readers what they think. Each post can have a link leading to your business blog of the day, relating to those posts.

FIVE RULES FOR FACEBOOK CONVERSATIONS

Remember "netiquette," the rules for acceptable online communication? We need a handbook, "Netiquette for Facebook," to show people how to behave civilly during a FB discussion, thread, or argument.

Rule #1: Don't directly say or even imply that the other person is stupid because you disagree with what he says.

Rule #2: When someone presents a link to a resource with data supporting their point, don't dismiss it simply by saying it is false, fake, or wrong. Why not? Because you don't know that for a fact. It's just your opinion. So say it's your opinion and back up your assertion with evidence supporting YOUR viewpoint. But just saying an article, Web site, study, or other proof from a credible source is B.S. without facts or logic to back you up is, well, a lot of B.S. on your part.

Rule #3: You cannot use logic and rational discourse to remove a thought from someone's mind that was not put there with logic in the first place. So don't even try to engage them. It is a fruitless endeavor and an enormous waste of your time and energy.

Rule #4: Don't state opinions as if they were indisputable facts. Opinion: filet mignon is better than chopped liver. Fact: Bob Bly likes chopped liver better than filet mignon.

Rule #5: As the writer Harlan Ellison states, you are actually not entitled to an opinion about everything and anything. You are entitled only to your INFORMED opinion. The average person is well-informed in only a handful of subject matter areas. But you see them on FB arguing and giving their opinions about everything and anything. Don't do that. The only way to know what you are talking about, said author Robert B. Parker, is to talk about only things that you know.

FACEBOOK

Facebook, in the first quarter of 2019, had 2.38 billion active users worldwide, according to Statista.com. This statistic covers all users who have logged in at least once in the last thirty days.

SproutSocial.com reports that, on a global level, India has

the highest number of Facebook users at 300 million, and is in first place over the United States, which has 210 million. You can go to either of these Web sites to get more information on demographics when deciding where your best target market group can be found, by platform usage and other associated criteria, such as age and gender.

• *Business page vs. personal page*

You may already have a personal page account with Facebook, where you have connected with family members and friends. Separate your personal life from your business life to be more professional when it comes to marketing your business.

Create a business page that is attached to your personal account.

The home page is where you create posts and type in your business name and set your logo. You will also see where you can promote your page and create event listings.

• *Add professional images and information*

Upload all of your high-quality images to your business page account—such as your brand logo, images for company history sections on what the company offers to its customers, your administrator profile picture—and set up messaging and contact information, too. You are guided by Facebook on each part. After filling out the information, you can start posting.

• *Develop a posting schedule*

Plan to add posts at least twice a week to begin adding readers and followers. Facebook is good at "nudging" you to add a post, so your business stays in the public eye. If you have the budget, use Facebook Ads to help bring in relevant readers interested in what you offer. You select the demographics of the target readers you want, and Facebook does all the rest. This can build your follower rates faster than if you were to not advertise at all.

SproutSocial.com suggests the number of characters to use in a post, including spaces between words and punctuation marks. If you do not want to spend time counting character spaces, insert your copy into the free social media character counter located on its page here: sproutsocial.com/insights /social-media-character-counter/.

- *Structure of a Facebook post*
  1. Start with a good attention-grabbing headline consisting of roughly five words.
  2. Write, at most, two or three paragraphs, with one or two short sentences in each, about 80 characters in total for your whole post.
  3. Keep your content brief, interesting, and always related to the headline.
  4. Add a topic-related image, photograph, or video.
  5. Add a link to your topic-related blog, or to an e-mail or newsletter sign-up page (optional).

Facebook posts I make are intended to be thought-provoking and also to elicit comments on the subject matter, both positive and negative. If you are a small business, a one-person sole proprietor, you can create interesting posts that grab readers' attention. As a business on a Facebook business page, create a post that does not give an opinion, but encourages readers to respond with their own viewpoints. See the samples below.

Robert Bly
May 9 · 🌐

Next time you kick yourself for making a mistake -- e.g., a typo on your resume, being late for an appointment, burning the roast -- be aware that more than 200 times a year, U.S surgeons operate on either the wrong patient or the wrong body part. A surgeon who once operated on my father's leg removed, in a different patient years later, the wrong part of that person's brain. (Source: Harper's Magazine.)

👍❤️😮 55   25 Comments 2 Shares

Robert Bly
May 8 · 🌐

According to an article in Industrial Equipment News (5/7/19), the lowest paid garment workers in the world are in Ethiopia. They earn $26 a month, while the minimum living wage in Ethiopia is about $110 a month. In comparison, Chinese garment workers make about $340 a month. Major clothing brands, among them H&M and the Gap, employee tens of thousands of Ethiopian garment workers, most of whom cannot support a family or even get by to the end of the month on $26. The world seems broken to me, with this being just one of dozens of examples.

👍❤️😮 58   29 Comments 5 Shares

This one got a lot of emotional response.

Robert Bly
April 29 · 🌐

As busy as you are, take time to visit your elderly relatives regularly. Many in nursing homes are bored and lonely, and a simple visit from family members brightens their day and reminds them they are still loved.

👍❤️ 119   22 Comments 7 Shares

LINKEDIN

The focus of LinkedIn is connecting with business professionals who want to contact other professionals and build business relationships. When you want to attract or connect with a certain type of business professional, have some knowledge of their area of expertise before you make a connection with them. Again, doing research will give you important information you can use to gain an initial contact and speak their "language."

This is not a place to chat with friends and family members. You will not find children here, so if you are marketing toys to parents and children, this platform may not work for you.

However, you may find professionals who can help you market your product, or a specialist in search engine optimization (SEO) who can help enhance your Web site and your advertising.

• *Creating a professional profile*

LinkedIn allows you to create a personal professional profile page. I have included a copy of my LinkedIn profile page to show one way to structure LI profiles that I and others have found effective. Here is the outline:

#1—Under my name at top is a one-sentence abstract of who I am and what I do. Note that it talks not just about me but, more important, about results I produce for clients.

#2—Instead of showing the standard head shot photo, I instead opted for an image of the cover of my book. Not only does it stand out because almost no one else does it, but it further establishes my brand as a recognized expert in my field.

#3—Scroll down a little to the paragraph "Copywriting for me is thrilling," which communicates my love of my profession and my objective, which is to win sales for my clients, not creative awards.

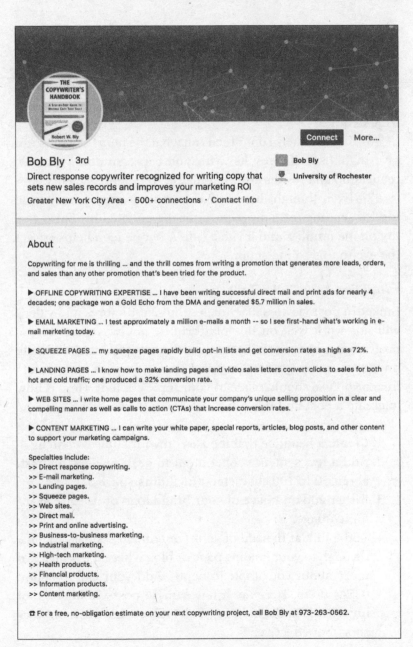

Bob Bly · 3rd

Direct response copywriter recognized for writing copy that sets new sales records and improves your marketing ROI

Greater New York City Area · 500+ connections · Contact info

Connect More...

Bob Bly

University of Rochester

About

Copywriting for me is thrilling ... and the thrill comes from writing a promotion that generates more leads, orders, and sales than any other promotion that's been tried for the product.

▶ OFFLINE COPYWRITING EXPERTISE ... I have been writing successful direct mail and print ads for nearly 4 decades; one package won a Gold Echo from the DMA and generated $5.7 million in sales.

▶ EMAIL MARKETING ... I test approximately a million e-mails a month -- so I see first-hand what's working in e-mail marketing today.

▶ SQUEEZE PAGES ... my squeeze pages rapidly build opt-in lists and get conversion rates as high as 72%.

▶ LANDING PAGES ... I know how to make landing pages and video sales letters convert clicks to sales for both hot and cold traffic; one produced a 32% conversion rate.

▶ WEB SITES ... I write home pages that communicate your company's unique selling proposition in a clear and compelling manner as well as calls to action (CTAs) that increase conversion rates.

▶ CONTENT MARKETING ... I can write your white paper, special reports, articles, blog posts, and other content to support your marketing campaigns.

Specialties Include:
>> Direct response copywriting.
>> E-mail marketing.
>> Landing pages.
>> Squeeze pages.
>> Web sites.
>> Direct mail.
>> Print and online advertising.
>> Business-to-business marketing.
>> Industrial marketing.
>> High-tech marketing.
>> Health products.
>> Financial products.
>> Information products.
>> Content marketing.

✿ For a free, no-obligation estimate on your next copywriting project, call Bob Bly at 973-263-0562.

#4—My capabilities and the types of work I do are denoted in a bulleted list with the items in all caps (e.g., CONTENT MARKETING) to make them stand out.

#5—Each area has a concise, one-sentence description so the list does not have a lot of text, looks very clean, and is easy to scan quickly.

#6—In the bullets I don't focus on what the item is, but instead give highly specific results, with numbers. Numbers increase readership and results are what matter to potential clients.

#7—Even though there is a button under my name at the top for sending me a message, after the bulleted list I also give my phone number and invite a call. A phone icon helps attract the eye to this call to action.

• *Building Your LinkedIn Post*

LinkedIn post viewers like images, but cat pictures and videos will not work well on this platform. It is always best to use professional images or, if you are artistically talented, to create images that are eye-catching and interesting. As always, any image you use should relate to your topic content. Here is how to create a post on LinkedIn.

1. Create a headline that focuses on your subject content.
2. Add a few sentences of content to grab readers' interest, about 50 to 100 characters (including spaces).
3. Either add an image of your brand logo or use a relevant topic image.
4. Add a link at the end of your content, so people can click through to your landing page or blog where they can learn more about your topic in depth. Add your call to action (CTA) there. Here are a few sample posts from some of my friends in the industry. You can see that posts are very short but effective.

Heather Lloyd-Martin
SEO Copywriting Trainer for Travel | B2B | Marketing |
Publishing. Business Coach. Keynote Speaker. OG SEO
10mo · Edited

Feeling like you have to publish a lot of content "because Google wants it that way?"
Good news -- you can relax. Here's why:

How Often Should You Publish New Content? - SuccessWorks
seocopywriting.com

Michael (Mike) Stelzner
CEO/Founder: Social Media Examiner & Social Media Marketing
World, host: Social Media Marketing podcast, author: Launch
1y · Edited

How to Create LinkedIn Video Ads https://lnkd.in/gc8DWx4

How to Create LinkedIn Video Ads : Social Media Examiner
https://www.socialmediaexaminer.com

TWITTER

You can use Twitter as a personal page or as a business page, or both. Twitter is a more informal platform and postings consist of short "blurbs" of up to 280 characters at most, along with a link. It depends on the content you want to share, but keep the character count down as much as possible, preferably not more than 100 characters. Concise content is easier to read when information runs about two sentences long.

• *Twitter hashtags*

Twitter hashtags are included at the front of a keyword or a phrase, which helps anyone searching for that topic to find your post, along with other posts fitting that trending topic. It is essentially a way to code your tweet.

For instance, #keto would help people find your tweet if they are interested in learning more about the keto diet.

The narrower and more focused the hashtag name, the more you'll attract the prospects you want. Therefore, if you sell keto diet information, #keto will bring you more qualified views than #weightloss or #diet.

Hashtags are not tweets. They are labels on tweets that tell Twitter users what your tweet is about. So if you want to reach people who hate or love Donald Trump, use #Trump.

Search a hashtag before you use it to see which version of it is most popular, so your post is found more readily in that category.

SUMMARIZING HOW TO USE SOCIAL MEDIA PLATFORMS

When you are starting a new professional page on a particular platform, spend time checking out how posts, especially popular posts, are being presented on the platform. Get a feel for what the "tone" of the platform is, so that you can meld with it, but still stand out in the right way through your posts.

If your goal is to use social media as part of an integrated multichannel marketing strategy to promote your business, the content can be a combination of business-related and personal.

As noted, the business content can give the reader data, links to content of interest, instruction, tips, news, or trends of interest to your target market. This content shows that you are an expert who delivers value.

The personal content is part of the online phenomenon known as transparency. People want to know more about you: who you are, your family, travels, hobbies, interests, activities.

I advise you to stay away from controversial topics such as religion, sex, and politics if you use social media to promote your business.

Why? Because it risks damage to your reputation and losing followers and potential customers. If you say that in your opinion religion is a bad thing and you do not believe in God or Jesus, what effect will that have on prospects who are devoted Christians? Giving such an opinion may offend and anger many of your friends, followers, and contacts.

Remember what happened to Salman Rushdie when he published *The Satanic Verses*, the reaction to which included serious threats against his life. While that is highly unlikely to happen in reaction to one of your tweets, even a single comment can make people irate and harm your reputation. And remember, once something gets onto the Internet, it becomes highly visible and may be extremely difficult to remove.

There are many more platforms available, such as Pinterest, Instagram, Snapchat, Flickr, Nextdoor (neighborhood focused), Foursquare, Myspace, Tumblr, and more. As a final mention, many of these platforms have phone apps that allow mobile phone viewers to connect with contacts on social media platforms throughout the day.

Always check your post to see how it looks through the phone app version of any social media platform. If something does not look quite right, fix it as soon as possible. Then recheck the post again until you are happy with how it looks, and then share your post.

RESOURCES

Sources for Royalty- and Copyright-Free Images: (Always read terms of use and check with the platform administration first)	
• Unsplash.com • Pexels.com • Pixabay.com • StockSnap.io	• Reshot.com • Foodiesfeed.com (for food pictures) • Picjumbo.com • Lifeofpix.com
Canva.com (photos, images, illustrations, icons, other elements for creative design) You can also resize images on Canva to fit the requirements for any social media platform. Check out the image templates listed for the social media platforms that you use.	
Character Space Counter Tool	
sproutsocial.com/insights/social-media-character-counter/	

16 ✒

WRITING FOR VIDEO

Video is taking over marketing and the world. According to a study by Cisco, in 2019 video will have accounted for up to 80 percent of all online traffic. And consumers are 85 percent more likely to buy your product after viewing your video. I have been writing video scripts continually since 1979 and in this chapter will share the best practices.

TYPES OF VIDEO SCRIPTS

Video scripts can range from a sixty-second commercial shown at halftime during the Super Bowl to a one-hour video sales letter (VSL). Here are a few types of scripts:

• *The sixty-second television advertisement*
These videos can also be cut down to thirty seconds or fifteen seconds for shorter viewing times, when several ads are run together during the program break. Under this category, you will see advertisements for brands of beer, other types of drinks, food, and restaurants and commercials for

car and home insurance, home improvement tools, and much more.

• *Explainer video script*

Explainer scripts are typically one to two minutes long and explain what a business does for its clients, how a new product works, or why you need a specific new service. One person is either on the video screen talking or is speaking in the background throughout the video. For example, a software-as-a-service (SaaS) company has come up with a new software platform geared toward dentists' offices that consolidates all parts of the business into one platform. The SaaS president opens the first scene by stating the problem dentists' offices have. Then the president offers a solution, and this is what viewers see in the video. The video shows the software in action, with typed lists of what reports can be pulled from the software.

• *Interviewing video script*

This can be done in several ways. The interviewer first develops a structure script for each part of the interview. This helps with planning a camera operation, such as moving from camera A to camera B at the right time. Think of an interview done on a news session, where a candidate for president is being interviewed.

Next, a list of leading questions is drawn up to ask the interviewee, and those are given to him or her in advance, so that the interviewee plans on what to say in the response. The responses can be written out as well, by the interviewee, so that everything is scripted for the time span allowed, say, fifteen minutes in total.

A teleprompter can be used for this, placed at and just behind camera level. This way, the interviewee remembers what he or

she wanted to say for that question, yet still speaks to the audience (the camera) as well as the interviewer.

• *Corporate script*

A president of a company wants to create a video about the
successful previous year's financial performance, so a script
is written to cover all aspects of the financial statement.
The president may start speaking while facing the camera,
but other video shots should pull in components of the statement created as charts and graphs to keep viewer interest
engaged.

   Alternatively, if the president comes off well on camera, the
main shot can be on the president during the full video, inter-
spersed with relevant graphs, tables, and charts.

• *Training script*

Many companies create training videos so that new employees
can get up to speed with using specific software that the company uses, and how to pull reports. Training videos also incorporate best practices, company culture, behavior expectations,
what is considered a firing offense, and more.

   These are only a few of the types of video scripts that you
might be hired to write, and more marketers are now creating
videos for their own Web sites, giving a more personal touch.
What was once the domain of corporations with huge budgets
for marketing services and products has now become so much
easier and affordable. Anyone can write and build a video if they
have the talent.

• *Online video script*

The average online video posted on a Web site home page
today is short, running two to three minutes. B2B videos
have an average run time of about four minutes, and about

half of viewers watch these videos in their entirety. Videos on second-level pages, especially those dealing with products and their applications, can go to five to seven minutes or longer.

As for script length, figure your narration at 120 words per minute. A ten-minute script would then have 1,200 words—the equivalent of five double-spaced pages in Word with 12-point Times Roman.

The best guideline for writing video scripts is: "One presentation, one topic." Your video should talk about only one product, one idea, or one offer. After all, you have a limited time to tell your story before viewer attention wanes and they click away.

HOW TO START YOUR SCRIPTWRITING PROJECT

In this section, I'll show you how to plan your script and then begin writing it. Let's say you are hired by an agency that is creating a commercial for SaaS, the software company that has developed a new software platform for all dentists' offices to use.

As part of the contract, it should be made clear that your client will provide you with all available information that you need to create the script, including any storyboards already completed, which can help guide your script.

• *Creative brief*
The creative brief that you get from your client outlines everything they have on the topic of the video, so you can build the script. This includes any discussions about how the video will be shot and who will be in it, such as hired actors or the employees of SaaS. Here is a typical list of what you want to know before creating the script.

- What is the message that this software company wants everyone to know? (buy the product or service, or sign up for something)
- What problem does this service or product solve for the customer?
- Will the video be shot inside or outside?
- Where can the customer get the product or service?

THE SCRIPT DEVELOPMENT

We will call the new software platform PantherWorks and the software company that produces it Biedermort. And let's say there will be one on-camera speaking actor. The video will take place in an actual dentist's office, although the name of the dentist or of the practice will not be acknowledged. The office is background material to fit the message. You will want to use an audiovisual format for the script. You should also know how many minutes the video will run for.

If your client has not created a storyboard or an outline, you can do so, just for yourself, to guide the script. We can call this an outline script, although the actual script is not yet written. See the example below.

Scene	Visual	Audio
1	Fade in for a picture of the software's logo called PantherWorks.	Music plays in the background as the logo or front face of the software pulls up.

2	Fade out, then in, where the speaker is standing in a dentist's office. There are two associates seated at their desks working on their computers.	The speaker begins talking about the common problem Biedermort had heard a lot about from dentists everywhere. States that the problem has now been solved.
3	Shot switches to a screen showing the first entry into the program showing where reports can be pulled up.	The speaker describes how PantherWorks is a fully integrated software platform. Any information can be easily called up from one single platform instantly.
4	The screen changes to several types of reports printed out and laid on a desktop. Schedule, Inventory, and Monthly Report of Income.	The speaker continues with showing how reports can be custom-designed to be pulled with only a little information input.
5	The shot moves back into the office where the workers are smiling and giving thumbs-up on the product. A Web site address is shown at the bottom of the screen.	The speaker turns to the camera and states to call a number for a consultation or to go to the Web site shown below on the screen.

Always keep in mind what the audience is seeing and hearing. Put yourself in their place and feel what they feel when seeing the video and hearing the speaker solve a problem for them.

HOW TO WRITE THE SCRIPT

Once you have the structure, you can start out by writing a sentence for each scene that informs what should be covered. That will help guide what you write for the script.

1. Here is what you should remember whenever you write any script for any type of video: know who your target audience is (i.e., dentists and office associates).
2. Always start with an introduction and make every word count. Get the message across in one to two sentences. Keep the total script to no longer than two pages with 100 to 120 words per minute.
3. Write concisely and effectively. Do not use fluff or big exotic words. Keep it simple.
4. Use the word "you" and speak conversationally to the audience.
5. Show what the problem was and then show how it was solved, or how it can be solved.
6. Show the outcome of how using the product or service makes life better and/or easier.
7. Give a call to action (CTA) and show how to get that product or service quickly, or how to sign up for something, such as an e-mail or a consultation.

AFTER YOU WRITE THE SCRIPT

Read it aloud and, if you want, record yourself reading it to see how it sounds when you play it back. Making a recording through your smartphone is an easy way to do this. You can time each section to see how it fits the visual scenes that will be in the video. The cadence of the script should have a natural rhythm and speed, not too fast, and not so slow that you fall asleep listening to it. Now we build the sample script, so you can see what one looks like:

TITLE: "Your Dentistry Office, Moving Faster and Better!"
LENGTH: Four (4) minutes
PRODUCT: PantherWorks Software Platform by Biedermort, Inc.

Scene	Visual	Audio
1	Fade in—logo visual for PantherWorks by Biedermort	(soft background music playing throughout the video) Hi, I'm James Faller for Biedermort and, today, we will show you how your office at your dentistry practice can operate faster and better than ever before. Does it take your associates 15 minutes to compile all the information you need for your next patient? That's just too long. And it is time and money wasted. You could be spending that time working with your patient instead. It's not your associates' fault. It is the tools they're working with.

| 2 | Fade out logo—fade in to speaker standing in a dentist's office. Workers at the computer. | In the last two years, we kept hearing about dentists and dental associates having problems with accessing too many databases to get the information they needed.

Patient history was a nightmare to pull together.

Treatments, recommendations, medical research, and office reports needed to be pulled daily. Too much time was involved, making office procedures very slow-moving.

So we, at Biedermort, got to work to solve the problem and came up with PantherWorks. The platform runs fast and sleek, and it is easy to operate. This will change your life. |
| 3 | A computer screen with the software opened on a selection page. | PantherWorks eliminates accessing multiple old, outdated databases.

Once all your information and data are updated and integrated, there is no more moving in and out of multiple databases, taking up too much time.

All the important information and data can be pulled up in one place, with just a few taps of the keyboard. |

4	Reports on desk: Schedule, Inventory, and Monthly Report of Income.	Once you hit the Enter key, it only takes just seconds to get your report out.
		We also customize reports especially for you, so you don't have to do that.
		Got a new report you want to pull every week? Let us know and we will create it for you and upload it onto your platform.
		It's fast, easy to do, and we provide initial training at the office for everyone, so the platform is up and functional immediately for everyone to use after training is completed.
		Training videos are available on our Web site, so you are never left without help. If you have questions, we will answer them for you.
5	Workers happy and giving thumbs-up . . . Fade out . . . A Web site address is shown at the bottom of the screen.	(speaker shakes hands with the dentist of the dentistry practice—speaker turns back to the camera) So, if you want to see what PantherWorks can do for you, give us a call right away at xxx-xxx-xxxx. We will schedule a time to come to your office and consult with you and your associates.

> Want to contact us online for more information and a phone call instead? Visit Biedermort.com/signup/ and connect with us there.
> We can't wait to help you and make a difference in your dentistry practice! Call xxx-xxx-xxxx now or send us a message online!

VIDEO SALES LETTERS (VSLS)

Video sales letters originally were created on a type of whiteboard screen. This is where you see a sentence typed onto the page, while a voice-over speaks the text as well. It is usually one sentence, maybe two sentences at a time for each slide.

These are presented as rather long videos and typically concern topics in the health or financial industries. They really can be about anything at all, but there is always a danger of making such a video carry on for too long, losing the viewer's attention along the way.

Video clips can be short, but for direct response marketing, video sales letters typically run fifteen to forty-five minutes or longer; the script is around 2,000 to 7,000 words.

A key difference between video sales letters and static (landing pages or print) sales letters is this: a prospect may read a conventional text sales letter several times and can go back to reread portions if desired. And they often do. But the prospect can only watch an entire video sales letter straight through; she has no ability to choose the portions she views.

That in mind, here are some guidelines for writing effective video sales letters:

1. **The way to begin is to grab audience attention** with a statement that breaks them out of their normal pattern. Surprise them. Shake them up.
2. **Tell an engaging story** that sweeps the listener along with it. Superstar marketer Michael Masterson calls this the "velvet slide."
3. **Keep is simple.** The "information density"—the number of facts per page—should be about 20 percent less than a text-based promotion.
4. **Use short sentences and especially short words.** I don't use any word longer than 9 letters.
5. **Use short paragraphs**—a couple of sentences is typical. This makes the text on the video easier to read.
6. **If you want to dramatize or prove a copy claim or fact, you can insert a chart or graph** into the video presentation. Even if the prospect has only a few seconds to view it, charts and graphs give the impression that your point is well backed up.
7. **You can concisely state the problem your product solves** in the lead of the video sales letter, but be sure to explain the solution within the first minute or two. If you wait too long to get to the solution, you risk having the prospect click away in boredom.
8. **Don't use more than two numbers in a sentence.** If you do, round off at least one of them.
9. **The tone of the copy should be positive and enthusiastic** because the prospect hears a voice reading the text. But it should also sound authoritative.

When I talk about video sales letters, invariably I hear the objection, "They're too long! I always click away. Who would sit there for thirty minutes and watch?"

But plenty of people do. How do I know? Testing shows

repeatedly that video sales letters usually generate higher conversion rates than static landing pages.

If you still object to video sales letters because you just don't like them, I quote this advice from ace copywriter Peter Beutel: "Don't let personal preference get in the way."

RESOURCES

The Voice Realm

Go here to upload your script into this time counter, known as the Voice Over Estimate, to see how long your script will be as a video.

https://www.thevoicerealm.com/count-script.php

Whiteboard Animation Videos

These are software platforms that allow you to create videos using preinstalled characters, backgrounds, items such as tables, chairs, clocks, and much more. You create your own scene by placing the components onto the page, and when you run it the platform will "draw" it.

VideoScribe: https://www.videoscribe.co/en/Whiteboard
-Animation

Renderforest: https://www.renderforest.com/whiteboard
-animation

Animaker: https://www.animaker.com/blog/how-to-create
-whiteboard-video/

Rawshorts: https://www.rawshorts.com/

Explee: https://explee.com/

If you want to create your own videos from start to finish, you can use one of the programs below.

Video Editing Software:
Windows 10 Video Editor program
Adobe Premiere Pro (comes with the Creative Cloud package or separate, if preferred)
Apple Final Cut Pro X (for Macs)
Adobe Premiere Elements (geared toward beginners)

17

WRITING FOR CONTENT MARKETING

Content marketing—giving away free information to build your brand, increase response to marketing campaigns, convert more online traffic, and educate the prospect on your technology, methodology, products, and services—is one of the hot trends in marketing today.

Other marketing methods also increasing in usage today include online video, social media, quick response codes (QRCs), search engine optimization (SEO), live online chat, and infographics. In August 2017, Apple announced that the company is making a $1 billion investment in original content.[1]

The term "content marketing" may have been coined in 1996, at a roundtable for journalists held at the American Society for Newspaper Editors by John F. Oppedahl. That would mean the name "content marketing" is over twenty years old.

But in fact content marketing has been used for far longer than that. It's only a new name for a vintage method. I personally have been doing content marketing for nearly four decades, and some marketers have been at it even longer.

I did my first content marketing campaign in 1980. At the time, I was advertising manager of Koch Engineering, an industrial manufacturing company owned and run by the late David Koch, who then, despite running for vice president of the United States on the libertarian party ticket, was relatively unknown. He later became a household name, one half of the infamous "billionaire Koch brothers."

One of the products we sold were various "tower internals," and one type of internal was the "tray." These are circular metal disks with capped openings on their surfaces. The trays are placed inside refinery towers to enhance the distillation of crude oil into kerosene, gasoline, heating oil, jet fuel, and other petroleum-based products.

Specifying the correct configuration for the design of trays for your particular refinery is a highly technical task, and the engineers who worked in the refineries needed instruction on how to do it correctly.

To assist and educate them, we produced a design manual that we dubbed the "tray manual." It cost us several dollars per copy to print and bind. The manual had stiff covers, spiral binding, and fold-out blueprint-style drawings showing the configurations of various trays. By the way, the tray manual was neither my idea nor my creation; it was already in use when I joined the firm.

The tray manual was wildly popular—by far our most requested piece of literature. The way it worked was this. First, by offering a valuable and relevant technical manual for free, we increased inquiries from the ad. Second, it helped the prospect specify the trade configuration he needed, and when he had done that following our design advice, naturally he ordered the tray from us, not from our competitors. Third, it helped establish Koch Engineering as a thought leader in refinery distillation.

Back then, we didn't call it "content marketing." We called it "giving away free information." The practice was the same. We just didn't have a name for it.

Content marketing has been used for well over a century. To test response to print ads, Claude Hopkins (1866–1932) offered free informational booklets in many of his ads.

And in 1916, Campbell's began promoting its soups with content marketing by offering free booklets of recipes that used Campbell's soups in the dishes.[2]

Back in those days, this free content was simply called "free booklets." In the later part of the twentieth century, marketers referred to them as "bait pieces," because the booklet or other free information offer helped "hook" prospects and turn them into leads.

Fig. 17.1: Free content offers are used as "bait" by many marketers to get leads from prospects. For this reason, free booklets and other free content were called "bait pieces." Today they are known as "lead magnets."

What is a Bait Piece?

Today the preferred term for "free content" is "lead magnet," the idea being that the tempting offer of valuable free information is like a magnet that draws people into your ad and gets them to respond and request the white paper or other free content.

There are all sorts of published opinions and tests on the

effectiveness of content marketing. But let me sum up my experience in just two simple points.

First, I can't remember the last time I did a B2B or B2C marketing campaign without a free content offer.

For B2B, the lead magnet is often the primary offer and what drives prospects to respond. For B2C, the free content is often a bonus report given as an added gift with purchase of the product.

Second, on average, adding the offer of a lead magnet to a B2B lead generation campaign can often double the number of inquiries—and often much more—versus the same campaign without the free content offer.

Plus, according to an October 3, 2016, poll by FierceCMO, more than four thousand *Forbes* readers found that branded content was 9 percent more effective than paid advertising at getting consumers to consider buying a particular brand.

In the good old days of B2B marketing, our primary offer was a "free color brochure" filled with sales copy about the product. It worked then. But today, prospects respond better if you also promise to send them free information that will be useful to them in their job.

THE 7 MOST COMMON CONTENT WRITING MISTAKES

1—*Mediocre writing.* Content writing is in many organizations at the bottom of the barrel as far as respect for those who do it and the value placed on it.

The reason: the more technical a skill (e.g., software engineering), the fewer people who can do it. But writing is a soft skill: everyone writes, as Ann Handley claims in the title of her book *Everybody Writes* (Wiley, 2014). But can they? And at what level?

Prolific author Harlan Ellison, who passed away in 2018,

once said the following to me: "[People think] they can drive a car more brilliantly than Fangio, and everybody else on the road is inept; they can screw like Don Juan and delight the g-spot every time; and they can write. Better than King, better than Dickens, better than Homer. When in fact these are three of the most difficult things in the world to do, and only a very few people do even one with grandeur, much less all three well."

2—*Mediocre research.* Increasingly content is "Google goulash." The writer uses Google to quickly research a few articles on the topic. He cobbles them together into a new article, one with no originality or firsthand knowledge, no wisdom, and no new thoughts or insights.

It can make good clickbait in some cases. But really, what's the point? All you are actually doing is adding to the cloud of "content pollution" growing out of control on the Web today.

3—*Taking the easy way out.* There are four levels of content, which from lowest to highest are *why*, *what*, *how*, and *done for you*.

The lowest form tells people *why* they should do something (e.g., "Why You Should Start an In-House Call Center").

The argument may be convincing and help readers make an important decision. But it provides no further help than influencing the reader's yes-no decision.

Next rung up on the content ladder is telling them *what* to do (e.g., "7 Steps to Planning and Implementing an In-House Call Center"). You get an action plan with the steps laid out. But you still have no idea how to do each step.

Climbing higher, our content tells them *how* to do it, though these are often tips rather than step-by-step instructions. Still, now we have actionable steps or ideas leading to a tangible result: a functional call center.

At the top of the content hierarchy is *done for you*. For

instance, if you tell the reader he needs prewritten scripts, you provide models or samples of telemarketing scripts that can be easily modified to fit the reader's business, saving her time and money.

So many content writers take the easy way out and tell the reader only what to do and why to do it. Stronger content shows the reader how to do it and, when possible, does some of the work for her.

4—*No interviewing or fact checking with subject matter experts (SMEs).* Especially for technical content or content about your company's proprietary methodology or systems, many content writers may have surface knowledge. But they often need a deeper dive to produce a particular content piece. SMEs can give them an explanation that is at least somewhat comprehensible and likely accurate.

5—*Content writers who do not understand the subject matter at hand.* Content writers who have a degree, training, or background in the subject matter should probably be on the team working on a project where their expertise would enhance their contributions.

For instance, I have a BS in chemical engineering, which gives me an advantage when writing in the chemical industry. I don't know the client's product in detail. But when I interview their SMEs, the engineers are immediately at ease with me because we have a common background and I speak their lingo.

6—*Not crediting your sources.* If you say in your article that 35 percent of U.S. companies have an in-house call center, your client will want to know the source of that statistic. If you found it on the Web, credit the source with the full URL. You can do this either in the copy or with a footnote.

Cite your source whether it is a trade journal, a technical paper presented at an association meeting, your client's own Web site, or an interview with one of its SMEs. If someone you interview gives you the information, you may want to track it down to where it resides on the Web and confirm its accuracy.

7—*The content is purely your subjective opinion.* Of course you can give your opinion. But the best opinions are evidence-based and supported by statistics, graphs, examples, logical arguments, and facts. As marketers, we cannot merely make our points; we must prove our points, lest our readers remain unconvinced.

THE 4 CONTENT FORMATS

There are four modes by which your prospects absorb your content: reading, listening, watching, and doing. Yet you do not know which mode the prospect prefers.

For that reason, you want to produce multiple pieces of content that, combined, cover all four modes of learning. That way, you have relevant content in the format your prospects like best. Many of these formats are listed in Table 17-1 according to the mode of learning they best serve.

Table 17-1. Content by mode of learning.

Reading	*Audio*	*Visual*	*Doing*
Books	Audio CDs	DVDs	Workshops
E-books	MP3	MP4 streaming videos	Classes
White papers	Podcasts	SlideShare	Boot camps
Blogs	Internet radio	Video	Retreats
E-newsletters	Speeches	Infographics	Conferences
E-classes	Seminars	Instagram	Software
Articles	Webinars	Rich media	Demos

It would take a separate book, not just this chapter, to cover in detail all the items in the table. So in this chapter, I have chosen to concentrate on three of the more effective content marketing tactics: white papers, blogs, and case studies. Earlier in the book we covered other key content marketing methods including video (chapter 16), social media (chapter 15), and public relations (chapter 14).

WHITE PAPERS

According to Constant Content, 50 percent of marketers say white papers are a valuable tool for lead generation. More than 49 percent of B2B buyers used a white paper to help them make technology purchase decisions.

Over the years, I've seen a number of direct-mail and e-mail tests in which offering a free white paper or other free content increased response rates by 10 percent to 100 percent or more. I do think, however, that we have to broaden our notion of how to use free content offers, which is essentially what a white paper is: free information designed to educate our prospects and motivate them to inquire about our product or service.

To begin with, I think it's not white papers themselves that are tiring but the name itself. "White paper" signals to some prospects a document that is an obvious selling tool. And with virtually every white paper in the world available for free, white papers have a low perceived value as a giveaway.

The solution is to keep using white papers in your marketing but to call them something else. The mailing list broker Edith Roman used to publish a print catalog of mailing lists. But instead of calling it a catalog, the broker called it the "Direct Mail Encyclopedia." Offering a free Direct Mail Encyclopedia helped generate more inquiries for its brokerage services.

Copywriter Ivan Levison calls his white papers "guides." Marketer David Yale uses "executive briefing." I'm partial to "special report." For consumer marketing, marketing expert Joe Polish suggests "consumer awareness guide," and for a B2B white paper giving product selection tips, I'd change this to "buyer's guide" or "selection guide." For a white paper giving tips or instructions on a process, I might call it a "manual." If you publish a print version that fits in a #10 envelope and is saddle stitched, you can call it a "free booklet."

Does what you call your lead magnet really matter? I think it does, because calling it a report or guide creates a perception of greater value—after all, thousands of publishers actually *sell* special reports and booklets for prices ranging from $3 to $40 or more. I often put a dollar price for the report in the upper right corner of the front cover, which strengthens the perception that the freebie has value; I don't think this would be credible on a document labeled as a white paper.

What about the complaint that prospects already have too much to read? I am reminded of a quotation from Rutherford Rogers: "We are drowning in information but starved for knowledge." There is more information on the Internet than you could process in a thousand lifetimes.

But good white papers don't merely present information; they offer solutions to business and technical problems. Virtually every sale you make is because someone thinks your product or service is the solution to their problem. A white paper can help clarify the problem as well as convince the reader that your idea or method is the best of many options for addressing it.

Every marketing campaign has an objective, yet if you ask most managers what the objective of their white paper is, they probably couldn't tell you. Too many see white papers as an opportunity to merely collect and publish a pile of research material they found on the Web using Google. To make your white paper successful, you must define the marketing objective before writing a single word.

For example, a manufacturer found that consumers were not buying their do-it-yourself (DIY) underground sprinkler kits, because home owners perceived installing the irrigation system by themselves as too difficult. Solution: a free DIY manual on how to install an underground sprinkler system in a single weekend. Clearly written and illustrated, the manual overcame the perception that this was a tough project, making it look easy.

In the pre-Internet era, bait pieces such as the sprinkler guide were mainly paper and ink. Thanks to the PC and the Internet, bait pieces can now be produced as PDF files and instantly downloaded online. But at the receiving end, they are usually printed by the prospect and read on paper.

It may be that what's wearing out is not free content, but the standard white paper format: pages of black ink on 8½ x 11–inch sheets of paper. To make your bait piece stand out, consider using alternative formats: DVDs, CDs, data on thumb drives, podcasts, webinars, tele-seminars, flash cards, stickers, posters, software, games, and slide guides.

A slide guide is a cardboard promotional item with a moving slide or wheel that allows the prospect to perform some simple calculation (e.g., convert inches to centimeters or determine the monthly payments on a mortgage).

Most white papers are six to ten pages—about 3,000 to 4,000 words—but you are not locked into that length. You can go shorter or longer, depending on the content you want to present and the marketing objective of the bait piece. The bait piece can be as short and simple as a list of tips printed on one side of a sheet of paper. Or it can be as long as a self-published paperback book.

Free content offers have been used effectively in marketing for decades, and rather than tiring, they have been given new life, thanks in part to the information-oriented culture spawned by the Internet. "Every organization possesses particular expertise that has value in the new e-marketplace of ideas," writes David Meerman Scott. "Organizations gain credibility and loyalty with customers, employees, the media, investors, and suppliers through content." [3]

9 STEPS TO MARKETING WITH WHITE PAPERS

This section shows how to plan a white paper marketing campaign for your product or service. Elements of the plan include:

1. Target markets—the groups of buyers who share a common problem, including their demographic and psychographic profile.
2. Problem identification—a clear definition of the pressing problem your product can help these buyers to solve.
3. Solution identification—why your product or methodology is a superior solution. Includes an evaluation of strengths and weaknesses of your product versus the competition.
4. Content—the type and format of the information you are going to provide these prospects in your marketing (e.g., online tutorials, regional seminars, standard white papers).
5. Media—where to reach these buyers (i.e., lists, databases, publications, Web sites, other media).
6. Tactics—means by which you will reach these prospects (i.e., direct mail, advertising, e-mail marketing, print advertising, radio spots, trade shows, and other marketing communications).
7. Schedule—quantities of promotions and when they are to run.
8. Budget—what it will cost.
9. Metrics—how you will measure results to evaluate whether the objectives have been achieved.

STEP ONE: DETERMINE YOUR TARGET MARKET

Your target market is the group of buyers who share a common problem, including their demographic and psychographic profile. Most marketers already have a pretty good idea of their target market. For instance, if you sell dental office equipment, your prospect is the dentist and his or her office staff.

Big corporations routinely spend thousands of dollars on expensive and elaborate market research studies designed to help them get inside the minds of their customers. These can include mail and online surveys, telephone interviews, and focus groups. Entrepreneurs running small businesses become worried that if they don't do this kind of expensive market research, they won't know how to reach their prospects and will fail miserably.

But for many small companies, the cost of even one study from one of the big market research companies would wipe out their entire marketing budget for the year. Relax. The good news is that focus groups and other formal market research studies are completely unnecessary.

"But how will I understand my customers?" you may ask. Simple: just use my colleague Michael Masterson's BDF formula, which stands for Beliefs, Desires, and Feelings. The BDF formula says that you can understand your prospect by asking yourself three simple questions:

"What do my prospects believe? What are their attitudes?"
"What do my prospects desire? What do they want?"
"What do my prospects feel? What are their emotions?"

There's little or no market research required, because you probably already know these things about your prospects. You really do! As Dr. Benjamin Spock used to say: "Trust yourself. You know more than you think you do."

For instance, a company that provides "soft skills" training to information technology (IT) professionals was promoting a new on-site seminar. It sent out a flyer with the title of the program as the headline: "Interpersonal Skills for IT Professionals." It generated less than half a percent response. (The offer was more detailed information about the program and registration.)

So the marketing manager and the owner brainstormed and asked themselves the BDF questions. Here's part of what they came up with:

- IT professionals BELIEVE that technology is all important . . . and that they are smarter than the non-techies they serve.
- IT professionals DESIRE recognition . . . respect . . . continuing opportunity to update their skill set in new technologies and platforms . . . job security . . . more money.
- IT professionals FEEL an adversarial relationship with end users . . . they are constantly arguing with them . . . and they resent having to explain their technology to us ignoramuses.

Based on this BDF analysis, the company rewrote the letter and tested it. This time, it generated a 3 percent response, outperforming the old mailing by 6 to 1. And one-third of those inquiries purchased an on-site one-day training seminar for $3,000. That means for every one hundred pieces mailed, at a total cost of about $100, they got three leads . . . and one order for $3,000 . . . a 30-to-1 return on their marketing investment.

Oh, and the headline based on the BDF analysis? It was this:

IMPORTANT NEWS FOR ANY IT PROFESSIONAL WHO HAS EVER FELT LIKE TELLING AN END USER, "GO TO HELL."

Says the company owner, "The BDF formula forced us to focus on the prospect instead of the product (our seminar), and the result was a winning promotion."

Amount of money spent on market research before the mailing? Not a dime.

STEP TWO: PROBLEM IDENTIFICATION

Next, you need a clear definition of the pressing problem your product can help these buyers solve. What are your customers most concerned about that your product can help them with? Or as my colleague Don Hauptman is fond of asking, "What's keeping these prospects up at night?"

Marketing reaches prospects on a deeper level when it starts with those prospects—their needs, problems, concerns, worries, fears, and desires—and then connects those needs and wants to the benefits the product delivers.

ONE THING CONTENT MARKETING CANNOT DO

White papers, and in fact all the marketing you do, cannot create a need or make someone want a benefit they do not already want. As Eugene Schwartz explains in his book *Breakthrough Advertising*:

"The power, the force, the overwhelming urge to own that makes advertising work, comes from the market itself, and not from the copy. Copy cannot create desire for a product. It can only take the hopes, dreams, fears, and desires that already exist in the hearts of millions of people, and focus those already-existing desires onto a particular product. This is the copywriter's task: not to create this mass desire—but to channel and direct it."

Content marketing does not, for instance, create the desire among IT professionals to keep their computer systems safe from hacking and computer viruses. It was not until that desire already existed as a major concern that sales of firewalls, anti-virus software, and other security solutions took off.

What you as a marketer can do in this instance is (a) dramatize the severity and urgency of the problem to create even greater awareness among IT professionals, and (b) educate them about the best, most reliable, and most affordable solutions for solving the problem.

For instance, SurfControl, a company since acquired by Websense, had a product that filtered unwanted Internet content. One of the goals of its content marketing program was to educate prospects about the dangers that unwanted Internet content, such as that delivered by spam and instant messaging, as well as use of the company computers for personal purposes, (e.g., checking stocks) pose to their networks and corporate productivity.

STEP THREE: SOLUTION IDENTIFICATION

Once you have clearly identified the problem, you want to offer a solution. In a conventional marketing campaign, this solution would clearly be the product or service you are selling. But in a content marketing campaign, we often position the white paper itself as a solution (albeit, a partial solution) to the prospect's problem.

So, for instance, if the prospect is a Web master struggling with the question of whether to spend a lot of his company's money on a content management system (CMS), a white paper on "How to Calculate ROI from Your CMS" may be just the thing he needs to make the decision.

Should your marketing materials focus on the product or the lead magnet? It's not always clear. But here's a rule of thumb that direct marketers have been using for decades with good results:

If you have an exceptionally strong free content offer, LEAD WITH THE OFFER in your copy. On the other hand, if the offer is not strong, lead with the prospect's problems and then offer the product as the solution. Therefore, I suggest the following guidelines:

- If your white paper is just average—meaning the content is either average or not of compelling interest to the prospect, or there is already a lot of similar information on the topic available—do not stress it in your advertising.
- If your white paper is superior—great quality content, valuable information, hard-to-get data, unique format or manner of presentation—consider stressing it early in your copy, perhaps even in the headline.
- If your product is similar to other products in its category, find an important aspect of the product that your competitors do not stress, and educate your prospects about this by offering them a free white paper explaining it.
- If your product is superior—more features, innovative technology, superior quality—devote a lot of your copy to making the case for its superiority, and then close with the offer of a white paper as an added incentive for prospects to response.

STEP FOUR: CONTENT

Here are a few more tips for writing white papers:

- The narrower the topic, the better.
- Tailor the content to the primary prospects (e.g., CEO, process engineer, plant manager).

• Craft the content so it helps move readers to the next step in the buying process.

What main points and secondary points should be covered? You can determine this by making a content outline. Show it to subject matter experts (SMEs) in the company. They will tell you what doesn't belong and add what you may have left out, as well as correct technical errors.

STEP FIVE: MEDIA

Where and how can you reach potential buyers—your target audience? To get results, you must promote your offer of a free white paper to prospects, and that is usually accomplished through some form of direct marketing.

Direct marketing through postal mail or e-mail is difficult unless you can obtain a list of prospects in your target market. Look around to see what's available in your target market with regard to mailing lists, databases, publications, Web sites, trade shows, conventions, professional associations, newsletters, e-zines, and other media. The more targeted your list, the greater the response rate to your marketing campaign.

On an episode of President Donald Trump's reality TV program *The Apprentice*, Trump gave the same assignment to two competing groups: create a bridal shop and hold an evening sale; whichever team had the higher sales would win.

Team A's marketing strategy was to print up flyers on the sale and hand them out at Penn Station during rush hour. Trump questioned the wisdom of this strategy, asking, "How many people are thinking of getting married when they get off the train to go to work in the morning?"

Team B's marketing strategy was to obtain a large e-mail list of New Yorkers who are getting married and e-mail a notice about the sale to the list.

I think you can guess the outcome: Team A's store was virtually empty. They had only a handful of shoppers, and sold just two dresses, grossing $1,000.

Team B's more targeted e-mail marketing strategy was the winner: they had people waiting in line to get into the shop, sold twenty-six dresses, and grossed more than $12,000 in sales, outselling Team A by better than twelve to one. (Sure enough, Trump fired Team A's leader that week.)

The point: the more targeted your media-mailing lists, online lists, banner ads, magazine and newspaper ads, radio and TV commercials, the more prospects who will download your white paper.

STEP SIX: TACTICS

Tactics are the means by which you will reach your prospects (i.e., direct mail, advertising, e-mail marketing, print advertising, radio spots, trade shows, banner ads, pay-per-click ads, joint ventures, and other marketing communications).

Part of your decision regarding tactics is governed by cost and availability. For instance, if there is no list you can rent of prospects with their e-mail addresses, you probably can't use e-mail marketing to reach them. Sometimes there is a mailing list priced at a reasonable rental cost of $100 per thousand e-mails. But if the list owner wants $1,000 per thousand, e-mail is not going to be economically feasible.

Another factor governing tactic selection is your prospects. E-mail marketing will not work if the majority of your prospects don't have access to the Internet—which, surprisingly, is still about half of the world's population.[4]

STEP SEVEN: SCHEDULE

A useful schedule has all project tasks and milestones (e.g., "first draft of white paper"), their due dates, and the people responsible.

Most white paper campaigns have multiple components and involve multiple contributors, reviewers, and approvers. Without a project schedule, including the tasks, steps involved in the task, the person responsible for each step, and the date the step must be completed, the likelihood of timely completion is remote.

STEP EIGHT: BUDGET

Budget is simply what the campaign will cost. To make a budget, you first make a list of the campaign deliverables.

For the white paper, your costs are copywriting, design, and—if it is a hard copy document—printing and binding.

There is also the cost of inquiry fulfillment, which refers to sending prospects who respond to the mailing the bait piece and other materials they requested. When you automatically fulfill requests for your white paper by sending a PDF via autoresponder, inquiry fulfillment is close to free.

However, don't forget to factor in the cost of your marketing campaign. Just because it is mainly digital doesn't mean it's free.

On the contrary, digital marketing can in fact be relatively expensive. Your spending on banner ads, Google ads, Facebook ads, e-mails to rented lists can easily run into thousands of dollars a month, per week, or even a day.

STEP NINE: METRICS

Determine your goals. Key metrics for white paper marketing campaigns include:

- Click-through rates to the white paper landing page.
- Conversion rates of click to white paper downloads.
- Inquiries from white paper recipients via e-mail or phone.
- Number of white paper recipients who are qualified prospects for the product.
- Percentage of white paper recipients who make a purchase.

BLOGS

Blogging, which in its most basic form is journaling online—although it has farther-reaching ramifications—has gained national prominence over the past two decades.

According to SoftwareFindr, there are more than half a billion blogs on the Web. Techjury reports that 77 percent of Internet users read blogs, and that adding a blog to your existing Web site can increase traffic by as much as 434 percent.[5]

Search engines like content, and when you blog, you're posting lots of new content to your Web site on a regular basis. Adding an active blog to your Web site will almost surely boost your search engine rankings.

Unlike articles and white papers, which are traditionally one-way communications (you write it, your subscribers read it), blogs are a two-way online medium, a means of starting a lively conversation about an interesting topic.

One effective blogging technique is to make a strong statement in your post, and then ask the reader for a response (e.g., I often end my posts with a question such as "What do you think?"). Another blogging technique that stimulates conversation is to withhold your opinion but ask readers for theirs.

If you are discussing an article you or another source has already published, be sure to put a reference to the original article in your blog post. Hyperlink that reference to the actual article online, if it's available.

Many business blogs are written in the voice of a single author who becomes familiar to the readership over time, building a relationship and trust.

Where appropriate, hyperlink a sentence or two in your posts to relevant material such as articles or Web sites covering the same topic as the post.

According to Orbit Media, the average blog post is about a thousand words and takes more than three hours to write. Your blog should have at least one new post per week.[6]

There are many blogging platforms. WordPress, an open-source software platform, is the most commonly used platform for creating blogs, and some hosts will set that up for you with just one click. WordPress comes with free and paid themes, but also check out others that can be used. For WordPress, there is the downloadable version you can get for free at WordPress.org. If you go this route, then make sure your hosting company supports the WordPress platform, and most do.

The other version is found at WordPress.com, where WordPress hosts your blogging page, but is very minimal in terms of extending it farther. Extra purchase options are a custom domain name and added storage. You cannot use advertising platforms, such as Google AdSense.

You will also run across the term "WordPress Theme Frameworks," which means that the WordPress version you downloaded from WordPress.org has been taken by a company of developers and recoded to be more efficient, using its own toolkits. Some charge fees to get their package, while others offer them for free, such as CherryFramework.com.

CASE STUDIES

According to copywriter Heather Sloan, case studies are often more effective than brochures and traditional sales collateral. Why?

"Everyone loves a story," explains Heather. "Never did this wisdom ring truer than in sales conversations and marketing pieces. Stories paint pictures. Stories evoke emotions. Stories are memorable. Stories give your presentations sticking power. The easiest way to tell a marketing story is by case study."

A case study is a product success story. It tells how a company solved a problem using a specific product, process, method, or idea. As with other marketing techniques, case studies fluctuate in popularity: while almost any company can profitably market with case studies, an informal survey of B2B Web sites shows that most companies don't take full advantage of the power of case study marketing.

While case studies need not adhere to any one formula, here are some guidelines.

The average case study is relatively brief: one or two sides of an 8½ x 11–inch page, or approximately 800 to 1,500 words. More complex or in-depth case studies can run 2,000 to 2,500 words.

An effective case study makes the reader want to learn more about the product it features. It's a soft-sell proposition designed to compel your prospects to request more detailed information. If you've mirrored the readers' problem successfully, the case study will propel them deeper into the sales funnel and closer to buying.

For the most part, case studies are not overly technical: they are written in a style similar to that of a magazine feature article. The intent of a case study is not to present in-depth minutiae and analytical data, but to briefly describe how a product or service can effectively address and solve a particular problem.

You needn't be creative or reinvent the wheel when creating a case study. Most case studies follow some variation of this time-tested outline:

1—Who is the customer?

2—What was the problem? How was it hurting the customer's business?

3—What solutions did they look at and ultimately reject, and why?

4—Why did they choose our product as the solution?

5—Describe the implementation of the product, including any problems and how they were solved.

6—How and where does the customer use the product?

7—What are the results and benefits they are getting?

8—Would they recommend it to others and why?

"We don't have formal guidelines for case studies," said Mark Rosenzweig, the former editor of *Chemical Processing*, a trade publication that has been running case study articles for decades. "Generally we're looking for a relatively recent installation, say within the last two years, of innovative technology. What issues prompted the installation? What did it involve? What results have been achieved? We're generally looking for 1,500 to 2,000 words."

Because case studies are presented in a story format, readers are naturally more inclined to take an interest—especially if the story has some sort of benefit to them. Unlike sales presentations, case studies are all about *showing* how a product or service works, rather than *telling*. Since the product benefits are extolled by an actual user—and not the manufacturer—the claims are more believable.

By using a satisfied customer as an example, a case study essentially demonstrates how well your product works. Rather than present a pile of facts and figures, you tell an engaging story that vividly shows your product's effectiveness.

An equally strong selling point is the level of empathy a case study creates between your prospects and your satisfied customers. People tend to identify with people like themselves.

Prospects feel far more at ease listening to their peers. They relate better, because they often share the same issues and problems.

Readers also believe case studies more than other sales literature. They are skeptical of ads and find brochures full of puffery, and even podcasts and company blogs can seem self-serving. But in a case study, a customer who has no motive or financial incentive to praise the product does so, creating instant credibility.

A survey by Forrester Research Inc. shows that 71 percent of buyers base their decisions on trust and believability. Relating your customers' positive experiences with your product is one of the best ways to establish credibility in the marketplace. Giving your customers confidence in what you're offering dramatically increases the likelihood they'll do business with you.

One of the best sources of candidates for case studies is the sales force. However, salespeople prefer to spend their time selling. They are often indifferent to marketing communications and view participating in case studies as an aggravation with no direct reward to them.

You can get salespeople excited about finding case study candidates by offering them tangible incentives: the sales rep gets cash, merchandise, or a travel incentive if her candidate is chosen and profiled in a case study. When offered a nice incentive, the sales force suddenly gets excited about the case study candidate search. The incentive does not have to be huge, but it should be desirable—a new iPod, for example.

To prepare the case study, a writer interviews the person in the customer organization who is most involved in the application. For a small business, this may be the owner; for a larger company, it could be a plant manager or engineer. Before the writer calls, the vendor salesperson or account manager handling that customer should call and make sure the customer is willing and even eager to participate. Case studies written about reluctant or hostile users are difficult to create and rarely successful.

During the interview, get as many good quotations as possible. Use these quotations in the case study text and attribute them to the person being interviewed.

Reason: the quotations in published case studies can do double duty as testimonials.

Tip: If the subject is not saying exactly what you want him to say, use the "So are you saying" technique. Say to the subject, "So are you saying that . . ." followed by the statement you want him to make. If he answers "yes, that's what I am saying," you can attribute your phrasing to the subject.

Often prospects are vague with their answers, and it is up to the interviewer/writer to wring the specifics out of the interview. Whenever possible, get the subject to give you numbers, so claims and results can be specific.

For instance, if the subject says the product reduces energy costs, but can't say by how much, pin him down: "Did it reduce energy consumption more than 10 percent? More than 100 percent?" He will give you a guesstimate, which you can use as an approximate figure (i.e., "The XYZ system reduced plant energy consumption by over 10 percent").

Before the case study can be released, the subject of the case study must approve and sign off on it. Keep these releases on file. If the subject takes a job with a different company, you may lose track of him. So you can't afford to lose track of his signed permission form. Otherwise, if your authorization to use the case study is questioned, and you can't produce a signed release, you may have to remove that case study from your site.

Ask subjects of case studies whether they are willing to serve as reference accounts. That way, a prospect whose needs relate to a particular case study can in fact speak with the product user featured in that case study. Check your reference account list periodically to make sure names and numbers are current; update as needed.

18 ✐

GETTING YOUR COPY WRITTEN

If you're a business owner or employer who doesn't write copy, today there are multiple options for getting your copy written. Some have been actively used for decades. Others were infrequent when I started forty years ago, but have exploded in popularity. A handful, most technology driven, are relatively new. In this chapter, we explore the options and how to best take advantage of each.

OPTION #1: WRITE YOUR OWN COPY

Back in the day, many clients wrote their own copy for these primary reasons:

- They already had a deep understanding of their product and their markets, and found it easier to use that market and product knowledge to write their own copy, rather than take the time to explain it to a copywriter who was not as conversant in their business.
- Clients did not value copywriting as a specialized skill. They

believed everyone can write. So why not write their own copy instead of paying a copywriter?

• The copy that came back from the professional copywriters they hired was not exactly as the client would have written it, or else contained mistakes ranging from technical errors to sales appeals that missed the mark. And they found it a frustrating nuisance to direct the copywriter to write the ad exactly as they themselves would have done.

In fact, you know your market and product better than outside writers and agencies. And some clients, especially today, when a plethora of copywriting courses are available, can gain considerable copywriting chops. For many of these copy-competent clients, they find that the best option is to write some of the copy themselves and assign other projects to staff or freelance writers.

As a rule of thumb, the copy-competent client may choose to write his own copy when:

• The product is highly technical and requires specialized background (e.g., an engineering degree) to understand.
• The client feels in the time it would take to bring a writer up to speed, he could write it himself.
• He wants it written in his "voice" and doubts that a writer could capture that voice.

The copy-competent clients may prefer to outsource the writing of a promotion when:

• The client doesn't have time to write the copy.
• The client does not have the desire to write the copy.
• The client feels his time is better spent on other tasks.

OPTION #2: OUTSOURCE

Many clients, however, either can't write their own copy, do not want to write copy, or do not have time to do so, and know they should instead focus on their core competencies—whether that's machine learning or circuit design. These clients often hire outside copywriters, either freelancers or agencies, for several reasons.

First, writing copy takes time. And busy executives realize that writing copy is not the highest and best use of their time.

Some view writing as an unwholesome mental chore to be avoided at all costs; it's just not in their wheelhouse.

Third, they find that professional writers produce superior copy.

This should neither surprise them nor give them an inferiority complex.

Think of it this way. I write copy sixty hours a week and have been doing so for forty years. For that reason, I'm probably a little bit better than most business owners and managers who have many other responsibilities and tasks to juggle.

A "little bit better" may not seem like much. But when promoting a consumer e-commerce product online, raising the conversion rate only a few percentage points can, in my experience, increase gross revenues by many hundreds of thousands of dollars or even more.

Writing in PR Daily, Jake Herway gives these tips on how clients can work more effectively with freelancers and independent contractors:[1]

- Consistently clarify expectations.
- Orient freelancers and their peers to the larger purpose and the goal.

- Give freelancers opportunities to communicate with client staff members to enhance productivity and build rapport.

OPTION #3: INSOURCE

Insourcing means you assign the copy to various people employed full-time at the company, typically those working in a marketing communications function. But some clients recruit others, including technical writers, public relations specialists, and sometimes engineers.

Unlike when hiring freelancers, who get a briefing, go away, and come back with a first draft, there are three advantages to insourcing.

First, while a freelancer may be working on half a dozen projects, the staff writer can be assigned 100 percent to yours.

Second, insourced writers have easier access to subject matter experts. These SMEs often have offices right down the hall. And some can enrich your knowledge by sharing their own stories, views, and specialized expertise that may not be in the copy briefing. They can also review your draft in progress and give you important direction on page 1 that may be reflected throughout the rest of the piece.

Third, most freelance copywriters sit alone in a room and write. Many corporations have multiple copywriters on staff. Members of the copywriting team can lend a helping hand to one another, from reading and reviewing rough drafts to helping one another come up with fresh campaign ideas.

The primary reasons many businesses today outsource their copy despite the above factors are these: (a) many business owners do believe copywriters possess specialized skills that result in high response rates and (b) they can easily test this outside copy against copy written by other sources. In some cases, they may test the new copy against the copy they already have been using to determine whether the fresh copy in fact produces improved results.

OPTION #4: SOFTWARE

Increasingly, robots and artificial intelligence (AI) software are taking over tasks and jobs once performed by human beings. Can this happen with writing?

According to an article in *Popular Science*, published just recently as I write the updates for this new edition,[2] a computer program coded by Sverker Johansson has written 2.7 million articles, accounting for 8.5 percent of the entries in Wikipedia.

Persado, an AI software company, has created algorithms that compare e-mail subject lines and their click rate. From this data, the software creates new subject lines. Based on data analysis, Persado subject lines almost always outperform those written by humans.[3]

WHY SOME CLIENTS DON'T RESPECT THEIR COPYWRITERS

Copywriters and their work are frequently criticized, and some writers get offended. Why do many copywriters "get no respect"? I can think of two reasons.

First, writing is more subjective than most other fields. An accountant can point to a ledger and prove that the books balance. A lawyer can back up her case with legal precedents and logical arguments.

Writing copy is not so cut-and-dried. There may be dozens of ways of writing an ad, each with merit. The copywriter can say he thinks his way is best. But he can't prove his ideas are superior. The client has to take it on faith . . . and few do.

Of course, there are guidelines for effective copy, presented earlier in this book, among other places. Unfortunately, many clients and writers are not aware of these rules. And without a clear idea of what makes good copy, how can the copywriter defend his work and say that it's good?

The second reason clients don't respect writers is that, way down deep, many clients fancy themselves better writers than their copywriters.

Doctors, lawyers, accountants, plumbers, mechanics, and software engineers deal in areas so technical and complex that their clients don't know enough to interfere. But everybody can write. (Even parrots and mockingbirds use language!) So there is less mystery to the copywriter's work, and clients are more confident that they could write the ad or letter "if only I had the time."

If you're hiring outside copywriters, here's a three-step recommendation to improve the relationship:

1. Hire the right copywriter for the job: someone who fits in with the product and your company.

2. Work with the writer on a professional basis. Treat the writer with the same respect you would your lawyer, accountant, or doctor. Stand back, and let the writer do her job.

3. Establish logical guidelines for reviewing copy. Base your review on these concrete standards, not on subjective or aesthetic judgments. And, above all, be specific in your criticism.

Let's look at each step of the plan in more detail.

HOW TO HIRE A STAFF OR FREELANCE COPYWRITER

How do you go about finding copywriters to hire on a staff or freelance basis? And how do you know which writer is right for your business? Here are ten tips for finding and selecting the best copywriter for the job at hand.

1. Ask around

Need to find a writer? The best way to find one is through referrals. Ask your friends, colleagues, and acquaintances to recommend writers they have used in the past.

The people most likely to know the name of a good copywriter include:

- Local advertising agencies and PR firms
- Magazine space reps and editors
- Printers, photographers, graphic artists, design studios, and other outside vendors
- Communications managers of nearby manufacturing and service firms

---

LOOKING FOR COPYWRITERS ONLINE

Most copywriters I know have Web sites, so you can find plenty with a Google Search.

The most important things you should look for: online portfolio of copywriting samples, copywriter's bio and credentials, client list, client testimonials, content (e.g., a blog or newsletter) displaying knowledge of marketing, and a sample agreement for copywriting assignments.

There are also a number of specialty "freelance Web sites" that help connect copywriters with clients. In my experience, these sites tend to attract hungry newbie copywriters who need assignments, and clients whose main concern seems to be finding writers who charge the lowest price.

---

2. Choose a writer with experience in your industry

There are three advantages to using a writer who knows your business. First, you'll spend less time briefing her and bringing her up to speed in your technology and your markets.

Second, because the writer already speaks the jargon of your industry, your employees will accept her more readily than they would an "outsider" who doesn't speak their language. This may be important if you want your managers and engineers to work closely with the writer.

Third, the writer may be able to vet your strategy or suggest new ideas based on her experience working with clients whose products are similar to your own.

Clients have asked me, "Do you have to be a software engineer to write copy on a computer account?" You don't, and many great computer ads have been written by writers who didn't know Pascal from Python when they started. On the other hand, a writer with programming experience does have a head start over the writer who has never written code.

The writer you hire doesn't have to be an expert in your particular product. (She won't ever know as much about your business as you do.) But she should have a feel for your industry and a knack for writing the type of copy you need.

For example, if you need a writer to write a brochure on your new Caribbean cruise package, don't insist that the writer have a portfolio full of color brochures or Web sites on Caribbean cruises. Chances are you won't be able to find such an individual. But you should look for a copywriter specializing in travel rather than one who is more at home with subscription mailings, annual reports, or fashion advertising.

In other words, don't insist that the writer have specific experience in your product line. Do look for a writer who specializes in your kind of advertising, be it travel, high-tech, home furnishings, or pharmaceuticals.

3. Hire someone in your league

Not all copywriting assignments require the same level of skill. Writing a bulletin board notice to sell your used Chevrolet doesn't take the same level of copywriting sophistication that writing a corporate ad campaign for Exxon does.

Copywriters also operate on different levels. There are high-paid specialists, middle-level generalists, and beginners to handle the easy stuff. These writers charge according to their level of skill, and you can save money by not overhiring for the job.

A marketing manager at a small industrial firm needed a cover letter to accompany a new brochure he was mailing to customers, sales reps, and regional offices. Because I have experience writing shorter letters and e-mails for B2B firms, my copy is often successful for these firms, and I charge accordingly—$1,500 minimum for a one-page letter.

4. Pick a writer whose style is somewhat in sync with your own

The conservative company, thinking that it's time to improve its image, hires the most creative digital marketing or branding agency in town.

The first ads come in. They're what you'd expect from a creative agency—creative. "A little too far out for us, though," says the conservative client. "Can you come up with something a little more dignified. We're just not sure about the dancing chemical drums."

"You're stifling our creativity!" screams the agency, which picks up the presentation, stamps out of the conference room, sends a bill, and refuses to work with the barbaric client anymore.

Moral of the story: an ad agency or freelancer is unlikely to convince the client to make a radical change in their way of doing business. So clients would do well to select copywriters whose approach and style are in tune with their own.

If you like hard-sell ads—ads with coupons, with benefits in the headlines, with price and where-to-buy information, with straightforward body copy that sells the features and benefits of the product—you probably won't like the ads you get from a copywriter trained on splashy "image" campaigns for national brands. After all, this writer may believe that an ad should have a "clever" headline and a glossy color visual, and that people "don't read long copy."

Well, he's not going to convert you to his point of view. And you're not going to waste your hard-earned ad dollars so he can win creative awards. The best bet is to stay away from each other in the first place. Hire a writer whose portfolio is full of your type of fact-filled ads. Let a company who wants "show-place" ads hire the creative guy.

Do you like long-copy ads or short-copy ads? Fancy color photos or plain-Jane graphics? Informational copy or emotional copy? Plain language or purple prose? Choose a copywriter whose style and "advertising philosophy" fit in with your own. You'll both be happier with the working relationship—and with the copy it produces.

5. Taking the first step

Let's say you have the name of a copywriter you want to hire. The first step is to phone or write her and ask to see background material on her copywriting services.

At the very least, you want to see samples of her work, a résumé or capsule biography, and a list of clients. Many experienced copywriters already have a standard information package prepared that contains all of this and more. Novices often have to be told what to send you.

Here are the things to look for when evaluating the freelancer's information package or Web site:

• *Is it well written?* If the freelancer can't promote himself effectively, how can he write copy for services and products with which he's not intimately familiar?

• *Do you like the sample work?* The samples represent what she considers to be her best copy. If you don't think they show promise, keep looking. This isn't the right writer for you, and asking to see more samples isn't going to change anything.

• *Look at the client list.* Make sure the copywriter has experience in your industry or in related fields. Don't hire a straight technical writer to write your new perfume ad. Find a writer who likes doing perfume ads and is good at it.

• *Did the copywriter include information on his fee rate and structure?* A true professional will give you his rates up front. He doesn't want to waste your time—or his—if you can't afford to pay him.

• *What related writing and communications experience does the copywriter have?* A well-rounded copywriter does more than write copy. What else has your copywriter written? Any books? Articles? Papers? Speeches? Seminars? Teaching experience?

• *What overall feeling do you get from the whole thing?* You've looked over the writer's material and chatted with her over the phone. Do her package and presentation say "professional" or "amateur"? Do you feel comfortable with the writer and confident that she can handle the job? Gut feelings are important. Go with your instincts.

6. *Don't expect something for nothing*

An amazing number of smaller companies will call me up and say, "We're a small manufacturer in South Jersey. We don't do much advertising, but we saw your ad and may need a one-page press release to announce our president's retirement next month. We'd like to meet with you to check you over. Can you come over this afternoon?"

I have news for you. Unless you're a major advertiser or ad

agency with a large project in hand, you are not going to see me. And why not? Because if I jumped in the car and spent the better part of the day visiting every small business that wanted a $750 press release, I'd have no time to write copy for my dozens of regular and higher-paying clients.

My point is: the copywriter, like a lawyer or doctor, is a professional. If you want his time, you must be willing to pay for it. Few copywriters give free house calls these days.

You may object and say, "But I want to hire you! Isn't a meeting the next step?"

It doesn't have to be. We can handle the assignment by e-mail, Skype, or Zoom.

"But I want to meet you!"

Fine. Come to my office and there is no charge. If I have to leave the office, though, I have to charge you for my time—if it's just an exploratory meeting. If you have an assignment for me, I'll include the meeting as part of my fee, provided we've already agreed that I'm going to handle the project for you.

As I've said, I may make an exception if you're a big advertiser or if you're dangling an attractive project in front of me. But it's unreasonable for most clients—smaller companies with infrequent copywriting assignments—to expect the copywriter to come running without compensation. The few projects they have to offer don't justify the time spent in travel and meetings.

Most copywriters will be glad to chat with you over the phone or in their office. But don't expect the copywriter to make an out-of-office trip to your plant or office unless you're willing to pay for a consultation. A writer who earns $1,000 to $2,000 a day or more isn't going to spend half a day chasing down a $500 assignment.

In the pre-Internet days, the major reason for copywriters to visit clients was to drop off their portfolio case of copywriting samples. But today many copywriters, myself included, post our samples on our Web sites (mine is www.bly.com), where anyone can see them at the click of a mouse.

7. Discuss fees up front

There's no point in talking if you can't afford the writer's rates. Save yourself a lot of time and find out fees up front.

Most writers can give you rough estimates of what they charge for different jobs: so much for an ad, so much for a sales letter, more for a brochure. Ask to see the copywriter's fee schedule, if she has one.

These estimates are "ballpark" figures only. The exact fee depends on the specific assignment. But the ballpark figures give you a good idea of what you'll pay for the copy you need.

If the copywriter charges by time instead of project, find out her rate for a week, day, half day, or hour. Ask how long she thinks your project will take. Multiply the number of days by the day rate to get the total cost estimate.

Also discuss deadlines up front. The top copywriters are often booked weeks in advance and cannot always handle rush jobs. Some prospects are shocked to learn that I can't write their ad overnight. They don't realize that I already have six jobs on my desk, all due in a few weeks.

Find out how much time the writer normally takes to do small projects (ads, letters) and large ones (Web sites, white papers, autoresponder e-mail sequences). If your deadlines are short, say so, and ask the writer if she can meet them.

Copy revisions should also be discussed up front. Are they included in the copywriter's initial fee or do they cost extra? How many drafts are included in the basic project price? How quickly can the writer make revisions? What happens if there is a change in the nature of the assignment? Are revisions still included? Is there a time limit in which revisions must be assigned?

Make sure you understand the writer's policy for revisions. Otherwise, it can become a problem area later on.

8. *Provide complete background information on the project*

Send the writer all the background information you can. With this material in hand, the writer can give the most accurate estimate as to what the job will cost. Without it, he is "flying blind" because he doesn't know how much research is involved, and his high estimate will reflect this degree of uncertainty.

You'll get the best price by giving the writer whatever information he needs to make an informed, accurate estimate of what the copy will cost.

9. *Get it in writing*

Put the fee, terms, deadlines, and a description of the assignment in a purchase order or letter of agreement.

A written agreement eliminates confusion and spells out what the client is buying and what the writer is selling. Too many buyers and sellers in all fields of business have gone to court because they made their deals orally. Don't make the same mistake. A written agreement protects both the client and the writer. So don't just shake hands on it. Put it in writing.

10. *Stand back*

Once you've hired the writer and given her the background material, stand back and let her do her job. Don't interfere; don't ask to "take a look at the first few pages"; don't badger the writer with constant "how's it going?" phone calls.

You've hired a professional. Now let the professional work. You'll get your copy by the deadline date or sooner. And it will be copy that pleases you and is effective in selling your product. If you need changes, the writer will make them. After all, that's what you're paying for.

One veteran copywriter says: "On the first draft, the client gets what he needs. On the second draft, the client gets what he wants. On the third draft, the client gets what he deserves."

TIPS ON WORKING WITH YOUR COPYWRITER

The best way to work with your copywriter is to leave him alone during the first-draft stage of the project. He knows what he's doing, and you trust him. Otherwise, you wouldn't have hired him in the first place.

But, even when the copywriter is working at a distance, it's important that the two of you start off with a comfortable, mutually agreeable working relationship. Copywriting is a partnership: you provide the information and direction, the copywriter provides the persuasive writing, and together you sell more of a product or service.

If one or both partners aren't happy, someone won't be doing his job with enthusiasm. And a job done without enthusiasm is a job done poorly.

Here are some suggestions for maintaining a good working relationship between client and copywriter:

1. Pay fairly

Pay fair rates for copywriting services performed. Remember, an underpaid worker is an unhappy and unproductive worker. Writers writing for extremely low wages rarely produce exciting prose.

Everything in life is negotiable, but only so far. A good writer with a steady business may take 10 or 20 percent off the price if your assignment interests her. But she can't afford to—and probably won't—go much below that.

A writer who needs the work may come very cheaply. But even if you sense you can get it for less, pay a fair wage. If you force the writer down to the bargain-basement price, she's not going to feel very good about your project. And you want your writer to be enthusiastic, not apathetic.

2. Pay on time

There are few things as unpleasant in business life as trying to collect an unpaid invoice. Unfortunately, it's not unusual for clients to be four, six, even eight weeks or more behind in their payments to their freelancers.

Pay on time—in thirty days—and the freelancer will get a warm glow inside whenever you call. Better still, get a check out in ten days or less, and the freelancer will try to perform miracles for you on your next ad or campaign.

3. Cooperate

Provide complete background information on the product, your audience, and your objectives. Be available to answer questions or give direction. Review outlines and rough drafts in a timely fashion.

One person from the client organization should be the contact between the company and the copywriter. It is inefficient for the copywriter to have to track down executives from half a dozen different departments of your firm, and this can result in conflicting instructions.

4. Don't waste time

Avoid unnecessary meetings. Maybe a meeting or two will be needed, but most of the writing and revision can be handled by e-mail and phone.

Don't feed information or revisions to the writer one piece at a time. Give him the background information or the instructions for the rewrite in one shot.

It is good manners not to keep people waiting when they have an appointment with you. This applies to copywriters, too.

To the copywriter, time is money. If you do not waste their time, your account will be profitable to them, and they will gladly devote themselves to giving you the best copy possible.

On the other hand, the more you waste the writer's time, the less profitable the project becomes. The writer might either devote less time to writing your copy or drop your account.

In general, writing copy should not require a great deal of contact between client and copywriter. The fewer number of contacts, the better. Meetings should never be more than two hours long and should follow a tight agenda. Phone conferences should be brief and to the point.

Not only will the writer save time (and possibly charge you less as a result), but you will save time, too.

5. *Let them hear from you*

The copywriter mails his copy and never hears from the client until the next project. His insides are twisted with worry. Did the client hate the copy or did they love it? Probably they loved it—no news is good news—but the writer doesn't know.

A kind word from a client—a quick phone call or a brief, one-line note of praise—can do wonders for the copywriter's ego. Writers seldom receive feedback on their work, even when the reaction is favorable.

A thank-you note will be much appreciated by the writer starved for praise and ego gratification. Sincere flattery can quickly put you at the top of the writer's "favorite clients" list. And the benefits of this—better service, better copy—are far in excess of the effort involved.

6. *Critique copy rationally*

"I don't like it" is a meaningless critique and a frustrating response for the copywriter to deal with.

The key to reviewing copy is to give specific, objective criticisms. Subjective and vague comments don't give the writer any guidelines for revision and often lead to hurt feelings, defensiveness, and a gradual collapse of the client-copywriter relationship.

Below are nine rules for reviewing and approving copy. They will eliminate bad feelings and misunderstandings and give the copywriter the guidelines he or she needs to rewrite the copy so that it will be acceptable and effective.

THE #1 MISTAKE IN CRITIQUING COPY

Simply put, you should not hire copywriters to write ads exactly as *you* would have written them if only you had the time.

Rather, you select a good copywriter whose style you like, then sit back and let them write it in their own natural style.

If there are rules or guidelines your company abides by (e.g., never just say your product is "better," but rather be highly specific about what makes it different and superior to other products in its category), make note of those errors in your copy critique. Even better would be to inform the writer about your rules and guidelines *before* he starts writing.

The key here is not to edit and rewrite strong copy from an experienced writer so that it sounds exactly like you would have written it. If you feel compelled to do so, don't assign the project to other writers. Instead, write it yourself.

There are two reasons for this. First, copywriters are not mind readers, so it's impossible for them to know exactly how you'd write the ad. Second, hamstring good writers, and they concentrate on trying to please you rather than writing copy that sells the product. And serving two masters, in this case you and the market, almost never works.

MORE WAYS TO REVIEW AND APPROVE COPY

Reading and reviewing copy is as much an art as writing copy is. Here are some other guidelines to help you review copy in such a way that you end up with the strongest promotion possible:

1. Be specific

Make your critique of the copy factual and specific. Show the copywriter where he went wrong—and how you want him to fix it.

Some examples of nonspecific versus specific criticisms:

Nonspecific:	Specific:
"Not enough pizzazz."	"Our product is the only one that offers these features. The copy should stress its uniqueness more strongly."
"The copy doesn't 'position' the product."	"Our process is 20 percent more efficient than the competition's. That should be in the headline."
"The ad is dull and boring."	"Put in less about the technical features and more about what the product can do for people."
"It doesn't tell the story we want to tell."	"Here are the four consumer benefits the copy should cover."
"I don't like it."	"This is a good start. But there are some specific changes I'd like to see. Let me tell you what I have in mind."

Remember, it is not enough to say you want changes in the copy; you must specify what those changes are.

This does not mean that you should do the copywriter's job and rewrite the copy yourself. It does require that you write down specific, factual changes and corrections you want made and give them to the copywriter so he can rewrite your copy to incorporate these changes.

And be sure to give these instructions in writing, not orally (unless they are very brief and very minor). The act of writing out your comments forces you to be more specific. Use Word's Track Changes or Comments feature to mark up the electronic draft; this makes your edits easier to read and eliminates the need for the copywriter to struggle with your handwritten notes.

2. The fewer levels of approval, the better

Who should have approval authority? A product manager. A technical expert, usually an engineer or scientist. The marketing manager. The sales manager. And the company president. But certainly no more than that.

Everybody has a different opinion of what should appear in an ad. By trying to please a committee, you end up with an ad that is too spread out, one that is weak and watered down, with no strong selling message or point of view.

Four or fewer reviewers is ideal. Six should be the maximum. Any more, and you are writing ads by committee—and committees cannot write effective ads.

When I write for small companies, my copy is usually approved by one person: the company owner or president. Some of my best copy has been published this way. If others in your organization want to see the copy before it is published, put them on a "cc" list of people who receive informational copies. These people can give you their opinion if they want to, but they have no right of approval or disapproval. Only a handful of team members should have a say over what the final content of the ad will be.

THE 25-50-25 PRINCIPLE OF COPY REVISIONS

About 25 percent of the changes made by the client improve the copy. Around 25 percent make the copy weaker. The other 50 percent make no difference either way.

My reaction? I make the 25 percent changes that improve the copy and thank the client for their careful review. I also make the 50 percent of changes that won't affect the copy's effectiveness one way or the other, and I do it without question or quibble.

For the 25 percent of changes that I believe will adversely affect the campaign's results, I voice my reasons why to the client. If they do not agree with me, I acquiesce pleasantly.

---

3. What about compliance?

Compliance means making sure your copy meets all the legal and regulatory requirements required by the federal government and its departments.

For instance, when writing copy to sell dietary supplements, you cannot say that your pill cures a disease. So you can't say your joint supplement cures or eliminates arthritis. You *can* say that your supplement supports optimal joint health. Even safer is to say it "can" or "may help" support optimal joint health.

I am not an attorney. I can't advise you on legal matters or compliance issues.

However, different companies nonetheless follow regulatory rules at varying levels. Some play it looser while others publish compliance copy as tight as a drum.

One experienced direct marketer told me his compliance rule: "For each 10 percent your copy gets closer to strict 100 percent compliance, your response rate drops about 10 percent."

4. Be civil

Some clients love to tear apart a writer's work. Others are merely insensitive. They don't realize that writing is a highly personal act, and writers take criticism on a personal level.

Adman Amil Gargano says that some people "take delight in browbeating creative people. These are people who have a very fragile ego and a difficult time handling rejection. You should comment on their work in a way that is thoughtful, considerate, and articulate."

You don't have to baby writers. Just remember they're people. And, like your own employees, they are quick to respond to praise and to insult.

Be tactful when you have to tell a writer that his work doesn't meet your standards. Don't say, "The copy isn't very good, and we need a total rewrite."

Rather, start with praise, then get to the defects. Say, "Overall you've done a good job in putting this together. Let me show you our reactions and the changes we'd like you to make."

Companies spend a great deal of money motivating employees. Outside vendors also respond to the motivators of praise, kindness, courtesy, and decency. Treat your copywriters well, and they'll give you their best.

My former boss at Westinghouse, T. C. Smith, has a smart and effective way for giving critiques. The first step is to say "What I like about this is" and then praise one or two of the strong points, which you can always find if you look hard enough.

Then you say, "If it were mine to do" and give your criticisms, sometimes referred to as "crits."

Copywriters are more accepting and less negative about the crits when you start with some words of praise first, as T. C. does in the example above.

5. Let writers write

"Good clients don't write copy," says Malcolm MacDougall, president of SSC&B. "Good clients know in their hearts that nobody from Harvard Business School ever wrote a great ad campaign. That is why they have an agency."

Let your writers do their job. Don't write or rewrite copy. If you want changes made, write out what these changes are. But don't make them yourself. Give them to the copywriter and let him redo the words.

Don't play schoolteacher or amateur grammarian. The copywriter is the expert on how to use language as a selling tool.

If you think the ad doesn't reflect your strategy and objective, say so. If there's a wrong fact, point it out. But don't change commas to semicolons or dot i's and cross t's. Leave writing to the writer.

6. Don't take opinion polls

One of my clients had me come up with two versions of a brochure cover. He made his selection by asking his mother, his father, his wife, his wife's parents, his grandfather, and several friends which they liked better. Cover "B" got more votes and that's the one he went with. Don't make the same mistake as my client. Ad copy should be judged by professional businesspeople, not by friends, relatives, and neighbors.

When viewing an ad layout or reading a piece of copy, amateurs judge the ad by aesthetics, not by whether it would move them to buy the product. They'll pick the pretty layout, the flowery, poetic-sounding copy every time. So, nice as these folks may be, their opinion of your ad shouldn't play a part in your approval process.

Some marketers circulate the copy, often on Google Docs, to many people, because they believe that the more opinions they get, the better this makes the copy.

I am of the same mind as another former boss of mine, David Koch. One day at the office, more than half a dozen of us were arguing about whether we liked a piece of copy or not.

Then David spoke up and asked us: "Do you know what a moose is?" We didn't know what to say, so David told us: "It's a cow designed by committee." From this, I formulated my own rule of copy review:

I have found that the quality of marketing copy is inversely proportional to the number of people who review it.

7. Read copy as a customer, not as an advertiser or as an editor

I worry when the client reads copy with pen or pencil in hand. It tells me he's reading the ad as an editor, and not as a buyer.

Instead, read the copy from the customer's point of view. Ask, "If I were my customer, would this ad get my attention? Does it hold my interest strongly enough to get me to read or at least skim the body copy? Would I remember the ad, want to buy the product, or be moved to clip the coupon and respond?"

Don't worry if the ad doesn't show a picture of the company president or talk about the new conveyor belts in the Kentucky factory. If the customer doesn't care, then you shouldn't, either.

8. Develop and publish guidelines for copy review

As I said, the copywriter can't read your mind. He can't know your corporate guidelines, your company's likes and dislikes, unless you tell him what they are.

Develop a set of rules and guidelines for your writers to follow. These rules should contain both mandatory stylistic requirements (for example, "The company name is to be set in all caps and followed by a registered trademark symbol") and suggested guidelines.

The suggested guidelines clue copywriters on the way you're used to doing things. (For example, you might prefer long, informative subheads in brochures rather than short, snappy ones.) However, the copywriter should consider these guidelines as suggestions only. Rules can be bent and broken to make the copy more effective.

You can enlist the aid of your freelance copywriter, advertising consultant, or ad agency in developing these rules and guidelines. Together you may decide to add new rules or delete those guidelines that serve no real purpose.

Ideally, copy guidelines should be formulated and refined based on analysis of tested data. For instance, one of my clients has found, through extensive testing, that headlines in half-page newspaper ads of 8 to 12 words generate the most orders. He has many other guidelines, also based on tested experience, that he uses to boost his ad response.

19

GETTING YOUR COPY
DESIGNED AND PRODUCED

THE ROLE OF THE COPYWRITER IN DESIGN

The copywriter's job is to come up with selling ideas. Many of the most important of these messages can be expressed primarily with words, though experience shows that a strong photo or drawing with a persuasive caption can improve ad effectiveness.

In the pre-digital era, many copywriters stated that the primary purpose of the layout was to make the copy easy to read. While older boomers (like me) still believe making copy easy to read is an essential component of design, many younger marketers make the graphics, pictures, and videos the center of attention.

The reason is twofold. First, they contend that consumers do not read copy, especially long copy. This erroneous assumption has repeatedly been proven wrong in countless digital and print tests. Or, rather more specifically, casual Web surfers and browsers don't read long copy, but prospects and buyers do.

Second, they have grown up in a digital, visual age. They subscribe to the old saw "one picture is worth a thousand words." They do not realize that the ads are stronger when a powerful visual is accompanied by words.

As noted, people who do not read your copy are usually not serious buyers, but rather browsers. Consumers who intend to buy read a lot of copy about the product—and without this detail, do not buy. Exceptions? Of course.

The visual supports, enhances, and explains the ideas in the copy, but the copy usually doesn't depend on the visual and can stand on its own, even in the digital age. Some concepts are best expressed only by a strong combination of images and pictures. For others, especially those that would benefit from demonstration, video may work best.

There are times when you, as a copywriter, need more than copy to get your ideas across. You may need photos to show the consumer what you are offering and make it desirable (e.g., travel, fashion, jewelry, cars, homes, and many other things that are most clearly communicated with pictures).

To guide both digital and print designers and graphic artists on how the copywriter wants the copy designed, he creates what is known as a *copywriter's rough*. As the name implies, this is a simple sketch used to communicate the layout the copywriter envisions, especially the positioning of headlines, subheads, banners, calls to action, videos, photos, and response devices.

I draw my copywriter's roughs in Microsoft Word, so I can easily insert them into the Word documents containing my copy. I also keep a subdirectory of files on my PC containing copywriter's roughs I have created for many different projects. Often the copywriter's rough for one project can be reused as is or with minor modification, saving me time and effort.

Some prospective clients ask, "Do you do the artwork also?" I reply, "I don't take photographs or do illustrations. If my concept depends on a visual, I'll either write a description of the visual in the copy or provide a copywriter's rough." See figure 19.1 for an example.

Fig. 19.1: Copywriter's rough layout for full-page magazine ad.

A freelance copywriter submits a copywriter's rough— typically a crude sketch just to show where the various elements go.

An agency writer turns his copy and copywriter's rough over to the art director for polishing. A good art director enhances the writer's visual concept by adding his own ideas and creativity to it.

Some agencies submit two or three versions of the layout so the client can select the one he likes best. To me, this is like having my lawyer say, "Which defense do you think I ought to use?" I believe the agency should select the version it thinks is best and submit this to the client. After all, the client is paying the agency to make judgments in the creative area.

Once the rough is approved, the agency may submit a more

polished drawing—the comp—before photos are taken and type is set.

Why do ad agencies go through the process of submitting roughs? Because of the cost of revisions. It is relatively inexpensive to make changes to a rough, especially with almost all art and layout done on computer these days.

ART DIRECTION FOR COPYWRITERS

Agency copywriters know they have staff artists who can put their layout ideas in polished form.

Freelancers don't. So the client can either hire a freelance graphic artist or rely on the company's staff graphics team.

There is no need for the freelancer to hire an artist; just let your clients know that you will be providing copywriter's roughs, not finished comps. If the client demands comps, and if you're willing to provide this service, you can hire an artist.

In return for supervising the artwork, you may add an extra charge for artwork to your bill. This charge can be based on a percentage of the cost of hiring the artist. Or it can be whatever fee you think is reasonable.

If all this talk of drawing and art has you, as a "pure" writer, a bit worried, stop worrying.

On nine out of ten projects I do not do a copywriter's rough or any other type of sketch. It's not necessary: either my concept doesn't depend on a visual or, if it does, the visual can easily be described in words in the manuscript I submit.

Only one out of ten of my ads or Web pages is so visually complex or dependent upon a visual that I need to sketch it out. And doing the crude sketch never takes more than ten minutes.

The computer has helped with this enormously. Reason: not every promotion needs an original layout. So the layout I draw for one project can often be recycled, as is, or with minor modification for other projects—saving me an enormous amount of time.

As mentioned earlier, I keep all the layouts I do for my various copywriting assignments in a folder on my PC labeled "layouts." They are all drawn in Microsoft Word, making them easy to incorporate into the Word documents I submit as copy to my clients.

Below is another sample layout from this folder. As you can see, a copywriter's rough is truly rough—this is a layout for a postcard. The copywriter does not design the finished piece; the layout is to show position of copy elements only.

Fig. 19.2: Copywriter's rough postcard layout.

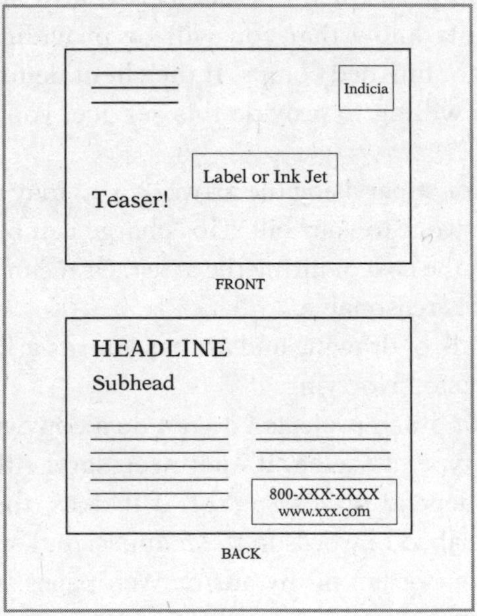

Here are a few more of my copywriter's roughs you may find interesting—even useful.

These are crude drawings, which you can do either using drawing software (e.g., Adobe Illustrator) or with a black marker on a sheet of paper.

Note that there is no attempt to dress them up and make them looked like a finished layout. That's the graphic designer's job, and she can do it better than you can. All that your copywriter's roughs do is show where you think each element should be positioned and the relative size and emphasis of each.

Fig. 19.3: Copywriter's rough for landing page.

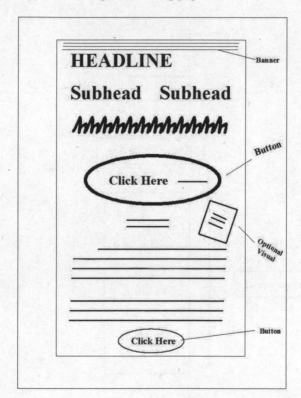

Fig. 19.4: Copywriter's rough for trifold brochure to fit on a rack or in a #10 envelope.

Trifold Brochure—letter size folded to form 6 panels

Front (Address) Panel   Back Panel

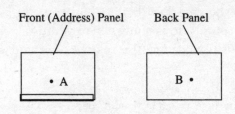

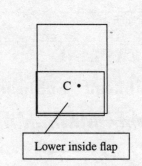

Lower inside flap

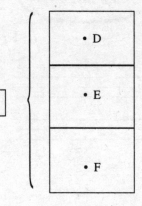

inside spread

10 TIPS FROM A TOP GRAPHIC DESIGNER

Veteran graphic artist Lori Haller says that by following the tips below, you can easily eliminate the most common graphic design mistakes from your marketing materials:

#1) Copy is KING. ALWAYS. PERIOD.

#2) Readability can make or break the campaign—online, print, always . . .

#3) Know your reader—deeply.

#4) Use fonts that are easy to read for your core audience. Small fonts are difficult for older audiences, as are column widths that are too wide.

#5) Stay on top of color trends. Your design can look outdated quickly.

#6) You have the ability to force the reader to read where you direct them.

#7) Get into the minds of the audience, into their shoes; become them, think like them, feel their pain, know what keeps them up at night.

#8) Read testimonials about the product, service, or guru . . .

#9) Order forms and cart pages must be easy to read, simple, and easy to understand. The reader does not want to feel tricked.

#10) Read the copy. Understand it. Get tight as a unit with the writer and make strategic plans together for success. Trust each other; share, bend, learn, and grow together. A solid team has a bigger potential to WIN—ALWAYS.

MORE DESIGN TIPS FOR COPYWRITERS

Here is a miscellany of graphic arts tips, rules, and techniques that every copywriter should know:

• First, there's the magic of the "Basic A" layout for magazine ads (fig. 19.5). This is the simplest, most standard layout: large picture at the top, headline underneath, body copy in two or three columns under the headline, logo and address in the bottom right-hand corner.

• Basic A is not spectacular, and some art directors consider it "old hat." But it's sensible, it draws the reader into the copy, and it's easy to read.

• You may want something different. Fine. But at least consider Basic A before going on to a more "creative" design.

Fig. 19.5: Copywriter's rough for Basic A ad layout.

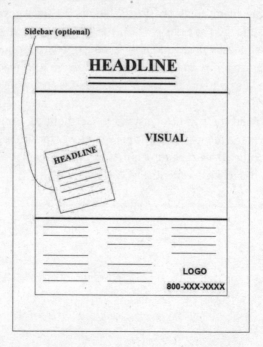

• A layout should have a single "focal point" where the eye goes to first. This is usually the visual; it can also be the headline.

• A layout should pull the eye from headline and visual through the body copy in logical sequence to the signature and logo. Subheads and bullets can help accomplish this.

• On a Web site, the visitor's eye goes to the upper right corner of the home page first. So that's a good location for a prominent call to action (CTA).

• Setting the headline in big, bold type helps draw attention to it. A powerfully written headline, splashed across a print or Web page in large letters, can be a real stopper.

• If you want the reader to respond to your ad, use a coupon. The coupon should appear in the lower right-hand corner of the ad; the ad should be run against the outer edge of the right-hand page. If a coupon borders the "gutter"—the fold running down the middle of a magazine or newspaper—people will not tear it out.

• If you want people to respond to your ad by phoning, set the phone number in large type at the end of the body copy. A toll-free number gets more calls than a pay number—even if you invite the reader to call on your pay number "collect."

• If you prefer an online response, include in large bold type the URL of the sales or landing page where the consumer can see and read more about the product, and also buy online.

• Photos usually make better visuals than drawings. They are more real, more believable, than illustrations.

• Full-color gets more attention and gives a better impression than black and white. But full-color is much more expensive to produce and to run in print.

• Online, color adds no cost. But put most of the copy in black type against a white background. Sparingly use red or another color to emphasize a word or phrase.

• In the hands of a skilled graphic artist, a second color can add to a brochure or ad's effectiveness. In the hands of an amateur, it can look chintzy and cheap. Be careful when using a second color in your layout.

• The simpler the layout, the better. Ads, PowerPoint slides, and Web pages with too many elements—small pictures, graphs, tables, charts, sidebars—have a complex look that discourages people from reading the copy. It takes a highly skilled graphic designer to produce a multielement ad that doesn't look cluttered and ponderous.

• The most important factor in selecting type is its readability. Type should be clear, easy on the eye, friendly, and inviting. Style is important—the choice of font is one of many elements that contributes to the image conveyed by the ad—but readability comes first. Always.

• Photos should be sharp, clear, and simple. If you have to choose between using a photo of poor quality or no photo, don't use a photo. Professional photography once was necessary in advertising. Today many people are capable of producing ad-quality photographs taken with the cameras in their smartphones.

• The best photos demonstrate a product benefit or make you think, "That looks interesting. I wonder what is going on here?" The latter type of photo has story appeal but doesn't tell the whole story; it leaves something to the imagination and arouses curiosity so that you will read the body copy to find out what the photo is about.

• Never do anything to make the copy difficult to read. Type should be set in black against a white background: not a tint, not white on black, not in color. I just saw an ad in which the copy was printed on a tablecloth and shot as a photo! Naturally, it was quite difficult to read.

Some ads and many Web sites, of course, are strongly driven by visuals, but even then, the visuals must complement the copy. One example that ran many years ago was an ad for United Technologies. The headline reads, "If you could punch this hole in a Sikorsky Black Hawk helicopter's gas tank, it would seal itself. In flight."

The visual is stark: a black circle five inches in diameter. To make the demonstration more dramatic, the ad is printed as an insert in the magazine on card stock.

The circumference of the black is perforated with a dashed line. Push on the black circle, and it pops out of the page, leaving the hole talked about in the headline.

PARTING THOUGHTS

Here are a few opinions I've developed on copywriters, art, and art directors:

Some copywriters try to add to their value in the marketplace by taking on a second skill. There are copywriter-photographers, copywriter–art directors, copywriter-narrators, and copywriter–television producers.

The logic makes sense. By hiring the dual-function copywriter, the client gets two services for the price of one.

In reality, the vast majority of A-level copywriters are those who write copy exclusively. People who do two jobs are usually not very good at either one. I know of only one or two exceptions, if that.

For example, all of the copywriter-photographers I know are mediocre writers and mediocre photographers. The reason may be that a skilled writer is so in demand that he has no time for picture taking.

But whatever the reason, I've rarely met a "combination copywriter" who was a truly first-rate writer.

Successful copywriters—at least the ones I know—are good at visualizing their ideas, but their visual concepts and layouts are always simple in design. The reason may be that copywriters don't have the drawing skills needed to express complex visual concepts on paper. So they stick to layouts they can illustrate with stick figures and squiggly lines.

Art directors, on the other hand, have the ability to do elaborate sketches, and so their layouts tend to be more sophisticated and complex.

A good art director can take a writer's simple concept and add graphic elements that enhance its selling power.

A clear-thinking copywriter can look at an art director's layout and see ways to make it cleaner, simpler, easier to read, and easier to respond to.

Designing ads is not the complex, mysterious task some people make it out to be. Laypeople believe, and artists encourage this belief, that there is some arcane formula of color combinations, type styles, photography, illustration, graphic elements, and positioning that creates ads with magical selling power.

Simple layouts are the best layouts. They are easier to conceive and cost much less to produce. And they are often the most effective.

A copywriter friend of mine wrote a small (6½ x 4⅞-inch) black-and-white ad selling a home-study foreign language course. The ad's layout is undistinguished: all copy except for a small line drawing of the study kit in the bottom right-hand corner. Yet this plain-Jane ad has produced sales of more than $5 million!

Words, not pictures, are the most important way of communicating great ideas. The Bible contains many thousands of words and not a single picture.

GLOSSARY OF ADVERTISING TERMS

Account—An advertising agency's client.

Account executive—An advertising agency employee who serves as the liaison between the agency and the client.

Ad click rate—Sometimes referred to as click-through, this is the percentage of ad views that resulted in an ad click.

Ad clicks—Number of times users click on an ad banner.

Ad views (impressions)—Number of times an ad banner is downloaded and presumably seen by visitors.

Address—A unique identifier for a computer or site online, usually a URL for a Web site or marked with an @ for an e-mail address.

Advertisement—A paid message in which the sponsor is identified.

Advertising manager—A professional employed by an advertiser to coordinate and manage the company's advertising program.

Affiliate marketing—A system of advertising in which site A agrees to feature buttons from site B, and site A gets a percentage of any sales generated for site B.

Affiliate program—An arrangement in which a company pays you a percentage of the sale for every online customer it gets through a link from your Web site to theirs.

Affinity Marketing—Marketing efforts—including e-mail promotions, banners, or offline media—aimed at consumers on the basis of established buying patterns.

Agora Model—Online business model in which you build a large opt-in e-list, and then drive sales by sending e-mails with product offers to your list.

Agora Publishing—A publisher of consumer newsletters credited with inventing the Agora Model.

Anchor—A word, phrase, or graphic image; in hypertext, it is the object that is highlighted, underlined, or "clickable" that links to another site.

Applet—An application program written in Java that allows viewing of simple animation on Web pages.

Art—A photograph or illustration used in an advertisement.

Art director—An ad agency employee responsible for designing and producing the artwork and layout for advertisements.

ASP (application service provider)—Third-party vendor that develops and hosts Internet and intranet applications for consumers.

AV—Audiovisual. A presentation with words and pictures. The most common digital AV are mp4 video files, which are typically posted on a server.

Avatar—A digital representation of a user in a virtual reality site.

B&W—Black and white.

Bandwidth—How much information (text, images, video, or sound) can be sent through a connection.

Banner ad—A banner is a small boxed message that appears atop commercial Web sites (usually the home page)—or on the first page of an e-zine—and is usually hyperlinked to the advertiser's site.

BBS (bulletin board system)—Software that enables users to log on to e-mail, Usenet, and chat groups via modem.

Billings—The fees an ad agency charges its clients.

Bleed—An illustration that goes to the edge of the page. Bleed artwork has no borders or margins.

Blue chip—A highly profitable company or product.

Boilerplate—Standard copy used because of legal requirements or company policy.

Book—See **portfolio**.

Bookmark—An easy way to find your way back to a Web site—just like a bookmark helps you keep your place in a book you are reading.

Bounce—This is what happens when e-mail returns as undeliverable.

Brand—The label by which a product is identified.

Brand manager—A manager employed by an advertiser to take charge of the marketing and advertising of a brand.

Branding—A school of advertising that says, "If the consumer has heard of us, we've done our job."

Broadband—A data-transmission scheme in which multiple signals share the bandwidth.

Broadside—A one-page promotional flyer folded for mailing.

Brochure—A booklet promoting a product or service.

Browser—An application used to view information from the Internet.

Budget—The amount of money the advertiser plans to spend on advertising.

Bulk mailing—The mailing of a large number of identical pieces of third-class mail at a reduced rate.

Bullet—A heavy dot used to separate lines or paragraphs of copy.

Buried ad—An ad surrounded by other ads.

Business-to-business advertising—Advertising of products and services sold by a business to other businesses.

Buttons—Objects that, when clicked once, cause something to happen.

Cache—A storage area for frequently accessed information.

Campaign—A coordinated program of advertising and promotion.

CGI (common gateway interface)—An interface-creation scripting program that allows Web pages to be made on the fly based on information from buttons, checkboxes, text input, and so on.

Chat room—An area online where you can chat with other members in real time.

Click—The opportunity for a visitor to be transferred to a location by clicking on an ad, as recorded by the server.

Clickbait—Copy or content posted on your Web site and stuffed with key words, for the sole purpose of attracting search engines. Google is wise to the practice and often ignores clickbait; it also penalizes you if the exact same content appears word for word on other sites.

ClickFunnel—A platform for creating and managing Web sites that takes visitors through your sales funnel online—a sequence of steps in a marketing campaign with the sole purpose of turning clicks into either leads or direct sales.

Click-through rate (CTR)—The percentage of users who click on a hyperlink (usually in an online ad or e-mail) to reach the Web page to which the link is attached.

Client—A company that uses the services of advertising professionals.

Clio—Advertising-industry awards given for the best television commercials of the year.

Collateral—Printed product information such as brochures, flyers, catalogs, and direct mail.

Considered purchase—A purchase made after careful evaluation of the product.

Consumer—One who buys or uses products and services.

Consumer advertising—Advertising of products sold to the general public.

Consumer products—Goods sold to individuals rather than to business or industry.

Contest—Sales promotion in which the consumer uses his skill to try to win a prize. Some contests require proof of purchase.

Conversion—Getting an online user to take a specific action, typically registering online in exchange for free content or purchasing a product from a Web site.

Cookie—A file on your computer that records information such as where you have been on the World Wide Web. The browser stores this information, which allows a site to remember the browser in future transactions or requests.

Copy—The text of an ad, commercial, or promotion.

Copy/Contact—An ad agency copywriter who works directly with the client instead of through an account executive.

Copywriter—A person who writes copy.

CPC—Cost per click.

CPL—Cost per lead.

CPM—CPM is the cost per thousand for a particular site. A Web site that charges $15,000 per banner and guarantees 600,000 impressions has a CPM of $25 ($15,000 divided by 600).

CPT—Cost per transaction.

CPTM—Cost per targeted thousand impressions.

Creative—Describes activities directly related to the creation of advertising. These include copywriting, photography, illustration, and design.

Creative director—Ad agency employee responsible for supervising the work of copywriters, art directors, and others who produce advertising.

Demographic overlay—Adding demographic data to a prospect or customer list by running it through the computer and matching it against other lists that already contain the data.

Demographics—Statistics describing the characteristics of a segment of the population. These characteristics include age, sex, income, religion, and race.

Direct mail—Unsolicited advertising material delivered by mail.

Direct response—Marketing that seeks to get orders or leads directly and immediately rather than build an image or awareness over a period of time.

Domain Part of the DNS (domain naming system)—Name that specifies details about the host. A domain is the main subdivision of Internet addresses, the last three letters after the final dot, and it tells you what kind of organization you are dealing with. There are six top-level domains widely used in the United States: .com (commercial), .edu (educational), .net (network operations), .gov (U.S. government), .mil (U.S. military), and .org (organization).

Downscale—Consumers on the low end of the social scale in terms of income, education, and status.

Drill down—A term used to express what a surfer does as he or she goes further into a Web site—deeper into the back pages, deeper into data.

E-commerce—Using electronic information technologies on the Internet to allow direct selling and automatic processing of purchases between parties.

E-list—A direct-mail list containing Internet addresses and used to distribute promotional messages over the Internet.

E-mail—An abbreviation for electronic mail, which is a network service that allows users to send and receive messages via computer.

E-zine—A part-promotional, part-informational newsletter or magazine distributed on the Internet.

Editorial—Those portions of a magazine's or newspaper's reading matter that are not advertisements, articles, news briefs, fillers, and other material produced by the publication's editors and writers.

Emoticons—The online means of facial expression and gestures, such as a smiley face: ☺ or :).

Eyeballs—The number of people clicking on and viewing a given Web site or page.

FAQ—FAQ is a commonly used abbreviation for "frequently asked questions."

Farm out—To assign work to an outside vendor rather than handle it in-house.

Feature story—A full-length magazine article.

Fee—The charge made by an agency or advertising professional to the client for services performed.

Firewall—A security barrier placed between an organization's internal computer network—either its IT system or intranet—and the Internet.

Flame—An intentionally crude or abusive e-mail message.

Floater—Similar to a pop-up or pop-under, except it is not blocked by pop-up blockers because it is part of the Web page or landing page HTML code. The floater is used to capture the visitor's e-mail address, usually by offering free content.

Forms—The pages in most browsers that accept information in text-entry fields.

Four A's—American Association of Advertising Agencies, an industry trade association.

Four color—Artwork reproduced in full color.

Fractional ad—An ad that takes less than a full page in a magazine or newspaper.

Freelance—A self-employed copywriter, photographer, artist, media buyer, or other advertising professional.

Frequency—The number of times an ad is delivered to the same browser in a single session or time period. A site needs to use cookies in order to manage ad frequency.

FTP (file transfer protocol)—A protocol that allows the transfer of files from one computer to another. FTP can also be used as a verb.

Full-service agency—An ad agency that offers its clients a full range of advertising services including creative services, media buying, planning, marketing, and research.

General advertising—Advertising that seeks to instill a preference for the product in the consumer's mind to promote the future sale of the product at a retail outlet or through a distributor or agent. This is the opposite of direct response advertising.

GIF (graphic interchange format)—A common compression format used for transferring graphics files between different computers.

Hack—To illicitly access a Web site to either purloin data, make unauthorized page changes, or shut the site down.

Hit—When a page request is made, all elements or files that comprise the page are recorded as hits on a server's log file.

Home page—The page designated as the main point of entry of a Web site or the starting point when a browser first connects to the Internet.

Host—A server connected to the Internet (with a unique IP address).

House organ—A company-published newsletter or magazine.

HTML—A coding language used to make hypertext documents for use on the Web.

https (hypertext transfer protocol)—A standard method of publishing information as hypertext in HTML format on the Internet.

https-SSL—https with SSL (secure socket layer) encryption for security.

Hyperlink—This is the clickable link in text graphics on a Web page that takes you to another place on the same page, another page, or a whole other site.

Hypertext—Electronic documents that present information that can be read by following many different directions through links, rather than just read linearly like printed text.

Image—The public's perception of a firm or product.

Impulse buy—A purchase motivated by chance rather than by plan.

In-house—Anything done internally within a company.

Industrial advertising—Advertising of industrial products and services.

Influencer—Someone who is widely followed on the Web and uses her popularity to influence her readers to buy various products and brands, often in exchange for free products and services from the marketer.

Inquiry—A request for information made by a potential customer responding to an ad or promotion.

Inquiry fulfillment package—Product literature sent in response to an inquiry.

Internet—A collection of approximately 60,000 independent, interconnected networks providing reliable and redundant connectivity between disparate computers and systems by using common transport and data protocols.

Internet domain name—The unique name that identifies an Internet entity.

Interstitial—An interstitial ad is an "intrusive" ad unit that is spontaneously delivered without specifically being requested by a user.

IP address (Internet protocol address)—Every system connected to the Internet has a unique IP address, which consists of a number in the format A, B, C, or D, where each of the four sections is a decimal number from 0 to 255.

ISP (Internet service provider)—A business that provides access to the Internet.

Java—An object-oriented programming language created by Sun Microsystems that supports enhanced features such as animation or real-time updating of information.

Jingle—Music and lyrics used in a commercial.

JPEG (joint photographic experts group)—A newer graphics format that displays photographs and graphic images with millions of colors, compresses well, and is easy to download.

Keyword—A word or phrase used to focus on online research.

Landing page—Any Web page designed to generate conversion or other direct action, as opposed to a page that just provides content or links to more content.

Layout—A drawing used to get a rough idea of how a finished ad, poster, or brochure will look.

Lead—See **sales lead**.

Lettershop—A firm that reproduces sales letters and other advertising literature.

Lift letter—A second letter included in a direct-mail package; the lift letter is designed to increase response to the mailing. Also known as a publisher's letter because it is primarily used in mailings that solicit magazine subscriptions.

Link—An electronic connection between two Web sites.

List broker—A person who rents mailing lists.

Listserver—A program that automatically sends e-mail to a list of subscribers. It is the mechanism that is used to keep new groups informed.

Load—Usually used with *upload* or *download*, it means to transfer files or software—to "load"—from one computer or server to another computer or server.

Log or log file—File that keeps track of network connections.

Login—The identification or name used to access—log in to—a computer, network, or site.

Logo—The name of a company set in specially designed lettering.

Lottery—In a lottery, winners are chosen by chance and must make a purchase to enter.

Madison Avenue—The mainstream of the New York City advertising community. Madison Avenue is a street that runs along the East Side of Manhattan; used in the advertising sense, the term "Madison Avenue" refers to agencies located in the heart of midtown Manhattan.

Mailing list—An online mailing list is an automatically distributed e-mail message on a particular topic going to certain individuals.

Market—A portion of the population representing potential and current customers for a product or service.

Marketing—The activities companies perform to produce, distribute, promote, and sell products and services to their customers.

Marketing communications—Communications used in marketing a product or service. "Marketing communications" includes advertising, public relations, and sales promotion.

Mass advertising—Advertising aimed at the general public.

Media—Any method of communication that brings information, entertainment, and advertising to the public or the business community.

Merchandising—Activities designed to promote retail sales.

Meta tags—Used to identify the creator of a Web page, what HTML specs the page follows, and the keywords and description of the page. Model of selling information products online.

Modem—A contraction for "modulation/demodulation," it is the device that converts a digital bit stream into an analog signal (and back again) so computers can communicate across phone lines.

Name squeeze page—A landing page, usually brief, designed to capture the user's e-mail address, either in exchange for an offer of free content or as a condition of allowing the reader access to copy on a landing page or other Web page. (Also known as a squeeze page.)

Native advertising—Advertising designed to look like editorial content.

Netiquette (Internet etiquette)—The rules of how to behave on the Internet.

Netizen—An active Internet user.

Newbie—A term to describe anyone new to an area, whether it be a particular forum online or the Internet.

Newsgroup—A discussion group on Usenet devoted to talking about a specific topic.

On speculation ("on spec")—Work that the client will pay for only if he likes it and uses it.

One-Time Offer (OTO)—A product offer you make to people, usually those who have just subscribed to your e-zine or joined your e-list, that they will see once and not again.

Opt in—To agree to receive promotional e-mails when registering on a particular Web site from the site owner and other companies to whom he or she may rent your e-mail address.

Opt out—To request that an e-list owner take your name off the list or at least make sure you are not sent any promotional e-mails.

Order page—When you click the Order Now button on a landing page, you are taken to an order page describing the offer and allowing you to place your order online.

Package goods—Products wrapped or packaged by the manufacturer. Package goods are low in cost and typically sold on store shelves.

Page—All Web sites are a collection of electronic "pages" formatted in HTML.

Page views—Number of times users request a page.

Pay-per-click—An advertising pricing model in which advertisers pay agencies based on how many consumers clicked on a promotion.

PDF files—Adobe's portable document format (pdf) is a translation format used primarily for distributing files across a network or on a Web site. Files with a .pdf extension have been created in another application and then translated into .pdf files so they can be viewed by anyone, regardless of platform.

Per diem—Fees charged by the day.

PI—Per inquiry advertising. Advertising for which the publisher or broadcast station is paid according to the number of inquiries produced by the ad or commercial.

Pop-over—A page that pops up on the screen when you visit a Web site or landing page, the purpose of which is to capture the e-mail address of the visitor, usually by offering free content.

Pop-under—A page that pops up on the screen when you attempt to leave a landing page or Web site without placing an order, the purpose of which is to capture the e-mail address of the visitor, usually by offering free content.

Portfolio—A presentation folder containing samples of your work. Shown to prospective employers when you are interviewing for a job.

Premium—Gift offered to potential customers as motivation for buying a product.

Press release—Written news information mailed to the press.

Product manager—A manager employed by an advertiser to supervise the marketing and advertising of a product or product line.

Promotion—Activities other than advertising that are used to encourage the purchase of a product or service.

Prospect—A person with the money, authority, and desire to buy a product or service; a potential customer.

Psychographics—Statistics relating to the personalities, attitudes, and lifestyles of various groups of people.

Pub-set—Ads designed and typeset by the publication in which they will appear.

Public relations—The activity of influencing the press so that they print (and broadcast) stories that promote a favorable image of a company and its products.

Publisher's letter—See **lift letter**.

Puffery—Exaggerated product claims made by an advertiser.

Pull—The response generated by an advertisement.

Red Book—Refers to both *The Standard Directory of Advertising Agencies* and *The Standard Directory of Advertisers*.

Reel—A reel of film or videotape containing sample commercials written by the copywriter.

Reply card—A self-addressed postcard sent with advertising material to encourage the prospect to respond.

Research—Surveys, interviews, and studies designed to show an advertiser how the public perceives his product and company or how they react to the advertiser's ads and commercials.

Sales funnel—A sequence of steps in a marketing campaign with the sole purpose of turning clicks into either leads or direct sales.

Sales lead—An inquiry from a qualified prospect.

Sales promotion—A temporary marketing effort designed to generate short-term interest in the purchase of a product. Coupons, sales, discounts, premiums, sweepstakes, and contests are all examples of sales promotion.

Space—The portion of a magazine or newspaper devoted to advertisements.

Special report—Free content offered as an incentive for the visitor to take action, typically either placing an order or giving you his e-mail address.

Split run test—Two versions of an ad are run in different copies of a publication to test the effectiveness of one version against the other.

Squeeze page—See **name squeeze page**.

Storyboard—Rough series of illustrations showing what a finished TV commercial will look like.

Sweepstakes—A sales promotion in which prizes are awarded by chance and the consumer does not have to make a purchase to enter.

Teaser—Copy printed on the outside envelope of a direct-mail package.

Trade advertising—Advertising aimed at wholesalers, distributors, sales reps, agents, and retailers rather than consumers.

Transaction page—An order page.

Two color—An ad or sales brochure printed in two colors, usually black and a second color such as blue, red, or yellow.

Type—Text set in lettering that can be reproduced by a printer.

Universe—The total number of people who are prospects for your product.

Upscale—Prospects at the upper end of the social scale in terms of income, education, and status.

Vertical publication—Magazine intended for a narrow group of special-interest readers.

Wire frame—A rough layout or diagram showing how a Web site home page or other pages are to be laid out; i.e., where the page elements such as headline, copy, CTA buttons, videos, and graphics should be placed on the page.

PERIODICALS

Advertising Age
685 Third Avenue
New York, NY 10017-4036
Tel: 212-210-0100
www.adage.com

Adweek
261 Madison Avenue, 8th Floor
New York, NY 10016
Tel: 212-493-4262 or 844-674-8161
www.adweek.com
Offers readers a blend of advertising news, features, how-to articles, insights, and columns.

B-to-B
Now published as part of *Advertising Age*
https://adage.com/section/btob/976

Chief Marketer
https://www.chiefmarketer.com

Direct Marketing
228 Park Avenue
Suite #88658
New York, NY 10003
Tel: 646-741-4771
www.dmcny.org

DM News
156 Fifth Avenue
New York, NY 10010
Tel: 800-538-5544
Fax: 212-925-8752
www.dmnews.com

PublicRelations Journal
120 Wall Street, 21st Floor
New York, NY 10005-4024
Tel: 212-460-1400
www.prsa.org

Sales and Marketing Management
Mach1 Business Media
P.O. Box 247
27020 Noble Road
Excelsior, MN 55331
Tel: 952-401-1283

Target Marketing
11049 Lakeridge Parkway
Ashland, VA 23005
Tel: 888-780-8300
https://www.targetmarketingmag.com/

ONLINE NEWSLETTERS

Ben Settle Daily Email
Regardless of whether you buy in to Ben's hard-hitting and unorthodox view of marketing, just reading his daily e-mail will make you a better e-mail writer.
www.bensettle.com

Bencivenga's Bullets
www.bencivengabullets.com
Master copywriter Gary Bencivenga's can't-miss e-zine based on his decades of tested results.

Business Made Simple Daily
Cindy Rayfield's daily video business tip.
https://www.businessmadesimple.com/daily/

The Copywriter's Roundtable
http://copywritersroundtable.com/
John Forde's superb e-newsletter on copywriting.

The Direct Response Letter
www.bly.com
My monthly e-newsletter on copywriting and direct marketing.

Excess Voice
https://nickusborne.com/newsletter/
Nick Usborne's e-newsletter on online copywriting. Informative and great fun.

Marketing Minute
www.yudkin.com/markmin.htm
Weekly marketing tip from consultant Marcia Yudkin.

Paul Hartunian's Million-Dollar Publicity Strategies
http://www.hartunian.com/
Great marketing e-newsletter focusing on publicity.

The Success Margin
www.tednicholas.com
Ted Nicholas's must-read marketing e-zine.

Total Annarchy
https://annhandley.com/newsletter/
Ann Handley's marketing e-newsletter.

WEB SITES AND BLOGS

The Advertising Show
http://theadvertisingshow.com/
Radio show on marketing.

American Writers and Artists Inc. (AWAI)
www.awaionline.com
Home-study courses and conferences on copywriting.

Copywriting Genius: The Master Collection
www.monthlycopywritinggenius.com
Regular reviews of winning promotions and interviews with the copywriters who wrote them.

Happy Earner
www.happyearner.com
Tom Woods on Internet marketing (and politics).

The Small Business Advocate
www.smallbusinessadvocate.com
Radio show and Web site dedicated to small business.

Warrior Forum
https://www.warriorforum.com/
An active online forum where copywriters and marketers discuss and debate all things marketing.

BOOKS

How to Write a Good Advertisement by Vic Schwab (Wilshire Book Company, 1962).
A commonsense course in how to write advertising copy that gets people to buy your product or service, written by a plain-speaking veteran mail-order copywriter in 1962.

My First 50 Years in Advertising by Max Sackheim (Prentice Hall, 1982).
Another plain-speaking, commonsense guide that stresses salesmanship over creativity, and results over awards. The author was one of the founders of the Book of the Month Club.

The Robert Collier Letter Book by Robert Collier (Robert Collier Publications, 1937).
How to write sales letters with numerous examples of classic mail-order letters.

Reality in Advertising by Rosser Reeves (Alfred A. Knopf, 1961).
The book in which Reeves introduced the now-famous concept of the USP (Unique Selling Proposition).

Breakthrough Advertising by Eugene Schwartz (Bottom Line Books, 2004).
A copywriting guide by one of the greatest direct-response copywriters of the twentieth century.

How to Write Advertising That Sells by Clyde Bedell (McGraw-Hill, 1952).
An in-depth guide to persuasive copywriting by an acknowledged twentieth-century master of the craft.

Tested Advertising Methods, 5th ed., by John Caples, revised by Fred Hahn (Prentice Hall, 1997).
An updated edition of John Caples's classic book on the principles of persuasion.

The 100 Greatest Advertisements: Who Wrote Them and What They Did by Julian Watkins (Dover, 1959).
A collection of one hundred enormously successful print ads with an analysis of what made each perform so well.

Confessions of an Advertising Man by David Ogilvy (Atheneum, 1988).
Charming autobiography of legendary adman David Ogilvy, packed with useful advice on how to create effective advertising.

Scientific Advertising by Claude Hopkins (Bell Publishing, 1920).
A book on the philosophy that advertising's purpose is to sell, not entertain or win creative awards—and how to apply this philosophy to create winning ads.

Method Marketing by Denny Hatch (Bonus Books, 1999).
How to write successful direct-response copy by putting yourself in the customer's shoes. Packed with case histories of modern direct-response success stories, including Bill Bonner of Agora Publishing and Martin Edelston of Boardroom.

Advertising Secrets of the Written Word by Joseph Sugarman (DelStar, 1998).
How to write successful advertising copy by a modern master of the space ad.

ORGANIZATIONS

American Writers and Artists Inc. (AWAI)
www.awaionline.com
Copywriting training.

Business Marketing Association
www.marketing.org
Association for business-to-business marketers.

Content Marketing Institute
https://contentmarketinginstitute.com/

Copywriters Council of America
https://www.linkedin.com/in/drandrewlinick

Data and Marketing Association
www.the-dma.org

Social Media Examiner
https://www.socialmediaexaminer.com/

Specialized Information Publishers Association
http://www.siia.net/Divisions/SIPA-Specialized-Information
-Publishers-Association

NOTES

CHAPTER 1

1 The Gary Halbert Letter, undated.
2 PR Daily, April 11, 2019.
3 "From Digital-First to Data-First: 2019 Marketing Predictions." Signal white paper, p. 2.
4 "Awash in Data," eMarketer Daily, April 12, 2019.
5 http://www.writingfromtheheart.net/writing-advice-from-john-mcphee/.
6 IAB Smart Brief, March 15, 2019.
7 Ibid.
8 https://merchdope.com/youtube-stats/.
9 eMarketer, April 12, 2019, p. 2.

CHAPTER 2

1 https://www.statista.com/statistics/273288/advertising-spending-worldwide/.
2 http://blog.cdnsciencepub.com/21st-century-science-overload/.
3 https://gowithfloat.com/2018/01/rapid-doubling-knowledge-drives-change-learn/.
4 https://www.forbes.com/sites/forbesagencycouncil/2017/08/25/finding-brand-success-in-the-digital-world/#2765ac66626e.
5 https://www.propellercrm.com/blog/cold-email-statistics.

CHAPTER 4

1 https://www.thedailymeal.com/eat/has-mcdonald-s-really-sold-billions-and-billions-burgers.
2 "The Writer's Life," AWAI, July 12, 2019.
3 Dr. Ralph Ryback, "From Baby Boomers to Generation Z," *Psychology Today*, February 22, 2016.
4 https://www.marketingteacher.com/the-six-living-generations-in-america/.
5 FourHooks, a Digital consultancy agency, *The Generation Guide—Millennials, Gen X, Y, Z and Baby Boomers*, April 26, 2015, http://fourhooks.com/marketing/the-generation-guide-millennials-gen-x-y-z-and-baby-boomers-art5910718593/.

CHAPTER 5

1 http://credibility.stanford.edu/pdf/Stanford-MakovskyWebCredStudy2002-prelim.pdf.
2 https://mason.gmu.edu/~montecin/web-eval-sites.htm.
3 Ibid.

CHAPTER 6

1 https://www.marketingcharts.com/featured-104785.
2 https://www.adweek.com/digital/iab-study-says-26-desktop-users-turn-ad-blockers-172665/.

CHAPTER 7

1 https://www.themailshark.com/resources/articles/is-direct-mail-dead/.
2 https://www.datatargetingsolutions.com/blog/2018/11/16/20-direct-mail-statistics-for-2019.
3 Talon Newsletter, July 2019, p. 1.
4 Robert Bly, *The Direct Mail Revolution* (Irvine, CA: Entrepreneur Press, 2019), p. 8.

CHAPTER 12

1 Daniela McVicker, PR Daily, "10 Mistakes That Will Doom a Startup's First Marketing Campaign," May 7, 2019.
2 Mequoda Landing Page Scorecard, Mequoda Library, Robert Bly, consulting editor.

CHAPTER 17

1 Content Marketing Institute, August 26, 2017.
2 *The Splendid Table*, an American Public Media (a.k.a. NPR) talk program: "Spaghetti à la Campbell," http://www.splendidtable.org/recipes /spaghetti-la-campbell.
3 David Meerman Scott, *Cashing In with Content* (Medford, NJ: Information Today, 2005), p. 8.
4 https://www.google.com/search?ei=rTnsXPmKLpCxgge3jobABA&q =what+percentage+of+people+have+internat+access+in+2019&oq=wh at+percentage+of+people+have+internat+access+in+2019&gs_l=psy-ab .3 . . . 40570.43093.45216 . . . 0.0.0.230.1019.1j6j1. . . . 0. . . . 1.gws-wiz. . . . 0i71j0i22i30.z7uCJHXxcyY.
5 https://techjury.net/stats-about/blogging/.
6 https://www.ragan.com/study-the-perfect-blog-post-length-and-how -long-it-should-take-to-write-2/.

CHAPTER 18

1 https://www.prdaily.com/why-and-how-you-should-engage-your-gig -workers/?utm_source=RDH&utm_medium=email&utm_campaign =RDH+(2019-06-03)&utm_content=article+title&utm_term=3.
2 https://www.popsci.com/article/science/bot-has-written-more -wikipedia-articles-anybody.
3 https://www.targetmarketingmag.com/article/can-a-computer-write -better-copy-than-you/all/.

INDEX

ABOUT THE AUTHOR

ROBERT W. BLY is a freelance copywriter specializing in business-to-business, high-tech, and direct response marketing.

He has four decades of experience writing ads, brochures, direct-mail packages, sales letters, publicity materials, e-mail campaigns, white papers, e-books, special reports, e-newsletters, banner ads, landing pages, squeeze pages, and Web sites for more than one hundred clients including Grumman, AlliedSignal, AT&T, IBM, Lucent Technologies, Medical Economics, McGraw-Hill, Philips Publishing, *Forbes*, KCI, Agora Publishing, Ken Roberts Company, and EBI Medical Systems.

Bob Bly has won a number of industry awards including a Gold Echo from the Direct Marketing Association, an IMMY from the Information Industry Association, two Southstar Awards, an American Corporate Identity Award of Excellence, and the Standard of Excellence award from the Web Marketing Association.

Robert W. Bly is the author of one hundred books including *The Digital Marketing Handbook* (Entrepreneur Press), *Complete Idiot's Guide to Direct Marketing* (Alpha Books), and *The New Email Revolution* (Skyhorse).

His articles have appeared in such publications as *Cosmopolitan*, *Chemical Engineering Progress*, *New Jersey Monthly*, *Writer's Digest*, and *City Paper*.

Robert W. Bly has taught copywriting at New York University and has presented sales and marketing seminars to numerous corporations, associations, and groups, including the Direct Marketing Creative Guild, Women's Direct Response Group, American Chemical Society, Publicity Club of New York, Social Media World, and the International Tile Exposition.

Bob has been a guest on dozens of radio and TV shows including CNBC and CBS's *Hard Copy*, and has been featured in periodicals ranging from *Nation's Business* to the *Los Angeles Times*.

He is a member of the Business Marketing Association, Specialized Information Publishing Association, and the American Institute of Chemical Engineers. His online newsletter, *Direct Response Letter*, goes to thousands of subscribers weekly. You can subscribe for free at www.bly.com/reports.

For more information on Bob's books, information products, consulting, and freelance copywriting services, contact:

Robert W. Bly
Copywriter
31 Cheyenne Drive
Montville, NJ 07045
Phone: 973-263-0562
Fax: 973-263-0613
E-mail: rwbly@bly.com
Web site: www.bly.com